WALKING IN TRUTH IN
A WORLD -OF-

LIES

COMMENTS

"Given a choice, most students prefer a true or false test over essay questions. Perhaps that's because with true or false questions there is at least a 50/50 chance of getting the right answer. However, guessing is risky. Far better to study the subject and know what is true.

Knowing what is true is never a matter of guessing; it's a matter of knowing. Solomon wrote 'Buy truth, and do not sell it, Get wisdom and instruction and understanding' (Proverbs 23:23 NASV). I can think of no better reason to encourage you to read Steve Gallagher's masterful essay on truth. Get it, read it, and I can assure you that you will get wisdom, and instruction and understanding on how to walk in the truth in a world of lies."

-DR. DENNIS FREY. PRESIDENT, MASTER'S INTERNATIONAL UNIVERSITY OF DIVINITY

"If God were to send a modern-day prophet to America, calling out against complacency and apostasy, I suspect he would sound a lot like Steve Gallagher. *Walking in Truth in a World of Lies* is a call of warning, but also of great mercy. Refreshingly clear, cogently reasoned, deeply researched, and compellingly presented; this book is like a drink of cold water in a desert for anyone who loves the truth. True believers will be strengthened to stand in the midst of a world of lies and compromise. The Church has needed a book like this for a long time! Thank God it's here."

-ISRAEL WAYNE, AUTHOR AND CONFERENCE SPEAKER

"I believe this book has come into the Kingdom for such a time as this. Never before has the enemy amassed such an arsenal of deception as today. Jesus warned

WALKING IN TRUTH IN
A WORLD -OF-
LIES

STEVE GALLAGHER

us that in the last days the love of many would wax cold. Blow out any candle and the wax will remain hot momentarily but gradually it will return to its previously hardened state. Such is the state of multiplied millions of believers today; the fire has gone out and relationship has been replaced by ritual, love by legalism and devotion by duty.

I believe this is Gallagher's finest work as it broadens its scope beyond the sex addict to the believer who feels comfortable in his lukewarmness and mediocrity. My prayer is that this book will find its way into every believer's home and will serve to awaken us to the enemy's diabolical devices. Keep a copy for yourself and buy one for your pastor and friend. You may well help avert a major spiritual disaster."
-DAVID RAVENHILL, AUTHOR AND ITINERANT TEACHER

"In *Walking in Truth in a World of Lies* Steve Gallagher has provided a Biblical, powerful and penetrating resource for those struggling with sexual addiction. Carefully researched, thoroughly scriptural, and well documented the author exposes an alarming problem while providing solutions that are biblical and practical. Building his case, step by step, the author's thesis is made even more compelling by his insightful description of the historical backdrop of how modern technology and sales techniques have become tools of deception in the battle against sexual idolatry and immorality. An enormously useful book in addressing an out of control problem in the church, that pastors will want to distribute far and wide in helping needy souls break free from the bondage of this addiction."
-JOSEPH M. JACOWITZ, PRESIDENT, FIRSTLOVE MINISTRIES
PASTOR, CHRIST BIBLE CHURCH

For books and other teaching resources please contact:

PURE LIFE MINISTRIES
14 School Street
Dry Ridge, KY 41035
(888) PURELIFE - to order
www.purelifeministries.org

Walking in Truth in a World of Lies
Copyright © 2020 by Pure Life Ministries.

ISBN/EAN 978-0-578-70764-8
eBook ISBN/EAN 978-0-578-70765-5

TO ED AND KARLA, TWO SINCERE LOVERS OF TRUTH:
CONTINUE TO GUARD THE TREASURE THAT
HAS BEEN ENTRUSTED TO YOU.

CONTENTS

APPENDICES

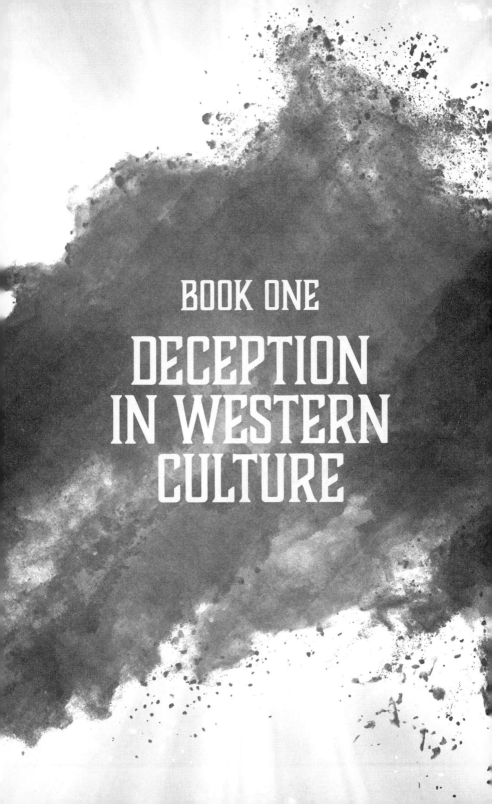

BOOK ONE

DECEPTION IN WESTERN CULTURE

"You live in a world of deception. In
their deception they refuse to know Me.
This is the LORD's declaration."

-THE PROPHET JEREMIAH[1]

INTRODUCTION TO BOOK ONE:
THE MANY FACES OF DECEPTION

You and I are being lied to on a regular basis. In fact, our entire culture is riddled with deception. Things have gotten so bad that we need a "Truth-O-Meter" to stay on top of what politicians tell us, a governmental agency (Food and Drug Administration) to oversee the preposterous claims made by advertisers, and a variety of independent websites to monitor the veracity of what we are being told by public figures—including Christian ministers!*

Satan uses every sort of duplicity to lead people away from Truth and into the tangled and confusing realm of Deception. Truth has been outrageously violated in every quarter. Book One will explore numerous aspects of American life that the enemy has infused with his falsehoods. But before we begin digging more deeply into the lies of our culture, let's take a better look at exactly what deceitfulness actually is.

DECEPTION IN HUMANKIND

The word deception could be defined as communication or behavior that is meant to leave others with a false impression. We encounter it in many forms in everyday life. Consider the following synonyms, each of which conveys a slightly different nuance of this concept:

---

* Wikipedia lists over 70 fact-checking websites that make it their mission to expose lies that are masquerading as truth.

+ Disinformation: "deliberately misleading or biased information; manipulated narrative or facts; propaganda."[2]
+ Doublespeak: "evasive, ambiguous language that is intended to deceive or confuse."[3]
+ Duplicity: "deceitfulness in speech or conduct, as by speaking or acting in two different ways to different people concerning the same matter; double-dealing."[4]
+ Fabrication: "to make up for the purpose of deception."[5]
+ Falsehood: "Contrariety or inconformity to fact or truth."
+ Fraud: "deceit [or] trickery... perpetrated for profit or to gain some unfair or dishonest advantage."[6]
+ Half-truth: "a statement that fails to divulge the whole truth..."[7] or using a portion of truthful information to make a lie seem more trustworthy.
+ Hypocrisy: "a concealment of one's real character or motives... a deceitful show of a good character, in morals or religion; a counterfeiting of religion."[8]
+ Lie: "a falsehood uttered for the purpose of deception; an intentional violation of truth."[9]
+ Scam: "a confidence game or other fraudulent scheme, especially for making a quick profit; swindle."[10]
+ Subterfuge: "an artifice or expedient used to evade a rule, escape a consequence, hide something, etc."[11]

These are some of the more common terms we are accustomed to encountering regarding deception, but there are actually quite a few others. The point is that deception is employed by others (or even by ourselves) in a wide variety of ways. I guess it could be said that there is a lie for every occasion.

Sometimes falsehood comes through brazen assertions or mendacious whoppers. Duplicity can come in the form of indirect influences meant to lead to wrong conclusions, whereas enticements are intended to lead one astray from the path of honest and upright behavior. Bald-faced lies are uttered by product pitchmen and half-truths by compromising preachers. Cover-ups, fake news, and disinformation permeate the political landscape on every level. People tell outright lies to each other, witnesses perjure themselves, and adulterous spouses cover their secret behavior. We are surrounded by every form of deception, from little white lies to audacious falsehoods.

Apparently, most people lie fairly regularly—at least when they are concerned about what others think of them. This assertion comes from a study conducted at the University of Massachusetts. According to this report, 60 percent of people lied at least once during a ten minute conversation—with the average number hovering somewhere between two and three stated falsehoods. [12]According to Robert S. Feldman, the psychologist who conducted the study:

> People tell a considerable number of lies in everyday conversation. It was a very surprising result. We didn't expect lying to be such a common part of daily life… It's so easy to lie. We teach our children that honesty is the best policy, but we also tell them it's polite to pretend they like a birthday gift they've been given. Kids get a very mixed message regarding the practical aspects of lying, and it has an impact on how they behave as adults. [13]

The reality is that lying is fairly ubiquitous amongst humankind. "Little white lies" intended to protect someone's feelings—"Your sermon was really powerful!"—are, perhaps, understandable.[†] However, other falsehoods are more serious, such as purposely misleading a prospective buyer about the defects of a used car or offering a disingenuous statement to a police officer.

When discussing people who lie, it is important to note that there is a huge difference between those who occasionally fudge on the truth and those who tell untruths on a regular basis.

Habitual liars are so accustomed to deceiving others that they actually get to where they can no longer differentiate truth from falsehood; or, at the very least, lose track of all of the lies they have told. Such people have been termed prolific liars, chronic liars, inveterate liars, and, at the extreme end, pathological liars. And who could forget New York Times columnist William Safire calling Hillary Clinton a "congenital liar"? "They delight in falsehood," observed David. (Psalm 62:4) In other words, habitual liars take great pleasure in propagating false narratives and perpetuating dishonest impressions.

People who practice telling lies to this extent have allowed a framework of deception to become established in their minds, distorting every encounter with reality into something foreign to the truth. These people tell falsehoods consistently and habitually, even when they have nothing to gain from such behavior. They are often quite adept at spinning colorful and convincing tales, invariably portraying themselves as either heroes or victims. Special agent John Douglas, who interviewed hundreds of

---

† Sometimes believers find themselves in situations where complete honesty would hurt another person. The Lord was the only one who ever maintained the perfect balance between truth and mercy. (John 1:14, 17) Mortals can only pray for discernment to know when and if less than full disclosure is appropriate. I will say that there have been many saints down through the ages who found it wise to be less than totally forthright in certain situations. Corrie Ten Boom (*The Hiding Place*) and Brother Andrew (*God's Smuggler*) are two who come to mind.

serial killers for the FBI, noted: "Sociopaths often did well on polygraph tests. If you have no conscience and can lie to other people without a problem, lying to a box isn't any big deal."[14]

AN UNEXPECTED DANGER

Let's face it; deception has become embedded in Western culture. The more a person is deceived, the less capacity he[‡] will have to discern truth. Many come to such a place of despair of being able to distinguish truth that they simply give up hope of ever really knowing what is genuine and what is false. Yet, there is a subtle peril that can be even more hazardous and harmful than the hopelessness of this mindset.

Being subjected to an unrelenting barrage of falsehood has a way of leaving people in a state of undetected cynicism. If a person's heart is spiritually unhealthy, he can become so distrustful of others that he disparages the intentions and motives of just about everyone. The more a person is deceived, the less trust he will have for others. Such a person can easily erect an imperceptible wall of mistrust in his heart toward everyone—including the Lord. Before long, Scripture comes under a cloud of suspicion; doubts about the veracity of God's statements become strengthened. An atmosphere of unbelief can hover over every aspect of the person's life. It is a very dangerous mindset to allow to fester because the Christian faith is built upon trust in and dependence upon the honest and upright character of God.

Cynicism has now become so rooted in American thought that even standards of honesty that have been established over

---

‡ Throughout this book I regularly use masculine pronouns. This is not a slight against the female reader. I just find that vacillating back and forth between the masculine and feminine forms or attempting to use a neutral term (e.g. they, them, their) makes for awkward writing and cumbersome reading.

many decades in our society are held in contempt. So how can believers find their way through this maze of deception? It must begin by taking an honest inventory of what our culture is actually telling us.

THE MANY FACES OF DECEPTION

"Postmodernism really isn't about 'truth,' it's about doing whatever is right in our own eyes."

-SHANE IDLEMAN[1]

"The church in its effort to become relevant has become irrelevant. It has decided to redefine itself in such clearly cultural terms to appeal to the culture that it can't confront the culture."

-OS GUINNESS[2]

ONE:
WALKING IN TRUTH IN
A POST-TRUTH ERA

Human beings are driven through life by appetite, desire, and lust. (Galatians 5:16, 24; 1 John 2:16) We pursue that which interests us—whether it is something as noble as knowing God, as innocuous as collecting stamps, or as evil as chasing sexual fantasies. Every human is propelled through the journey of life reaching for those things which he desires.

When considering the subject of truth, one must take into account the fact that *a person's perspective about truth will be heavily clouded by what he wants it to be.* The one who hungers for righteousness will tend to be very open and amenable to God's truth. On the other hand, a sex addict, for instance, would be very vulnerable to the falsehoods of antinomianism—the errant belief that grace frees the Christian from the gospel's demands for holy living.

It is this appetite for that next experience, possession, or attainment that creates the perfect breeding ground for deception. In large part, human beings are willing to believe anything, as long as it caters to what they want. The enemy, fully understanding this human tendency, has become very adept at creating belief systems with just enough plausibility to make them credible. These fabricated religious systems keep people by the millions from coming into a saving knowledge of God.

That's bad enough, but—perhaps worse—they also create so much confusion and uncertainty in the religious realm that, without the aid of the Holy Spirit, not even the stoutest seeker would have the wherewithal to ferret out the truth.

In this postmodern era, interest in the spiritual life is waning in favor of a secular viewpoint that seems much more reasonable and tolerant to young people than what they consider to be the self-righteous, narrow-minded, and even violent world of religion. Many take this idea even further than simply questioning the status quo.

In 2016 the Oxford Dictionaries named "Post-truth" as Word of the Year. "Post-truth" has been defined as the phenomenon in which "objective facts are less influential in shaping public opinion than appeals to emotion and personal belief."[3] In this era, truth is being replaced with feelings and personal experiences. The bedrock of objective truth is eroding with each passing year. The media isn't helping truth's cause either, as Katharine Viner observes:

> It seemed that journalists were no longer required to believe their own stories to be true, nor, apparently, did they need to provide evidence. Instead it was up to the reader – who does not even know the identity of the source – to make up their own mind. But based on what? Gut instinct, intuition, mood?[4]

The public is increasingly favoring the more tolerant philosophy of humanistic relativism. People think everyone's opinions and ideas should be considered "relative to differences in perception and consideration. There is no universal, objective truth according to relativism; rather each point of view has its own truth."[5]

Much of this vein of thinking can be laid at the doorstep of Friedrich Nietzche who was convinced that a person's beliefs are neither right nor wrong. He dismissed the ethical system of Christianity as a "slave morality" followed by fearful and weak people. According to his thinking, an emotionally healthy person would reject the Christian ethic and create his own.

This perspective is becoming increasingly more popular in our day. The Christian community has not exactly been the beacon of integrity one would hope for in this deceptive atmosphere. Our weakened spiritual condition not only hinders us from presenting a convincing argument for the veracity of Scripture, but it has also fueled the skepticism of the world. The lack of love and godliness in the lives of professing Christians* leave unbelievers simply shaking their heads in self-righteous disgust.

There was a time when the world gave the Church a certain degree of begrudging admiration, but it seems that Christianity is quickly losing favor with unbelievers. In a 2019 article entitled, "In U.S., Decline of Christianity Continues at Rapid Pace," the Pew Research team shared the following:

> In [our] telephone surveys conducted in 2018 and 2019, 65% of American adults describe themselves as Christians when asked about their religion, down 12 percentage points over the past decade. Meanwhile, the religiously unaffiliated share of the population, consisting of people who describe their religious identity as atheist, agnostic or "nothing in particular," now stands at 26%, up from 17% in 2009.[6]

This downward trend will undoubtedly continue as new generations come of age, creating a vacuum which the relativism of humanistic thinking is quickly filling. I could

---

* I use the terms, "professing Christians" and "churchgoers" to describe people who claim to be believers but who probably do not actually know the Lord.

envision a typical Westerner going on a rant about the claims of Christianity that might sound something like this:

> How can you Christians be so sure that what you believe has any kind of validity whatsoever? If I went to the Far East, there are some 375 million Buddhists who would swear they know the way. If I spent time in India, nearly a billion Hindus would claim that their religion is the right one. If I traveled to the Middle East or North Africa, 1.3 billion Muslims would assert that they are the guardians of truth. I don't see any reason to think that you know more than all of those people!
>
> Who's to say which of these religions is right? I seriously doubt that truth is even discernible. There are so many different opinions about spiritual matters. Who can say what is real and what is fake? Let's face it: truth is relative.
>
> And besides, your lives don't show that you really believe what you claim to believe. If you were really convinced you knew the truth, you would practice what you preach. Anymore, it's hard to tell the difference between Christians and non-Christians.
>
> I think I would rather trust the wisdom of my college professor who once said that truth varies from individual to individual. He claims that one person's truth is not necessarily another person's truth. He believes people just shape their realities to suit themselves. We make truth to be what we want it to be. He would tell you that the world's greatest problem is all of these different religious groups claiming that they alone are right and everyone who disagrees with them is wrong. It is much better to think of truth as something that is relative to a particular situation or person than to speak of it in absolute terms.

I just think that every human should have the right to decide for himself what his truth is and others shouldn't have the right to push their beliefs onto him. That arrogance only causes discord within humanity. In fact, I'm almost to the point of believing we would be a lot better off if we banned people from proselytizing others. If they want what you are offering them, they can show up at your church on a Sunday morning and check it out for themselves!

I think that diatribe is a fairly accurate picture of the quickly emerging mindset in the United States, Canada, and most of Europe. Isaiah could have been speaking about our culture when he lamented, "Truth has stumbled in the public square, and honesty cannot enter. Truth is missing..." (Isaiah 59:14b-15a CSB) Every time Truth has attempted to take a stand in the public forum of Western thought, it has been shouted down and overthrown. (cf. Romans 1:18) If Christianity is going to make a difference in this world, something radical must change in the Church.

"WHAT IS TRUTH?"

Pilate could have been representing the masses of Western youth who are currently grappling with this very question. He actually asked his famous question ("What is truth?") in response to the most wonderful words he had ever heard. Jesus had just explained, "For this I have been born, and for this I have come into the world, to testify to the truth. Everyone who is of the truth hears My voice." (John 18:37) But Pilate did not have "ears to hear." His life had been characterized by a ruthless climb to the upper echelons of the Roman political world. Uninterested in this Jewish rabbi's version of truth, he, like so many today, chose to mold his concept of truth around his desires and ambitions.

Still, the question he posed at that historic moment is one which every thinking person should earnestly and solemnly ponder. The answer begins with the Hebrew word for truth: *emeth*. The root word from which *emeth* is derived is *aman*, a term that is often used to describe something firm and immoveable, such as the pillars of the Temple. (2 Kings 18:16) In the OT, the truth of God does not fluctuate with human whims but is considered to be fixed and secure. Because of this underlying root concept, *emeth* is frequently translated as faithful (or some derivative), revealing the necessity of comprehending its underlying meaning when considering the biblical view of truth.[†]

The *Theological Wordbook of the Old Testament* explains how vital it is to understand this double meaning:

> This very important concept in biblical doctrine gives clear evidence of the biblical meaning of "faith" in contradistinction to the many popular concepts of the term. At the heart of the meaning of the root is the idea of certainty. And this is borne out by the NT definition of faith found in Hebrews 11:1 ["Now faith is the assurance of things hoped for, the conviction of things not seen."]. The basic root idea is firmness or certainty.[7]

This perception really comes out in the book of Psalms where "the God of truth" (Psalm 31:5) is called a "rock" by the various writers some twenty times. You get the sense of His "firmness" and "certainty" in their lives through verses such as this one: "The LORD is my rock and my fortress and my deliverer, my God, my rock, in whom I take refuge… my stronghold." (Psalm 18:2) That is the God of truth a person can trust and depend upon!

---

† See Appendix # 1 for a fascinating study of truth and its correlation with faith.

Why are all these linguistic technicalities so important? It is necessary to grasp this because it refers to the determining factor involving our eternal destiny. *Without biblical truth as its foundation, there can be no saving faith.* God's truth is only granted to the utterly sincere person who seeks it and responds to it. There is only one narrow path that arrives in the celestial city while there are many deceptive roads which lead to hell. Those who put their trust in some past experience or a flimsy belief in a watered-down version of the gospel very well may find out to their horror on that great Day that they never really belonged to Christ. (Matthew 7:21-23)

Before we leave the OT concept of truth, I want to substantiate this sense of the firmness, stability, and trustworthiness conveyed by *emeth* by comparing it to its counterpart. There are actually twenty different word groups that describe various facets of deception in the OT.‡ The term that heads the list is *sheqer*, which is "used of words or activities which are false in the sense that they are groundless, without basis in fact or reality."[8] Thus, the psalmist exclaims, "You have rejected all those who wander from Your statutes, for their deceitfulness is *sheqer* ["groundless, without basis in fact or reality."]." (Psalm 119:118)

Interestingly, the primary Greek word for truth is *aletheia*, which takes a different slant than that of *emeth*. It is derived from *alethes*, which is a compound of the Greek prefix "a" (corresponding to the English prefix "un") and the word *lanthano*, meaning concealed or hidden. So *alethes* literally means unconcealed. If you were describing a person of *alethes* you might say he was transparent, having no pretense, falseness, or duplicity. This sense is carried forth in the more common Greek term *aletheia*.

---

‡ See Appendix # 2 for a deeper study of these terms.

Recall what Jesus told Pilate in John 18:37, "For this I have been born, and for this I have come into the world, to testify to the *aletheia* [that which is utterly without pretense, falseness, or duplicity]. Everyone who is of the *aletheia* [who lives with this same quality of sincerity and genuineness] hears My voice." Pilate, steeped in the Roman system with all its false gods, could only come up with the lame response, "What is truth?" He was so full of deceit himself that he could not comprehend that the veritable Rock of truth from time immemorial was standing right in front of him. If his heart had been open to the truth, his life could have been radically and eternally changed.

Before we move on from this profound question ("What is truth?"), let's briefly consider the meaning of truth in the English language. One dictionary says that it is the "actual state of a matter: conformity with fact or reality."[9] That is the sense Americans have of the word truth, but there is a vital issue lying behind this definition that few consider: Who is the arbiter of the "actual state of a matter"? The problem is that every human's version of reality is determined by the whims, lusts, and pride of his own fallen nature. In the end, truth can only be delineated by someone who is uncontaminated by sin; someone who has access to all of the facts—those both in the physical and spiritual realms; someone who is omniscient and omnipresent. The only person who can properly define truth is Jesus Christ. Therefore, truth is reality as Jesus sees it, and those who wish to understand it must immerse themselves in His thoughts, words, and teachings.

WALKING IN TRUTH

We might as well come to grips with the fact that, aside from a major revival, America has passed the point of no return. Our pleasure-laden culture has made people so self-indulgent that they have little interest in eternal values. No wonder Truth is so undervalued in the U.S.

When I consider the solidity inherent in the word *emeth*— as it relates to our culture of humanistic relativism—the picture that forms in my mind is an immense mountain called Truth standing immovable and unshakeable in the midst of a wildly churning sea of uncertainty.

In his book, *The Truth War*, John MacArthur writes about the western mindset of our day:

> Postmodernism in general is marked by a tendency to dismiss the possibility of any sure and settled knowledge of the truth. Postmodernism suggests that if objective truth exists, it cannot be known objectively or with any degree of certainty. This is because (according to postmodernists), the subjectivity of the human mind makes knowledge of objective truth impossible. So it is useless to think of truth in objective terms. Objectivity is an illusion. Nothing is certain, and the thoughtful person will never speak with too much conviction about anything. Strong convictions about any point of truth are judged supremely arrogant and hopelessly naïve. Everyone is entitled to his own truth.[10]

I attest to the reality of his conclusion, but the battle which concerns me is not so much the cultural war—which has long since been lost. My concern is with the unseen yet very real battle raging within the sacred halls of Christianity. I see God's truth losing ground within two great bodies of professing Christians.

The first group is made up of those who are involved at some level with the movement known as the Emergent Church. Like the humanistic culture which it is married to, it is known for questioning the age old traditional understanding of the Christian life. I will address this in greater detail later, but for now I want to mention it in passing because it has created an opening in the evangelical movement for deception to influence the minds of millions of church youth. Sacred truths that were held as unshakeable a few decades ago are all now up for discussion.

The prophet Jeremiah lived in a similar period during the demise of the nation of Israel.§ At that time, the Lord beckoned, "'Stand by the ways and see and ask for the ancient paths, where the good way is, and walk in it; and you will find rest for your souls.'" (Jeremiah 6:16) We desperately need the Lord to raise up a Jeremiah to speak this word in the fire of God today!

The second group is made up of those churchgoers who know and hold to all the traditional doctrines, faithfully attend church services, and identify themselves as Christians, but who do not really live out the truth in their daily lives. This group's apathy toward Christianity is just as concerning to me as those caught up in the Emergent movement. Even in the Fifties A.W. Tozer identified this growing trend: "Millions of professed believers talk as if [Christ] were real and act as if He were not. And always our actual position is to be discovered by the way we act, not by the way we talk."[11] Or, as the Apostle Paul put it in his day: "They profess to know God, but by their deeds they deny Him…" (Titus 1:16)

If there is one thing I have learned for myself over the years it is that I must immerse myself in truth: think the truth, speak the truth, and, perhaps most important of all, live the truth. Truth must be something more tangible than an ethereal belief system. If the truth of Scripture is not a powerful force in my life, directing the way I think, speak, and act, then my witness for Christ will be meaningless and will even do damage to the name of the Lord and His kingdom.

---

§ This period of Israel's history is examined in greater detail in Book Three, Chapter One.

WALKING IN TRUTH IN A POST-TRUTH ERA

By the time the Apostle John wrote his three epistles and shared the great Revelation, the first century was drawing to a close. Deception had already made strong inroads into the Church—the institution that is supposed to be the depository of the Truth of God. Heretics and false teachers swarmed through the Christian community. Sincere but naïve believers, having been taught the importance of mercy and hospitality, were inviting these traveling apostates into their homes. (2 John 10) Church leaders were not standing up against their false teachings. In fact, Jesus had to rebuke the leadership of the churches in Pergamum and Thyatira for allowing such wolves to ravage their flocks. (Revelation 2:14, 20)

However, there *were* sincere believers who were committed to the Truth, no matter what it might cost them. One was a man living in Asia Minor named Gaius. In his third epistle, John encouraged him, "Beloved, I pray that in all respects you may prosper and be in good health, just as your soul prospers. For I was very glad when brethren came and testified to your truth, that is, how you are walking in truth. I have no greater joy than this, to hear of my children walking in the truth." (3 John 2-4)

Art Katz once told his listeners that in this last statement John was actually expressing the heart of God. I absolutely agree that this describes the Lord's feelings about His children. However, it begs the question, "What does it mean to 'walk in the truth'?"

The concept of walking to describe life's journey is a fairly common metaphor in Scripture. The Lord used it to describe a person's daily behavior: the way he acts and the way he lives. In short, you could say that it is a way to illustrate a person's lifestyle.

This really comes out in John's first epistle when he wrote, "If we say that we have fellowship with Him and yet walk in the darkness, we lie and do not practice the truth; but if we walk in the light as He Himself is in the light, we have fellowship with one another, and the blood of Jesus His Son cleanses us from all sin." (1 John 1:6-7)

As I touched on earlier, I have a great concern about the millions of professing Christians who hold to traditional orthodoxy but whose lives are more closely attuned to the spirit of the world than to the Spirit of truth. What does truth mean if it does not describe the reality of something? In this passage from his first epistle, John is telling his readers that they can profess Christ, but if the reality of their lives is that they are united to the darkness of this world system, they are only deceiving themselves. He reiterated this in Revelation when he said that, "everyone who loves and practices lying" will be barred from the New Jerusalem. (Revelation 22:15) As Matthew Henry posited, "The best evidence of our having the truth is our walking in the truth."[12]

This brings us full circle to the underlying premise of *emeth*: both truth and faith must be established in a person's heart for him to be saved. Or to say it negatively: a false-hearted Christian is not a genuine believer, whatever he may claim about himself. It is not possible to have faith in God and walk in deception. God is truth and we must be one with this Spirit of truth. If we are in fact united with the spirit of this world, we are deceived.

The Lord could have been speaking to us when He told Jeremiah, "You live in a world of deception…" (Jeremiah 9:6a CSB) and all those lies are affecting you and me far more than we realize. We must not—cannot—allow our hearts to be taken by the prevailing deceptions of our day. We must face the truth and live in the truth. However, to successfully accomplish this, we must first come to grips with some of the more blatant forms of deception coming forth from our culture.

WALKING IN TRUTH IN A POST-TRUTH ERA

"When a well-packaged web of lies has been
sold gradually to the masses over generations,
the truth will seem utterly preposterous
and its speaker a raving lunatic."
-DRESDEN JAMES[1]

"Let us never forget that truth, distorted
and exaggerated, can become the mother
of the most dangerous heresies."
-J.C. RYLE[2]

TWO:
HAS THE ACADEMIC SYSTEM BEEN LYING TO YOU?

There was a time when Christianity undergirded and pervaded every aspect of American society, including the educational structure. The Bible was not just an acceptable textbook for history and literature; it was the authoritative source for teaching character and morality. Noah Webster, known as "the schoolmaster of the republic" and author of the famed Webster's Dictionary, maintained that "education is useless without the Bible."[3] At least through the early part of the 20th century, biblical imagery, stories, passages, and lessons were incorporated in most of the popular textbooks.[4] The Lord's Prayer was commonly recited at the start of each school day and Christian belief and practices permeated academia.

But from the earliest days of the nation's founding, a competing philosophy was at work. The Enlightenment had swept through Europe and its influence was prominent in shaping the work of the Founding Fathers. The Enlightenment "advanced ideals such as liberty, progress, toleration, fraternity, constitutional government, and separation of church and state."[5] But more importantly, Enlightenment philosophy was "centered on the sovereignty of reason and the evidence of the senses as the primary sources of knowledge."[6] In other words, human intellect, natural reasoning, and the scientific method were considered superior to biblical truth and Christian faith.

With so many coming to the American colonies to escape religious persecution, the effect of this "humanist emphasis on science and reason in politics, the natural world, and learning, didn't take hold in schools until the 20th century."[7] But gradually Christianity was marginalized in the education arena and eventually replaced by a new enlightened and progressive system: Socialism.

At first glance, socialism is a theory that any conscientious person could endorse or even get excited about. If enacted, in its purest form, the idea is that it would instantly right the wrongs of society and put an end to poverty, starvation, deprivation, and most of the violence in which the world languishes. According to its proponents, socialism is the one political system that would answer the world's woes and bring it into a social utopia.

This belief system underlies and essentially controls the academic realm. The idea that people groups of all backgrounds— religious, socioeconomic, racial, ethnic, gender, and even sexual orientation—can live together in harmonious equality is a very powerful concept to the idealistic minds of young people.

Socialism sounds marvelous, but we really need to take a deeper look at the realities of socialism (i.e., the truth about it versus its advocates' spin) and how it is being used in our education system. Let's begin with a definition. According to Webster, socialism is "a system of society or group living in which there is no private property" and "in which the means of production are owned and controlled by the state."[8]

While the basic concept of socialism has been contemplated since ancient times, it really began to take root during the Industrial Age. As innovative production methods flourished, capitalist economies grew quickly. Men who owned modest manufacturing companies suddenly found revenues flowing into their coffers at an astonishing rate. Men like John

Rockefeller, J.P. Morgan, Henry Ford, Andrew Carnegie, and Cornelius Vanderbilt became the new titans of capitalism. Others were not far behind them.

These men were compelled by an insatiable lust for money and power. Perhaps their ambition would have been tolerable if it was only a matter of ingenious methodology, but it was more than that. These men "who oppress the poor, who crush the needy" (Amos 4:1), achieved their status at the expense of others. The laborers of the working class were expected to toil away for long hours in difficult working conditions while being paid just enough to keep them and their families from starvation.

Because of this gross injustice and inequality, the concept of socialism took hold in American culture. Social champions spoke of a better world, where prosperity would be for all to enjoy—not confined to a handful of ruthless men. Hope sprang up in the hearts of the downtrodden when they heard that there could be an escape from their endless merry-go-round of backbreaking work and squalid living conditions.

A SHIFT IN THE WORLDVIEW OF ACADEMIA

Not surprisingly, the academic realm proved to be a fertile breeding ground for socialist philosophy and the leftist propaganda it has birthed. "If you look at how to change society, well, one of the things you obviously do is you go after the next generation," comments Lt. General Jerry Boykin, former commander of Delta Force. "And you do that through the educational system. And that's exactly what has happened to us."[9]

Even when I was a child, the curriculum from which we were instructed was offered in a climate that was, for the most part, politically neutral. But those days are long gone. Today, nearly every course offered in both lower and higher education is laden with socialistic concepts, and, as I said before, this line of thinking finds a receptive audience amongst idealistic youth. In a thousand subtle ways, educators are pushing various aspects of the liberal agenda. Children are no longer taught to be grateful to be a part of the world's greatest nation; they are now taught to consider themselves citizens of the global village. Rather than thinking in terms of pursuing the American dream,* today's young people are taught to save the planet. Instead of offering a belief system with the moral underpinnings of Christianity, our youth are taught to discard such old-fashioned ideas in favor of humanism.

Perhaps the radicals of the Sixties and Seventies are to blame for the new mindset that has become entrenched in academic circles. I cannot say, but what is clear is that this new thinking has increasingly taken over our schools. In short, the minds of our children have been captured by leftist propaganda.

"In 1980, there was approximately 40% of Americans that were conservative, 10% liberal and 50% undecided," says film producer Curtis Bowers. "And since our numbers are showing that they [socialists] are capturing 85% of our young people each year through the educational system, this is how it plays out. In 2012, America was divided: 30% conservative and 30% liberal with 40% undecided... And by 2036, it will be 10% conservative and 70% liberal and 20% undecided. This is simply demographics."[10]

THE ALL IMPORTANCE OF DIVERSITY

The catch phrase in modern socialism is "diversity." Webster's Dictionary defines this term as, "the condition of having or being composed of differing elements: especially the inclusion of different types of people (such as people of different

---

* In the following chapter I will expose the deception that lies latent in that message as well.

races or cultures) in a group or organization…"[11] That is the strict definition of the word, but consider what one college says about it:

> The concept of diversity encompasses acceptance and respect. It means understanding that each individual is unique, and recognizing our individual differences. These can be along the dimensions of race, ethnicity, gender, sexual orientation, socio-economic status, age, physical abilities, religious beliefs, political beliefs, or other ideologies. It is the exploration of these differences in a safe, positive, and nurturing environment.[12]

It sounds rather utopic, does it not? It is so encouraging to see that religious beliefs of individuals are tolerated and accepted "in a safe, positive, and nurturing environment." But we all know that is simply not factual. A more honest evaluation of this new society is that in socialistic circles Christians are treated with the same type of disdain as the Jews of pre-war Germany.

No, the reality of "diversity" is something far different than the smooth explanation viewed above. One of the core beliefs of socialism is that there are minority groups that have been mistreated and therefore should be provided extra benefits. It is, in short, bias in reverse. White heterosexual males are at the bottom of the new social pecking order. Towering over them in this system are females, people of color, and non-heterosexuals, i.e., a Latina or African American lesbian would presumably find herself at the top of this hierarchy.

The reality of the socialism of Western academic circles is the belief that white America has, at best, taken advantage of minority groups; at worst, it has subjugated and abused them.[†] The typical thought that reigns in academic circles is that the onus is on white Americans to correct past wrongs through reparation. This is usually presented in regard to African Americans, but my guess is that it will only be a matter of time before it will cross into the ranks of the homosexual community as well.

So huge is the socialistic concept of diversity that it has even become the de facto litmus test of hiring teachers. In California, arguably the most "progressive" state in the U.S., most campuses require teaching applicants to submit a "contributions to diversity" statement as a part of their application. According to Kate Hardiman of the University of Notre Dame:

> The [National Association of Scholars] notes that many schools now link to articles explaining how to craft a diversity statement, which include affirmations that a professor will "keep the white students from dominating all classroom discussions," or "reflect a commitment to queer visibility," or teach students "not to thoughtlessly reproduce the standard white and Western model of legitimate knowledge."
>
> A focus on "racial oppression, sexism, homophobia, transphobia, ableism and other commonly recognized forms of oppression" has also been outlined as good fodder for diversity statements, according to a column in Inside Higher Ed.[13]

THE INCONTESTABLE FACT OF EVOLUTION

No examination of the current condition of the academic field is possible without touching on the theory of evolution—a belief system that is now totally entrenched in academia.

---

† There is truth to this, of course. Also true is the fact that 90% of this thinking is a thing of the past and opportunities and prosperity are open to people of color like never before.

HAS THE ACADEMIC SYSTEM BEEN LYING TO YOU?

It has been nearly a century since the comparatively simple arguments were offered by William Jennings Bryan and Clarence Darrow in the Scopes "Monkey" trial. In a criminal trial, jurors are mostly concerned with the prosecution's ability to establish a motive for the crime and evidence that would support its case. If the Scopes trial were held today, I would imagine that an honest jury would want to know if any scientific evidence has come forth during the past century that supports evolution. They would also want to look into any motives Darwin or his supporters might have to propagate their theory.

Let's consider the evidence together. The first thing the jury would encounter would be the difference between empirical science and historical science. The truth brought forth in empirical (or operational) science is built on experimentation. Historical science, on the other hand, is based largely on the presuppositions of the scientist (i.e., he builds his case on what he wants the outcome to be). Dr. Dana Sneed explains the difference between the two:

> If a scientist pours vinegar into a *papier-mâché* volcano filled with baking soda, the volcano will erupt with fizzy lava. This will happen each time, no matter how many times he repeats the experiment. No matter the scientist or his system of beliefs, we can trust his claim that vinegar reacts with baking soda.
>
> Not all that we call science, however, is operational science. While operational science focuses on what can be observed in the present, historical science uses scientific processes to gather and observe evidence in the present to determine what happened in the unobservable past. Because the past is not observable or repeatable, conclusions are more dependent on interpretations, assumptions, and presuppositions.

> Presuppositions refer to an individual's basic beliefs…
> The way a person interprets evidence is based on this
> set of presuppositions, his worldview. Even the most
> objective scientist has a worldview that will affect how he
> interprets evidence.[14]

The truth is that by now the enormous advancements in
science should be able to devastate creationist science with
irrefutable facts supporting evolution. But actually, just the
opposite is the case. John MacArthur has invested considerable
time studying this debate. Consider one point he discovered
regarding the claims of evolution:

> Every living organism has in it, DNA. DNA is genetic
> material and on that genetic material in every living thing
> is a code and that is an operative code. And that living
> organism, whether you're talking about a cell or whether
> you're talking about a large man and everything in between,
> all of that operation of every living thing is dependent on
> that encoded information. And listen to this, every different
> living thing has a completely different code.
> Darwin had no clue about that. There was no genetic
> study when he wrote his *Origin of Species*. He didn't know
> anything about DNA. He didn't know anything about
> chromosomes. He didn't know anything about genetics. It
> didn't exist as a science. He was just describing what he
> thought he was seeing…
> The big issue that is bringing down evolution is the
> study of the origin of information; it's called information
> theory. Where did the information come from? Where did
> the code come from? A monkey has a monkey code, and
> the DNA, and the chromosomes, and the genetics just
> keep making the monkey behave like a monkey. There's no

code in there to turn the monkey into a man. There's no such thing as jumping out of your species.[15]

The truth is that there is no evidence supporting Darwin's theories that could pass muster before a jury of impartial citizens. To get at the actual truth of what lies behind this theory, the jury would need to look into the motive of its proponents.

Scripture teaches that the material universe was created by an intelligent Designer of infinite intelligence and inexhaustible power. Mankind was created in His image with the capacity to enter into and maintain a relationship with Him.

However, atheism is the prevalent belief system dominating the fields of both education and science. Since these people are convinced that there is no God, there must be some other explanation as to the origins of the universe. Although Darwin expressed his misgivings about the theory he was putting forth, he staunchly held to it because the alternative to him was unthinkable. "I am determined," John MacArthur quotes him as saying, "to escape from design and a personal God at all costs."[16]

Now we are getting to the real issue. People do not want to be held accountable for their actions. It is precisely what the Creator Himself said, "This is the judgment, that the Light has come into the world, and men loved the darkness rather than the Light, for their deeds were evil. For everyone who does evil hates the Light, and does not come to the Light for fear that his deeds will be exposed." (John 3:19-21)

The real issue involved in the debate has nothing to do with scientific facts; it has to do with belief. Those who choose not to believe in God have concocted a different reality that supports the godless lifestyle they wish to pursue. They ignore the lack of credible scientific evidence to support evolution because they are determined to find an explanation—any explanation—other than creationism.

INDOCTRINATION

A massive deception has overtaken the educational system of the West. Its adherents absolutely believe what they teach. In fact, many liberals—at least in a purely human way—sincerely and earnestly believe their doctrines. They are so convinced that they see no point in considering views that lie outside their current perception.

It is this deep conviction of their beliefs that embolden them to espouse their views on young people. "Teachers have a captive audience of malleable young minds for several years," says Auguste Meyrat, an English teacher from the Dallas area. "They may not have figured out how to make students smart and productive, but they can at least make them submissive and obedient."[17]

Most children enter the system with a neutral outlook on political matters, but, unless their parents are taking the time to teach them biblical truth, chances are they will emerge from this twelve-to-eighteen-year program thoroughly indoctrinated in socialistic beliefs. Meyrat continues:

> While indoctrination involves pushing a certain opinion, it is also much more. It is the comprehensive effort of passively disseminating a particular viewpoint. The passive aspect is key. People who are indoctrinated with a certain narrative or ideology do not arrive at the intended conclusions through their own thinking, but hear the same thing repeated in a million different ways until they finally take it as unquestionable truth.
>
> Because indoctrination happens in the absence of thinking, many teachers who engage in indoctrination do so unconsciously. They themselves take what they're given and pass it along without thinking. Ideologues often intervene at this level by writing the scripts for

teachers, which is how LGBT advocacy and anti-Semitic fabrications become included in their lessons.

Thoughtlessness is essential. ... A person who really thinks will eventually reason himself out of the things he heard at school. ...

In such a system, thinking is only the articulation of opinion; it has no bearing on truth. This means that people don't really need to think critically and understand why they believe what they do. They just need to have the right viewpoint and force others to conform like they've been forced to conform. They engage in arguments where the loudest voice wins because no one's points are better than another. They pressure instead of persuade.[18]

The education system not only discourages honest discussion about different viewpoints, it simply does not allow it. Christian teachers who attempt to present a different perspective than the status quo are usually ostracized by other teachers and their administration. Likewise, brave students who attempt to question what they are being taught are nearly always silenced by the teacher. The icy response and hostile stares of indoctrinated classmates complete the suppression.

BULLYING TACTICS

There was a huge shift in the academic realm during the Sixties. It was then that the enemy successfully introduced the radical leftist beliefs that had already taken root in a handful of universities such as UC Berkeley. The takeover was pretty much complete within twenty years.

Prior to this coup, disagreement about social issues was typically handled in a civil manner. This was undergirded by the basic conviction that winning an argument is not the most important priority. Truth, along with the desire to treat one's opponent with respect, trumped victory in a debate.

This all changed in the Sixties when political activists, taking a page from the communist playbook, showed up in political events with bullhorns meant to disrupt the program of their political opponents, and blast the audience with their radical, leftist viewpoints. Their methodology was so effective that it is still employed today.

Alexander Riley of Bucknell University is concerned about what is happening in our school system. He explains how these methods are employed at universities to quell any opposition to the "diversity" belief system they espouse:

> This shout down culture rejects the old academic virtue of wide-ranging civil debate and embraces what is claimed, typically without argument, to be a superior method for settling debates: the emotional, personal indignation of the morally self-righteous.
>
> In the shout down worldview, calls for argument, evidence, and civility in disagreement are rejected as impediments to the more fundamental business of determining the rank of various historically aggrieved parties and catering to their emotional needs. Certain groups have suffered historic indignities and offenses, and members of those groups must be allowed to determine what is and what is not within the purview of debate according to the measuring stick of their outrage. If their outrage is sufficient—in their own subjective estimation, of course—then they have a right to shout down and physically intimidate to the point of shutting down those who adhere to the ideas that outrage them.[19]

Part of the issue is an arrogance built into the liberal mindset. That superior attitude, in turn, gives them the "right" to look down on those who disagree with them. "They aim not to provide a considered alternative to the ideas to which they object," Riley continues, "but only to prevent, through self-righteous incivility and the implicit threat of violence, the very expression of those ideas."[20]

The "implicit threat of violence" is a relatively new tactic which gained prominence when Donald Trump began holding enormous political rallies during his campaign for the presidency. It was then that masked thugs began showing up in different settings to intimidate and even attack anyone wearing a hat or shirt sporting the slogan, "Make America Great Again."

Another movement that began in Europe during the Sixties is Antifa (short for "anti-fascist").[‡] Ostensibly, their purpose was to counter Far Right groups such as skinheads and Nazis, but they have since taken on anyone with conservative values— no matter how mainstream those values might be.

While some antifa use their fists, other violent tactics include throwing projectiles, including bricks, crowbars, homemade slingshots, metal chains, water bottles, and balloons filled with urine and feces. They have deployed noxious gases, pushed through police barricades, and attempted to exploit any perceived weakness in law enforcement presence.

Away from rallies, they also engage in "doxxing," exposing their adversaries' identities, addresses, jobs and other private information. This can lead to their

---

‡ As I write this, riots are occurring in cities across America in response to the unfortunate death of George Floyd while in police custody. What began as peaceful protests, largely initiated by the African American community, quickly escalated into full-blown riots partially due to incitement from Antifa operatives. This clandestine organization has one overruling purpose: the overthrow of capitalism in favor of socialism.

opponents being harassed or losing their jobs, among other consequences.[21]

The current supercharged environment within Western schools will only become increasingly more charged with hatred and violence as the spiritual forces of darkness grow in strength. It is all part of a massive program of deception being orchestrated in the foul regions of hell.

This deception has long been embedded in academia and in the political landscape of Europe. It is now quietly, imperceptibly yet irresistibly, moving across America. Each generation that has emerged in the past fifty years has grown increasingly more liberal and more deceived. Yesterday's generation has become today's leaders. Every year our culture takes a further step into this deception. And, although it has a different face and comes with a different lure, it is also strongly at work within the commercialism of our day.

HAS THE ACADEMIC SYSTEM BEEN LYING TO YOU?

"Nothing can deceive unless it bears a plausible resemblance to reality... No one can deceive you unless he makes you think he is telling the truth."

-C.S. LEWIS[1]

"Propaganda is as powerful as heroin; it surreptitiously dissolves all capacity to think."

-GIL COURTEMANCHE[2]

THREE:
HAS BIG BUSINESS BEEN LYING TO YOU?

We live in an age of lust; lust for possessions, lust for experiences, lust for pleasure, and lust for entertainment. How did American culture go from simplicity and moderation to a frenzied pursuit of pleasure and possessions? And how did it come about that the American Church bought into this carnal and world-loving mindset?

For the better part of 6,000 years, people lived unhurried and uncomplicated lives. Even in the U.S., the pace of life remained fairly relaxed well into the 19th century. Most Americans lived on farms and spent the majority of their waking hours working in the fields. When they did make a trip into town to get supplies, it was done with their work-horse and wagon. In those days, a person's value tended to come from the quality of his character; his happiness was found in contentment, and many turned to God to find meaning in life.

But change was in the air. The Industrial Revolution of the 19th century opened the door for serious advancement in industry. The tycoons I mentioned in the last chapter led America into a new and exciting era. Inventors like Thomas Edison, Alexander Graham Bell, and the Wright Brothers opened the door into amazing new technologies. By the end of the century the U.S. was on the cusp of tremendous change.

Those innovations provided aspiring businessmen the ability to manufacture products in mass quantities. Their only dilemma now was how they could induce ordinary citizens to buy their merchandise.

In the past, if a merchant wanted to market his product, he would take out an ad in the local newspaper. These ads did not prove to be very effective, however. Hundreds of them could be found crammed together in the back of the newspaper in small print. But as the country approached the 20th century, savvy businessmen began finding ways to present their products with imagery—not just pictures of their products, but images that conveyed the sense that their goods would bring happiness to people's lives.

Gone were the days of simple living with all its tedium. America was undergoing a complete transformation as a nation. The U.S. became the first country in the world to develop an economy built on mass production and mass consumption.

Shrewd retailers learned early on that the key to success was found in their ability to market their goods. They figured out that it was the aggressive promoters who moved merchandise. These agents of progress learned to stir up desire in people by creating an association of their goods with comfort and pleasure.

Religion, moral values, and contented living were being replaced by a new, exciting lifestyle found in places like department stores, theaters, dance halls, and amusement parks. From our modern vantage point, these places seem like pretty tame fare, but in that day, when there was very little in life to entertain, this was a giant leap into a life of pleasure. Subsequently, interest in church began to wane, becoming little more than an obligatory intrusion into their increasingly busy lives.

As America entered the 20th century, marketing experts were in demand by retailers wanting to draw people into their department stores. Beautifully staged displays began appearing in large, bright showcase windows. Advertisements, filled with imagery showing the good life began appearing in newspapers. American housewives were told that they needed to keep up with the latest fashions and those who did not were made to feel like old maids, out of touch with the "in crowd."

The American culture was rapidly coming into a lifestyle built on coveting lust. A new way of thinking was taking hold in people's minds; gone forever were the days of simple contentment. In their place was a life of constant, unrelenting striving for more and more and more. This pursuit of pleasure and possessions fostered restlessness and stress and, when left unsatisfied, frustration, and resentment.

THE MARKETING OF FASHION

In 1861, John Wanamaker and his brother-in-law Nathan Brown opened a men's clothing store in Philadelphia named Oak Hall. For years Wanamaker had been contemplating innovative ideas about how to accomplish his dreams. Now he had the opportunity to put them into practice.

At the time, it was typical for customers to haggle with store owners over the price of goods—a practice that can still be seen in open air markets around the world. But Wanamaker was a professing Christian and he believed if everyone was equal in the eyes of God, then they should receive equal treatment in sales prices. So he inaugurated the business philosophy, "One price for all," inventing the price tag as part of it. Patrons would no longer feel like they had to argue with intimidating merchants to get a fair price on a product.

Another of his innovations was offering a money back guarantee. This was unheard of at the time and, as word got out, people began flocking to the little haberdashery. Later he would gain even more trust when he printed fliers showcasing his wares—another first. He was also the first retailer to place full-page ads in local newspapers to promote his products. "The time to advertise is all the time," he would say. And over time his honest business dealings paid off. Once people realized he delivered on what he promised, sales soared.

In 1868 Nathan Brown died and the following year John Wanamaker opened a second store. His business continued to flourish and in 1875 he purchased the freight depot of the Pennsylvania Railroad. He converted it into "The Grand Depot," which housed numerous specialty shops, thus becoming the first department store of Philadelphia.

Other innovations followed. In 1876 he opened an in-store restaurant and two years after that installed electric lights—something unheard of at the time. To keep inventory high and prices low, he created February "Opportunity Sales," July "Midsummer Sales," and in January 1878 the first "White Sale." He also hired a team of fashion experts who would travel to Europe every year for the purpose of acquiring trendy clothing considered to be in vogue. His persistent marketing campaigns convinced record numbers of people that they needed to stay up with the latest fashions if they wished to get ahead in life.

The Wanamaker Department Store became known as a palace of consumption that transformed the shopping experience into an exciting event. Trumpeted as "the largest space in the world devoted to retail selling on a single floor," the store featured 129 circular counters that ringed a central gas-lit tent for the demonstration of women's ballroom fashions. In time, he became known as "the greatest merchant in America."

He was a creative innovator, a merchandising genius and a proponent of the power of advertising. It would be hard to argue with his boast: "I single-handedly revolutionized the retail business in the United States."

HAS BIG BUSINESS BEEN LYING TO YOU?

John Wanamaker was a professing Christian who gave generous sums of money and verbally advocated for the cause of Christianity. However, his enduring legacy was how he used his profound influence as the nation's leading retailer to induce Americans to abandon their old traditions and buy into the life of consumption he aggressively advocated. So while he was honest in business, he was also guilty of promoting one of the devil's greatest lies: that fulfillment is only found in the dazzling offerings this temporary world provides.[3]

THE EMERGENCE OF PUBLIC RELATIONS

Perhaps you have never heard of the next subject of examination, but I can assure you that it was with good reason that *Life* magazine designated him as one of the "100 most influential Americans of the 20th century."

In 1891, Edward Bernays was born into the same Austrian family that produced Sigmund Freud.* Within a few years his family moved to New York, where he would major in agriculture at Cornell University. Whatever his interest had been in farming, by the time he graduated, his interest had changed to journalism.

Over the next several years, his writing became increasingly more involved in promotion, at one point acting as opera singer Enrico Caruso's press agent. His reputation in marketing grew, eventually earning him a place on Woodrow Wilson's Committee on Public Information. During World War One, his efforts were focused on building support for America's involvement in the war.

It was about this time that he began to take a closer look at the writings of his famous uncle. At the foundation of

* He was the double nephew of Freud: his mother was Sigmund's sister, and his father was the brother of Freud's wife.

Freud's beliefs was the notion that there is a subconscious area of the mind with which people are not in touch. Building on this, Bernays arrived at the conclusion that the masses could be "herded" into following the suggestions of a skilled promoter. He would later share those thoughts in his 1928 book, *Propaganda*:

> The conscious and intelligent manipulation of the organized habits and opinions of the masses is an important element in democratic society. Those who manipulate this unseen mechanism of society constitute an invisible government which is the true ruling power of our country. We are governed, our minds are molded, our tastes formed, and our ideas suggested, largely by men we have never heard of... It is they who pull the wires that control the public mind.[4]

It was this revelation that inspired him with the idea that if people could be manipulated into supporting war, they could be persuaded to see the value of peace. His time with Wilson's Committee on Public Information (CPI) had a great effect on his perceptions:

> There was one basic lesson I learned in the CPI—that efforts comparable to those applied by the CPI to affect the attitudes of the enemy, of neutrals, and people of this country could be applied with equal facility to peacetime pursuits. In other words, what could be done for a nation at war could be done for organizations and people in a nation at peace.[5]

Upon returning to New York, Bernays opened a public relations firm and busied himself with drumming up new business. He christened his method of promotion "the engineering of consent." Edward was a natural born salesman. When he coupled his own talents with the insights he received from Freud, he was able to manipulate the masses with devastating results.

During the following years, manufacturing giants such as General Electric, Procter & Gamble and the American Tobacco Company lined up to hire him. Perhaps a smattering of examples will better bring out just how effective were his methods.

In the election of 1920, Republican Warren Harding, along with his vice-president designate Calvin Coolidge, was elected president. Harding died of a heart attack in 1923, leaving the presidency to Coolidge. But the new commander-in-chief's dull personality and lack of ability to deliver a moving speech meant he faced an uphill battle if he were to win the upcoming presidential election. Edward Bernays was the perfect pitchman to change his stiff image.[†]

In 1924 Bernays set up a vaudeville "pancake breakfast" for Calvin Coolidge to change his stuffy image before the 1924 election. Entertainers including Al Jolson, John Drew, Raymond Hitchcock, and the Dolly Sisters performed on the White House lawn. The event was widely reported by American newspapers, with The New York Times running the story under the headline "President Nearly Laughs."[6]

Thanks in large part to Bernays' work, Coolidge won the presidency, but perhaps Bernays' most famous exploit was his promotion of Lucky Strike cigarettes. At the time, it was considered scandalous for a woman to smoke cigarettes—at least in public. This was a vice reserved for men only. It was

† In 1933, when told that Coolidge had died, satirist Dorothy Parker quipped, "How can they tell?"

the American Tobacco Company who first recognized that with the right marketing, half of the nation's untapped adult population could be enticed into smoking their cigarettes. They hired Bernays.

After studying the situation, he went to work. His first order of business was to launch an advertising campaign promoting the idea that being thin was the sign of beauty in women. He perpetuated this idea in print publications using photographs and paintings. The second step in his campaign was to foster the idea that smoking cigarettes curbed a woman's appetite. Medical authorities were hired to substantiate these claims. All of this was tied to the Lucky Strike brand.

His efforts accomplished the desired effect, but he still had to deal with the social stigma attached to women smoking in public. Feminists were already clamoring for the right to vote and arguing that females should be allowed the same rights as men. Bernays used this growing sense of female discontentment to argue the case that women had every right to smoke as did men.

At New York City's 1929 annual Easter parade, he arranged a demonstration featuring a number of sharp looking young women openly smoking. Tying smoking into the women's suffrage movement, he called cigarettes "torches of freedom." The subsequent ads he scripted gave the sense that a woman who smoked was more powerful and independent. The campaign became the stuff of legends.

Other devastatingly effective campaigns followed. Bernays would be remembered as the advertiser who could most effectively sublimate people into buying the products he promoted.

He would later look back over his achievements with great satisfaction. Throughout his long career as "the father of public relations," he maintained the premise that the "masses" are driven by the subconscious and that the key to getting them to do what one wants them to do is to appeal to that lower drive—something the Bible calls "the flesh."

"If we understand the mechanism and motives of the group mind," he once posited, "is it not possible to control and regiment the masses according to our will without their knowing about it? The recent practice of propaganda has proved that it is possible, at least up to a certain point and within certain limits."[7]

THE UPSHOT OF WANAMAKER AND BERNAYS

The groundbreaking innovations of John Wanamaker and Edward Bernays helped to usher the American public into an entirely new way of living. The first twenty years of the 20th century brought with it enormous societal changes. The "Roaring Twenties" proved to be the decade of decadence for both Americans and Europeans. This freefall into corruption was largely stymied by the Great Depression and World War Two, but with Western economies rebounding after the war, the good times began to roll once again.

In the Fifties, the increase of prosperity led city dwellers to begin moving in mass to the suburbs. The Sixties took this prosperity to unimagined heights, allowing people to indulge the lusts of their lower natures in inconceivable new ways. The sexual revolution introduced soft-core pornography and promiscuity into the U.S. The emergence of an entire subculture through illicit drugs deeply impacted the national attitude toward authority. It was a dramatic change from which the world could never recover.

These changes did not stop in the Sixties. Two more lines were crossed in 1973 when abortion was legalized and the adult entertainment industry was brought into mainstream America. All of this set the stage for the launching of the internet twenty years later. Technology has brought a level of corruption into our nation that would have been unimaginable in past centuries. It is all built on the lie that fulfillment can be found through indulging the flesh.

When a foundation of deception becomes embedded in a culture, smaller lies become more ingestible.

FALSE ADVERTISING

At first glance, it might not seem that deceptive practices occasionally employed in marketing should be anything with which to be overly concerned. But in reality it affects us more than we realize.

In 1946, President Harry Truman signed into law the Lanham Act. This bill was necessary to protect businesses from counterfeit trademarks and other fraudulent practices. Over time, this legislation was broadened to protect the consumer, as well. Today, this protection is afforded American citizens through the following legal enactment:

> Any person who... misrepresents the nature, characteristics, qualities, or geographic origin of his or her or another person's goods, services, or commercial activities, shall be liable in a civil action by any person who believes that he or she is or is likely to be damaged by such act.[8]

Unfortunately, the legal redress afforded in this consumer protection is not enough to stop many dishonest businessmen. The fact is that we are being lied to on a regular basis from many advertisers. Most of it simply leaves viewers and readers with an exaggerated sense about the value of a product. But there are also blatant lies coming our way more frequently than we might realize. "Your Dictionary" offers the following examples of misleading advertising methods:

+ Hidden fees - These are extra fees not specified in the advertised price, such as activation fees for cell phones or pre-delivery inspection charges on a new car.
+ "Going out of business" sales - This entails raising the prices from merchandise that was already on sale and then marking them down.
+ Changing the measurement units and standards - An example is changing from pounds and ounces to metric to hide the fact that the product was downsized.
+ Fillers - Food often has fillers to increase its weight, like meat injected with broth or brine...
+ Inconsistent comparison - This includes comparing a product to only the competitors it can beat.
+ Misleading illustrations - An example is showing the product in a picture as being bigger than it actually is...
+ Angel dusting - This is adding a very small amount of something beneficial so it can be labeled as such, like a cereal that contains 10 essential vitamins and the actual amount of them is less than one percent of the Recommended Dietary Allowance.
+ Bait and switch - This is advertising one product and substituting a similar product at a higher price, claiming the advertised product is unavailable or sold out.[9]

The truth is that this sort of deception is played out in front of us every day. The American public has become numb to being targeted with so many half-truths, exaggerations, and outright lies. We may not be able to discern each lie individually, but rather than insisting on holding businesses to higher standards, we just accept some level of dishonesty as normal.

This growing sense of mistrust brought about the overwhelming success of Amazon and smaller web-based companies such as Trip Advisor. The entrepreneurs who founded these businesses created sections for customer reviews, providing ratings and descriptions from an objective buyer's perspective. Consumers wearied by the incessant lies of ad men flock to such sites.

Services such as these have certainly helped alleviate consumer concerns, but they only go so far. For instance, customer ratings are not featured on television commercials, a medium which creates subliminal trust for products through repeated exposure. Moreover, a whole cottage industry has arisen whereby companies are able to buy fake reviews for their products.

Television, radio, and the internet are all involved in the overwhelming barrage of deceptive messages coming our way. To get to the bottom of this spiritual conspiracy, we must go back in time once again to examine the origins of the modern day media.

HAS BIG BUSINESS BEEN LYING TO YOU?

"Suppose someone invented an instrument, a convenient little talking tube which, say, could be heard over the whole land ... I wonder if the police would not forbid it, fearing that the whole country would become mentally deranged if it were used."

-SOREN KIERKEGAARD (C. 1813-1855)[1]

"Weak men may be content to echo the popular cries of the day. It is too often the mission of the servant of God to contradict these familiar voices."

-WALTER FREDERIC ADENAY[2]

FOUR:
HAS THE MEDIA BEEN LYING
TO YOU?

It was not a spiritual giant who predicted the technological future you and I call home, but actually two godless writers of the early 20th century.

By the time he was in his mid-thirties, Aldous Huxley had witnessed tremendous changes in his world. Inventions, innovations, and a massive, multi-nation war were quickly altering the landscape of the world. It seemed that the changes were coming so rapidly that he could not keep up with them.

With a certain foreboding, he took up his pen in 1931 and wrote a futuristic novel that was both compelling and disturbing. *Brave New World* described earth far into the future. It would be a dystopian society* run by an elite intelligentsia that would manipulate the masses through classical conditioning.

Eighteen years later, George Orwell penned his classic *Nineteen Eighty Four*, offering a different view of the future. He foresaw the time coming when Big Brother would be watching and controlling everything we do.

In his book, *Amusing Ourselves to Death*, Neil Postman offers the following comparison of the two:

---

* Utopian and dystopian describe societies with opposite conditions: Utopia is a world where everything is good; dystopia is a world that is undesirable or frightening.

What Orwell feared were those who would ban books. What Huxley feared was that there would be no reason to ban a book, for there would be no one who wanted to read one.

Orwell feared those who would deprive us of information. Huxley feared those who would give us so much that we would be reduced to passivity and egotism.

Orwell feared that the truth would be concealed from us. Huxley feared the truth would be drowned in a sea of irrelevance.

Orwell feared we would become a captive culture. Huxley feared we would become a trivial culture, preoccupied with some equivalent of the feelies, the orgy porgy, and the centrifugal bumblepuppy. As Huxley remarked in *Brave New World Revisited*, the civil libertarians, rationalists who are ever on the alert to oppose tyranny "failed to take into account man's almost infinite appetite for distractions."

In *1984*, Orwell added, people are controlled by inflicting pain. In *Brave New World*, they are controlled by inflicting pleasure.

In short, Orwell feared that our fear will ruin us. Huxley feared that our desire will ruin us.[3]

In spite of their strong sense of foreboding about the future, both Huxley and Orwell would be astounded to see where the technology of our day has taken us. While it is true that Huxley's version more aptly describes the world we currently live in, it seems that we are quickly entering an Orwellian era where cameras are installed everywhere we go; where facial recognition tracks our every movement; where our personal data is gathered and available for the government to access anytime they wish.

To better comprehend how we arrived where we are, we must briefly return to the past century.

THE BIRTH OF TELECOMMUNICATIONS

One of the chief differences between humans and every other species of animal is the capability for sophisticated communication. God created us with this ability so we could maintain a viable relationship with Him and also interact with other people.

The aptitude to read and write goes all the way back to ancient times, but communication over long distances would not be developed until the early part of the 19th century. The invention of the telegraph, with the code developed by Samuel Morse, created the first telecommunication system in the world.

In the 1860s, a man named James Clerk Maxwell proved that light waves traveled through space. This groundbreaking discovery led other scientists to the conclusion that they could actually send audio signals through the air.

It was around 1900 that Serbian-American scientist Nikola Tesla[†] and Italian physicist Guglielmo Marconi each played major roles in producing the first broadcasts. Two events occurred in succeeding years that revealed the extent of the breakthrough in radio transmissions. In the Russo-Japanese war of 1904-1905, the Japanese navy, using radio equipment purchased from Marconi, were able to receive intelligence as to the exact location of the Russian fleet, which was quickly decimated in the Battle of Tsushima. Seven years later, the Titanic sank in the Atlantic, but, through the use of radio transmissions, ships in the region were able to receive the Titanic's distress signals and rescued 711 passengers who otherwise would almost certainly have drowned.

---

† The electric car developed by Elon Musk was named after Nikola Tesla in recognition of his accomplishments.

All of this was done through the wireless transmission of simple Morse code signals. Innovative breakthroughs by Canadian Reginald Fessenden and Edwin Howard Armstrong allowed transmitters to send out more than dots and dashes. These advances soon led to transmitting voice and music over the airwaves.

In 1920, KDKA in Pittsburgh became the first commercial radio station to go on the air. By the end of the Roaring Twenties, there were hundreds of radio stations operating throughout the United States. In 1934, the Federal Communications Commission (FCC) was established. This served to bring some order to the growing field of broadcasting. Radio Corporation of America (RCA) wasted no time building a monopoly in radio through its subsidiary, the National Broadcasting Company (NBC). The FCC eventually stepped in and broke up this monopoly, forcing NBC to launch out on its own and making way for the American Broadcasting Company (ABC) to be formed.

In the meantime, advertisers were quick to jump into this new kind of communication.

The first recognized form of radio advertising came in early 1922 when AT&T began to sell toll broadcasting opportunities, in which businesses could underwrite or finance a broadcast in return for having their brand mentioned on air. Later that year, the New York radio station WEAF was the first station to run an official paid advertisement...

By 1930, almost 90% of radio stations in the United States were broadcasting commercials. This ushered in the golden age of radio, which lasted from the early 1930's through the late 1940's. Stations were generating enough revenue to support their operations and increase their offerings. As the demand for ads began to rise, stations began pre-recording the commercials instead of presenting them live...[4]

With the advent of television, the radio industry experienced an initial drop-off in listenership as families now began to gather around the big box of tubes with the tiny screen set up in the living room. By the mid-Fifties, most radio stars had transitioned to television. However, as the automobile industry boomed, car radios provided new life for the medium, ensuring radio would have a niche in American culture for decades to come.

To this day radio plays a vital role in shaping public attitudes:

+ Although other media and new technologies now place more demands on consumer's time, 95% of people still listen to the radio every week.[5]
+ U.S. Internet radio listening is also growing rapidly, rising from 12% in 2002 to over 50% in 2015.[6]
+ Although consumers have more choices today, a 2009 study reported that 92% of listeners stay tuned in when commercials break into their programming.[7]

TELEVISION—A HUGE STEP TOWARD A BRAVE NEW WORLD

No sooner had the broadcasting of audio signals been conceived than man was already working feverishly to transmit imagery across the airwaves. As early as 1911 a Russian named Boris Rosing was attempting the feat. But it would be another sixteen years before a 21-year-old man named Philo Farnsworth would actually accomplish it. One day he astounded the world when he was able to broadcast and receive on a crude screen the image of a simple line.

RCA, having been the pioneer in the production of radio stations and the radio sets which would retrieve their broadcasts, was also forward looking enough to invest $50 million in the development of television broadcasting. By 1939, this new industry had matured sufficiently to transmit a telecast of New York's World's Fair, including a speech by President Franklin Roosevelt. Just as they had done with radio during the previous decade, RCA began manufacturing the first television sets, offering a picture tube that was five inches by twelve inches.

Early television was quite primitive. All the action at that first televised baseball game had to be captured by a single camera, and the limitations of early cameras forced actors in dramas to work under impossibly hot lights, wearing black lipstick and green makeup (the cameras had trouble with the color white). The early newscasts on CBS were "chalk talks," with a newsman moving a pointer across a map of Europe, then consumed by war. The poor quality of the picture made it difficult to make out the newsman, let alone the map. World War II slowed the development of television, as companies like RCA turned their attention to military production.[8]

It was in 1947 that television broadcasting began in earnest. Over the next few years, many new programs premiered, such as *The Texaco Star Theater* with Milton Berle and a children's show called *Howdy Doody*. News shows were also featured in those early days. CBS News offered Douglas Edwards while NBC News was anchored by John Cameron Swayze. Radio stars such as Jack Benny and Milton Berle were quick to move to the new media. The first program that dominated was *I Love Lucy*, which aired from 1951 to 1957. Television sales skyrocketed from 6,000 sets in 1946 to nearly twelve million five years later as word spread about this new source of entertainment. By 1955, half of American living rooms had TV sets in them.

One of the longest airing TV programs has been *The Tonight Show*, which commenced in 1954 hosted by Steve Allen. Jack Paar took over three years later and Johnny Carson five years after him. Game shows (*The $64,000 Question*) and dramas (*Kraft Television Theater*) provided other genres to fill out broadcasting schedules.

And who could ever forget how a personable John Kennedy captured the White House from the hands of an awkward looking Richard Nixon in the first airing of a presidential debate? A few years later, war correspondents in Vietnam would forever strip away romantic notions of war when they showed the harsh realities U.S. soldiers were facing on the other side of the world. In the early Seventies, sitcoms such as *All in the Family* and *M.A.S.H.* helped usher into American culture a new standard of values and ethics that openly challenged traditional morality.

Cable television opened up an entirely new system of communication. In 1975, HBO became the first cable network to grab a share of the audience. It was soon followed by TBS, ESPN, C-SPAN and CNN. The emergence of satellite technology later made it possible for hundreds of networks to reach the lucrative American audience from around the world. The quality of network broadcasting persistently improved while its reach continued to expand.

There is no question that the advent of media has put into the hands of Satan a tremendous tool with which he can control the world's thinking. The "prince of the power of the air" has an ingenious system at his disposal whereby he can pump his message into the homes and hearts of people worldwide. The devil has always been a master of mixing falsehood in with truth and he does this on a regular basis through the media.

Political news is especially susceptible to being manipulated. For example, in response to the coronavirus pandemic, President Trump called for March 15, 2020 to be a National Day of Prayer. His proclamation referenced three passages from the Bible, including this statement: "As your President, I ask you to pray for the health and wellbeing of your fellow Americans and to remember that no problem is too big for God to handle. We should all take to heart the holy words found in 1 Peter 5:7: 'Casting all your care upon him, for he careth for you.' Let us pray that all those affected by the virus will feel the presence of our Lord's protection and love during this time. With God's help, we will overcome this threat."[9] This wonderful call from our president received little or no coverage in the news media. What was widely reported was this unsolicited comment by Governor Andrew Cuomo several weeks later, as cases in New York (the deadliest hotspot in the U.S.) showed remarkable improvement: "The number is down because *we* brought the number down. God did not do that. Faith did not do that. Destiny did not do that. A lot of pain and suffering did that" (his emphasis).[10] And in a CNN interview the next day, Cuomo reiterated his stance: "Our behavior has stopped the spread of the virus," he claimed. "God did not stop the spread of the virus."[11] That is one blatant example of how the enemy mixes his message into a factual news report. Of much more importance is the many subtle ways the enemy propagates his message: creating suspicion about subjects such as creationism; promoting the idea of living for the things this world offers; casting doubt on God's existence or His character, and so on.

Satan is using the media to bombard mankind with his value system and most Christians are willing to allow this to happen. We are unquestionably being lied to in a myriad of ways through the media.

THE FAKE IN FAKE NEWS

President Donald Trump regularly uses the term "fake news" to describe unfair or negative comments about him, but it was actually popularized in 2014 by Craig Silverman, media editor of BuzzFeed News. According to Wikipedia, fake news "is a form of news consisting of deliberate disinformation or hoaxes spread via traditional news media (print and broadcast) or online social media."[12] Whoever coined the term, there is a lot of it and it comes in various forms and from different sources.

It seems that the mainstream outlets for both print and broadcast journalism have always leaned left, but over the past twenty or thirty years the shift has become more dramatic. As in the case of the teaching profession, it is apparent that there is a liberal mindset embedded within the press corps. Have you ever noticed how often the "expert" being interviewed by the news reporter is another journalist, or worse, a biased activist? Instead of presenting a balanced view on any given issue, opposing viewpoints are discouraged or even forbidden. Occasionally the opposing viewpoint is presented, but it is usually a skewed or exaggerated version of that opinion.

In conjunction with promoting a liberal slant in the news, polls and statistics are manipulated to push whatever view the news authority prefers. I once heard someone say that "nothing determines public opinion like a public opinion poll"—in other words, people haven't thought about or decided what they believe on a topic until they hear the results of some poll.

Instead of gathering information and weighing the issue, they tend to accept the majority opinion as their own. There is an instinctive desire to be in the majority; after all, who wants to be an outcast?

Having said that, there is more to the "fake" in fake news than manipulating statistics and adding a liberal bias to stories. From the very beginning, newscasts in America have been first and foremost concerned with profit. Coverage of a gruesome death in the Bronx in an 1880s newspaper was only printed for its titillating effects. In other words, the point of it was and is to entertain. As Neil Postman brought out in his book, news stories (with the possible exception of political news) were never meant to convey information that has a personal and pertinent effect on our lives.

No matter what is depicted or from what point of view, the overarching presumption is that it is there for our amusement and pleasure. That is why even on newscasts which provide us daily with fragments of tragedy and barbarism, we are urged by the newscasters to "join with them tomorrow." What for? One would think that several minutes of murder and mayhem would suffice as material for a month of sleepless nights. We accept the newscasters' invitation because we know that the "news" is not to be taken seriously, that it is all in fun, so to say. Everything about a news show tells us this—the good looks and amiability of the cast, their pleasant banter, the exciting music that opens and closes the show, the vivid film footage, the attractive commercials—all these and more suggest that what we have just seen is no cause for weeping. A news show, to put it plainly, is a format for entertainment, not for education, reflection or catharsis.[13]

HAS THE MEDIA BEEN LYING TO YOU?

My wife and I have not had network television in our home since 1985, but if I want to stay up on what is happening, I generally go to the Fox News website to peruse the headlines. One thing I have noticed is how little focus Fox gives to general news stories. The featured story of the day is nearly always politically based—and always with a conservative slant.‡

Actually, it seems that most of the shows on Fox are more geared toward controversy than straight news reporting. This format originated on *Crossfire*, a current events debate program that began airing on CNN in 1982. Writing for *The Washington Spectator*, Matt Taibbi says, "*Crossfire* trained us to see our world not just as a binary political landscape but as one permanently steeped in conflict."[14] He goes on to add the underlying point in all of this controversy:

> We've discovered we can sell hate, and the more vituperative the rhetoric, the better. This also serves larger political purposes.
>
> So long as the public is busy hating each other and not aiming its ire at the more complex financial and political processes going on off-camera, there's very little danger of anything like a popular uprising...
>
> The news today is a reality show where you're part of the cast: *America vs. America*, on every channel...
>
> Fox nailed the formula of the modern news story. Forget just doing a cable variety show with conservatives and liberals engaged in ritualized fighting. Why not make the whole news landscape a rooting section?[15]

Taibbi is making the point that news departments are more concerned about the increased ratings such antagonistic

‡ Of course, this only counters the heavily left-leaning fare seen on CNN and other mainstream media outlets.

programs garner than they are about presenting legitimate news stories. No matter how you look at it, ultimately, news is printed and broadcasted to make a profit—not to present an impartial and trustworthy narrative of something significant occurring in the world.

Whether it is Fox or CNN, the main fare you will receive will be a report meant to appeal to a right- or left-leaning audience. The bottom line is that time devoted to preferred stories by conservative and liberal reporters is time that is not spent presenting relevant and honest depictions regarding events occurring in the world.

BIG BUSINESS INFLUENCE

Another reason to distrust information coming through the media is because broadcast news is now in the hands of mega-corporations. In 1986, General Electric bought NBC. In 1996, the Walt Disney empire purchased ABC. In 1999, Viacom paid $36.5 billion for CBS. In 2019, Fox Corporation purchased 21st century Fox, creating a new mega-conglomerate called "New Fox."

Is this something that should concern us? I think so. Consider the following story detailed on a documentary entitled *Shadows of Liberty*.

Roberta Baskin, Chief Correspondent of CBS News from 1992-1997, discovered the hard way that there are stories reporters do not have the freedom to investigate. It began in August of 1996 when she and a film crew flew to Vietnam to investigate a Nike factory using cheap labor. The feature won her the DuPont Award for investigative excellence. It was not long before her employer sent her back to the Far East to do a follow-up.

While in the middle of production, she was unexpectedly ordered to squelch the show. Baskins relates, "I got a call from my executive producer who said, 'The story is not going to air. It's been taken off schedule. There's some sort of deal being made between Nike and CBS News for the upcoming winter Olympics.'"[16]

After seeing "correspondent after correspondent" sporting jackets with Nike logos emblazoned across the shoulders, she fired off a 2-page letter to Andrew Heyward, President of CBS News (with copies also to Dan Rather and other executives), complaining that CBS reporters were essentially walking billboards for a company she had so recently exposed.

Brian Healy, who was a producer for CBS News from 1972-2010, agreed with her assessment. "CBS News was paying an enormous amount of money for the rights and so by definition they would be seeking out commercial sponsors who would pour lots of money into it so they could recoup the millions they would be paying for the rights to the Olympics."[17]

Not long after she sent the letter to Heyward, she was removed from her position as the chief correspondent for CBS News. "It wasn't an ordinary transfer, a change;" Healy says, "it was a demotion. And it was a demotion to send a message."

"CBS had crossed this incredible line," Baskin recalls "How do you trust serious stories when you're seeing the reporter wearing a bunch of logos?"

Yes, and that is exactly the point of including this internal squabble amongst newscasters. When news organizations are controlled by powerful corporations, it is inevitable that fair reporting will eventually be compromised.

THE DANGER OF MEDIA INFLUENCE

There is no question that radio and television have played enormous roles in the disintegration of American morality. The effects of the media are powerful in shaping American life.

Few inventions have had as much effect on contemporary American society as television. Before 1947 the number of U.S. homes with television sets could be measured in the thousands. By the late 1990s, 98 percent of U.S. homes had at least one television set, and those sets were on for an average of more than seven hours a day... It is significant not only that this time is being spent with television but that it is not being spent engaging in other activities, such as reading or going out or socializing.[18]

Nowadays, most homes have two or three TVs, sometimes taking up entire walls. Furthermore, just in case they are out when their favorite show comes on, they can watch it on their tablet or smart phone.

It cannot be stated strongly enough the enormous spiritual implications that television has had on our nation. It has been used by the enemy to establish a corporate consciousness which determines the rules of life. It has created a cultural consensus about what are acceptable and unacceptable norms of living. It tells us how we should think, how we should live and what should be important to us. When will Christians come to grips with the fact that they cannot trust the information being transmitted through the media—whether it is a newscast, a drama, or a sitcom? Each program carries the agenda set forth by the values of Hollywood. Billy Graham once exhorted believers to beware of the effects of television:

I think television is having a detrimental effect on Christians. They are no longer sensitive to sin... TV has brought the night club into the home along with violence and sex—things which Christians looked upon ten years ago with abhorrence... Christians are generally becoming desensitized, and I can cite case after case where they now watch these things on TV without feeling any tinge of conscience.[19]

Although the potential would have been there to influence people toward the Truth, we must not forget that "the prince of the power of the air" (Ephesians 2:2) is the one who presides over the airwaves. He has his own twisted version of truth. It was for good reason that Isaiah warned, "Woe to those who call evil good, and good evil; who substitute darkness for light and light for darkness..." (Isaiah 5:20) That biblical warning accurately represents the values presented on television.

This is why I have written extensively about the need for believers to show extreme caution about subjecting their minds and hearts to secular programming. It is based in falsehood and its influences are powerful.

As influential as television and radio are on the hearts and minds of humans, another media has emerged which may very well become even more formidable.

"Honesty is the rarest commodity in the 21st century. No one looks to the political class or journalists for truth these days. The average Joe seems to spend most of their time peddling a ludicrous, flawless Facebook version of their lives. The peer pressure of political correctness forgoes truth for the sake of groupthink."

-STEWART STAFFORD[1]

"Society has become so fake that the truth actually bothers people. Who wants or needs the Truth? Lies are so much more useful to people in their day-to-day lives."

-ADAM WEISHAUPT[2]

FIVE:
HAS THE INTERNET BEEN LYING TO YOU?

Troy and Malcolm are both currently serving time in California prisons, but I can remember a more innocent time when the three of us—along with a few other friends—used to play touch football on our street in Sacramento. Then, seemingly out of nowhere, drugs began appearing and all three of our lives took a ruinous route that left us spent and disillusioned at an early age. The next forty-some years for them were spent in and out of prison.

In many ways it was tough growing up in the close quarters of our neighborhood. Kids were regularly sized up and tested with no place to hide. Sure, we had fun, we talked, we played, we argued, we fought, and sometimes we got in trouble together. But at the end of the day we knew each other on an intimate level simply because we spent a lot of time together.

Those are the days of a bygone era. Today's young people grow up in a vastly different world. The neighborhood in which they spend most of their time is called cyberspace. Addresses are no longer associated with streets and house numbers; they now end with .com. Interactions with peers do not occur so much out on the streets but through text messages and posts. The painful give-and-take world of personal relationships is now largely avoided through this new form of social interaction that occurs almost exclusively through apps on their iPhones.

Young people have become increasingly more emotionally detached from each other, unable to relate on intimate terms. Friends are merely profiles, quickly "liked" and then just as easily "unliked."

This virtual form of interaction is also making it increasingly easy to project a false image of themselves—conveying to others the person they imagine themselves to be. Of course, the worst scenario in the mind of a teenager is doing something to embarrass himself. So, rather than facing the awkwardness and stresses of real-life conversations and encounters—where shallow façades would be exposed—today's world allows young people to create their own reality through complimentary pictures and selective comments. What young people are offering others is an illusion—a flattering image of themselves which they want others to buy into.

Young people wishing to be seen in the most favorable light are not limited to putting on their best face, either. There are now online services which will help approval-needy individuals oversell themselves by exaggerating the number of "likes" they've accumulated on their social media accounts. Consider the following:

> On Instagram, manufacturing fake followers is a ubiquitous tactic, one that's churned out at least 95 million near-perfect human forgeries for you to brush past in the digital hallways, unaware. You can buy them in droves from dozens of services online, or even from a coin-operated vending machine created by artist Dries Depoorter. He calls his fame dispenser "Quick Fix": a wall-mounted box with an Arduino and a keyboard, where visitors can type in their social media handles and select what faux honorific they'd like to receive—likes or follows, starting at just one euro, delivered instantly.[3]

HAS THE INTERNET BEEN LYING TO YOU?

Today's youth intuitively understand that they are not the only ones hyping themselves—everyone is doing it! Life on the internet is teaching them that honesty is not the best policy for gaining the recognition and approval of others. Successfully playing the deception game is the way to get ahead.

THE BIRTH OF THE INTERNET

We live in a world that Aldous Huxley and George Orwell could not have conceived. Their imagination could only take them so far back in the Thirties and Forties. They had pieces of the puzzle—faint as they may have been—to what the world would become in the 21st century. However, they were missing a huge piece, which another contemporary of theirs more clearly imagined.

In 1936, H.G. Wells envisioned the day when a world brain would become a central repository of mankind's knowledge. "The whole human memory can be, and probably in short time will be, made accessible to every individual," he wrote. "It need not be concentrated in any one single place. It need not be vulnerable as a human head or a human heart is vulnerable. It can be reproduced exactly and fully, in Peru, China, Iceland, Central Africa, or wherever else seems to afford an insurance against danger and interruption."[4]

As remarkable as it is to grasp, Wells envisioned a world brought together by the internet. Of course, the internet would not even be conceived until the Cold War of the Sixties. It was invented by the U.S. Defense Department for the purpose of having a technology that would make it possible to disseminate information even in the event of a nuclear attack.

Scientists employed by the U.S. government created computers that were able to share information with each other. Once this was accomplished, they set up host computers at four locations in the U.S. and in 1969 the first host-to-host message was sent between UCLA and the Stanford Research Institute.

By 1972, there were at least fifteen such sites and it was then that the InterNetworking Group was created to establish standards for networking. Over time this formed the working name we have all come to know: the internet. It was also about this time that email was first used in controlled settings.

January 1, 1983 is considered the official birth day of the internet because it was then that a universal language was established which allowed different kinds of computers on different networks to talk to each other. By the following year, there were a thousand hosts on the Internet. The Domain Name System (DNS) was introduced that year, paving the way for the dot-com world we currently live in.

The general public gained access to the Internet on July 16, 1986 when the first Freenet came on-line in Cleveland. Between 1987 and 1989 the number of hosts increased from 10,000 to 100,000.

With the development of the World Wide Web in 1991, there was no stopping the rapid expansion of the Internet. No longer did users need to learn complicated commands in order to access the information on the internet. They only had to download an internet browser, such as Netscape in order to access information on the web. Other countries began joining the internet, thus taking the first steps toward globalization.

One of the most important events came in 1995 with the provision of dialup access to the internet by new international service providers (ISPs) such as America Online (AOL), thus giving millions of ordinary folks a chance to surf the web.

By 1996, the number of hosts approached 10 million in 150 countries worldwide. As of January 2019, there were nearly two billion websites. China leads the world with some eight hundred million users; the U.S. is second with 320 million and

Russia follows with 109 million users. In 1995, approximately 1% of the world's population had an internet connection. In 2018, that number was 40%—and rising.

THE TWO RISING GIANTS

By the end of 1996, there were some 36 million users of the internet worldwide. And it was in that year that two Stanford PhD students named Larry Page and Sergey Brin teamed up on a project to better understand the inner workings of the internet. Page was a computer science major while Brin was a mathematician. After months of trial and error, the team created an internet search engine they called Google, a name they hoped would reflect the idea of huge numbers of users.* Within two years of its startup, Google had indexed some 60 web pages. As the number of users grew, Brin and Page started focusing on ways to make a profit from their efforts. Rather than cluttering the homepage of Google with ads, they began selling keywords to advertisers, beginning at $.05 per click. The finances of the newly formed company soon began rolling in.

Google was by no means the only search engine operating at the time. Yahoo, Ask Jeeves and others were offering their services, but they were basically indexes of websites hosted throughout the internet. By focusing their attention on algorithms, Brin and Page figured out how to list websites found in any given search by the amount of traffic they were receiving. It was this page ranking ability that began to separate them from the pack in those early days.

Today, Google dominates the cyber-search landscape, processing somewhere between seven and ten billion search queries per day, while accounting for 68% of all searches.

---

* The name Google is taken from a mathematical term for 10 to the 100th power; or essentially a number so large as to become incomprehensible—a prescient depiction of the vast quantity of information now available on the web.

Facebook (FB) is a social networking service that is responsible for connecting billions of people worldwide. Its boast is that it serves a public function by allowing people to stay in touch with family members and friends wherever they might be in the world. It also allows people with similar interests to unite together behind their cause.

Each profile functions more or less as a personal public relations page. The user presents himself to the world through pictures, videos and printed content. Visitors can respond to each post with various reactions, the most famous being "like" and "unlike." Unquestionably, FB has forever changed the way people of the world communicate with each other.

Facebook's founder Mark Zuckerberg was raised in a Jewish home in White Plains, NY. By the time he was admitted entrance into Harvard, he had already established a reputation as an internet whiz, capable of building online games and websites. He quickly found himself in hot water with school officials when he created a website of Harvard students called Facemash, which paired up the pictures of students with the question, "Who is hotter?" He was later forced to offer a public apology saying that what he did was "completely improper."

The following semester, in January 2004, Zuckerberg was approached by three other students about joining them in building a social networking site called Harvard Connection. Zuckerberg stayed with them long enough to learn the functions of their project and then created his own website he called, *thefacebook.com*.[†]

In just three years, by late 2007, it was estimated that Facebook was worth some $15 billion. During the next five years, the number of users increased from 100 million to 1

---

† By all accounts Zuckerberg stole their ideas which he used to create Facebook. The other students eventually sued him and were awarded 1.2 million shares of Facebook stock.

billion people—a number that has since more than doubled. Today, the social media giant is worth over $600 billion and has acquired over 70 rival (or potential rival) tech companies, including WhatsApp and Instagram, to ensure its ongoing dominance of the social media market.

KNOWING YOU AND SELLING YOU

Somewhere along the way, the Google team realized that their real ability to make money was in the data they were logging on individual users. It began with the premise that by tracking and storing information such as what subjects the user searched for, what websites the user visited, what products the user purchased online, and so on, they could create a profile of the person's interests and needs. Then they could sell that information to companies who would populate websites the person visited with ads about their products.

According to Dr. Robert Epstein, Google soon figured out how to branch out in order to retrieve even more of our personal data.

They were getting a lot of information from people using the search engine, but if people went directly to a website, uh oh, that's bad because now Google doesn't know that. So they developed a browser, which is now the most widely used browser in the world, Chrome. By getting people to use Chrome, they were able now to collect information about every single website you visited whether or not you were using their search engine. Of course, even that's not enough because people do a lot of things on their mobile devices... So Google developed an operating system, which is called Android, which on mobile devices is the dominant operating system. Android records what we're doing even when we are not online. As soon as you connect to the internet, Android uploads to Google a complete history of where you've been that day, among many other things. It's a progression of surveillance that Google has been engaged in since the beginning.[5]

According to Dylan Curran, a data consultant and web developer, Google possesses an amazing amount of information about individuals. If a person has location tracker turned on, they know where you are and where you have been physically. In fact, they have a timeline of all your travels, both near and far. They know every subject you have searched for—even if you have deleted it.

Google stores information on every app and extension you use. They know how often you use them, where you use them, and who you use them to interact with. That means they know who you talk to on Facebook, what countries are you speaking with, what time you go to sleep...

This is one of the craziest things about the modern age. We would never let the government or a corporation put cameras/microphones in our homes or location trackers on us. But we just went ahead and did it ourselves...[6]

Google knows what YouTube videos you have watched. They have an inventory of your bookmarks, emails (coming and going), contacts, photos you have taken, items you have purchased and things you have considered purchasing.

Using all of this data, Google has created a profile of you— your age, address, gender, hobbies, interests, career, health, political leanings, emotional struggles—in short, practically everything that describes you as an individual. This information is sold to the highest bidders, ostensibly to serve you by offering you the sort of products you would be interested in.

Like Google, Facebook is also a surveillance website. They too store every bit of information they have gleaned during the time you spend utilizing their service. Every text, photo or audio message you have ever sent or received is filed away in their records. It too forms a profile of you, based on the things you have written about yourself and the conversations you have had with others. It does not stop there, either. They keep track of the time, device, and location every time you log in to Facebook. Dylan Curran shares the extent of their surveillance of your life:

> The data they collect includes tracking where you are, what applications you have installed, when you use them, what you use them for, access to your webcam and microphone at any time, your contacts, your emails, your calendar, your call history, the messages you send and receive, the files you download, the games you play, your photos and videos, your music, your search history, your browsing history, even what radio stations you listen to.[7]

If our privacy issues were only a matter of the two giants, perhaps greater pressure would be exerted to curtail their activities. But the truth is that there are a host of other sites also surveilling us. Dating services, health care providers, credit card companies, department stores, and so on are all in on this financial bonanza.

Selling personal information has become big business in cyberspace. Of course, all of this is hidden from the average internet user. And let's face it, people are so busy and stressed out that they do not have the time or energy to deal with it. I can understand this laissez-faire attitude among unbelievers because they are part of the world system lying in the bosom of the evil one. What is difficult to fathom is the lack of concern

Christians show about it. We are quickly moving into Orwell's dystopian world of *Nineteen Eighty-Four*, and we seem to be so wrapped up in the world that we no longer care. Considering where this world is headed, this apathy is ominous news.

UNDUE INFLUENCE

Unfortunately, this control over our lives does not end at data gathering. One of the hidden dangers of using Google is the amount of misplaced trust we have given to it. Let me explain. When we do a search, we have come to trust that Google is going to give us the best choices available. Even more helpful is the little box at the top of the list that offers simplified answers to whatever questions we pose. All of this—perhaps rightly so—builds our trust in Google's ability to deliver what we are looking for.

What we often do not realize is that Google is also functioning as a filter, sifting potential results and ranking them on our behalf. This means criteria for filtering and ranking the search results must be established, criteria that is inherently influenced by the beliefs and worldview of those who establish it. And there has been enough evidence over the years to demonstrate that Google indeed has a liberal agenda, suppressing or favoring data, even blacklisting some sites, as it uses its search engine dominance to influence trusting users. "We're talking about a single company having the power to shift the opinions of literally billions of people without anyone having the slightest idea that they're doing so," says Robert Epstein.[8]

When it comes to online searches conducted around the world, Google far surpasses every other search engine. They have an enormous amount of power to influence world events as well as simple decisions we make every day. They are using us, manipulating us, and deceiving us. What is worse is that there is so little we can do about it.

WEB OF DECEPTION

While mega tech companies such as Google and Facebook use underhanded methods to make a profit from their users, other entrepreneurs use downright deceptive practices to gain attention, improve their image, or make money.

There are numerous ways of buying clout on the internet, anything from purchasing fake product reviews, fake "followers," and fake "likes," to employing experts or even "bots" to actively bolster your business's ranking in search engines. In the internet age, the drive for success in business has more to do with winning the battle for views, likes, and comments than on the quality of one's products or services.

Beyond the cutthroat competition for online consumers, there are more sinister characters operating in the shadows of the World Wide Web. There are a surplus of shams, hoaxes, and scam sites looking to steal credit card data, blackmail users by threatening to expose illicit online activities, and even outright steal a person's very identity. And then there is the secretive "Dark Web" where all manner of illegal activities, primarily involving drugs and sex, are transacted.

Such fraudulent practices are not limited to individuals who are in it for the money, either. Take Amina Arraf, for instance. She was a 35-year-old lesbian in Syria who posted a blog over the course of several years detailing her struggles under the regime of President Bashar al-Assad. Her ongoing, moving account captured the hearts of readers around the world. Then in 2011 the unthinkable happened: she was kidnapped. This brought international outrage, provoking various news outlets to investigate. The truth soon came out that Amina Arraf was actually an American peace activist named Tom MacMaster who had concocted the persona to further his own narrative about needed changes in the Middle East. It was all a hoax and it was a wakeup call to surfers that they can never really know what is true and what is false in the murky world of the internet.

And herein lies the greatest danger of the internet. In an environment where the false is presented side-by-side with truth as if they are deserving of equal consideration, the user has to decide for himself what is reliable and true. The task is made all the more daunting by the fact that what was once dubbed the "information superhighway" has degenerated into an information bazaar—like a crowded third-world market, with a few honorable laborers displaying their wares in an atmosphere teeming with profiteers and hucksters. And yet this flea market of facts, pseudo-facts, and artificial realities has become the go-to source for truth. In short, the internet serves as the bible for the post-truth culture.

It doesn't take much to see how the internet has taken mankind into new depths of deception. How far will it go? One only needs to read the book of Revelation to see where we are headed, and it will be the most loveable and trustworthy politician the world has ever known who will lead us there.

HAS THE INTERNET BEEN LYING TO YOU?

"What luck for rulers that men do not think."
-ADOLF HITLER[1]

"The consent of the governed is basic to American democracy. If the governed are misled, if they are not told the truth, or if through official secrecy and deception they lack information on which to base intelligent decisions, the system may go on—but not as a democracy. After nearly two hundred years, this may be the price America pays for the politics of lying."
-DAVID WISE[2]

"Look, all administrations, all governments lie, all officials lie and nothing they say is to be believed. That's a pretty good rule."
-DANIEL ELLSBERG[3]

SIX:
HAS THE POLITICAL SYSTEM BEEN LYING TO YOU?

While no political system is failproof or without its problems, I suppose the American democratic experiment of the past two hundred plus years has been about the best in the history of mankind.* However, the freedoms of democracy have also left us vulnerable to corruption and deception.

In a democratic society, government is made up of elected officials and long-term employees, i.e., bureaucrats. These career government workers are presumably made up of people that represent mainstream America, both Democrats and Republicans. And when things are as they should be, they are not overly concerned about the politics of government. Regrettably, recent events have shown that political bias can work its way into the bureaucratic world; thus the 2016 election campaign call to "drain the swamp."

Politicians, on the other hand, are nearly always either Democrat or Republican, leaning toward liberalism or conservatism. These men and women play to their base, meaning that they tend to vote along party lines when issues arise in Congress. They consider their ideology to be the right

---

* That unfortunately includes the only theocracy the world has ever known. The unbelief and rebellion of the Jewish people ruined all the good the Lord wanted to bring forth from the nation of Israel.

one and are very motivated to win this cultural battle over the future direction of our nation.

When considering the deception in our government, I see two basic camps. First, there are politicians who bend the truth or tell outright lies to win the debate with their political opponents. The second group is the politicians in office (i.e., presidents) who lie to the American public regarding their performance.

POLITICAL FALSEHOODS

In Chapter Two, I discussed the subject of debate and how a shout-down mentality has arisen, mostly within the ranks of radical liberals. This line of thinking is based in the belief that the end justifies the means; winning the argument is more important than being civil and honest. If the rules of the game mean win-at-any-cost, our society is in peril of becoming anarchistic or controlled by a tyrant willing to use any means to silence all opposition. The attitude that winning is more important than truth and integrity is at the root of a great deal of the deception that regularly comes forth from politicians.

I did a spot check on the website *politifact.com* to see what politicians have been telling us lately. The following whoppers represented by Politifact's "Truth-O-Meter,"[†] show what has become all too common in the American political field:

---

† The Truth-O-Meter is Politifact's editorial tool to "reflect the relative accuracy of a statement." The tool offers six ratings: 1) True – the statement is accurate and there's nothing significant missing. 2) Mostly True – the statement is accurate but needs clarification or additional information. 3) Half True – the statement is partially accurate but leaves out important details or takes things out of context. 4) Mostly False – the statement contains an element of truth but ignores critical facts that would give a different impression. 5) False – the statement is not accurate. 6) Pants on Fire – the statement is not accurate and makes a ridiculous claim.

HAS THE POLITICAL SYSTEM BEEN LYING TO YOU?

+ "In 2018, Biden lauded Paul Ryan for proposing cuts to Social Security and Medicare."— Senator Bernie Sanders on January 9, 2020. (This statement deemed "false" by the *Truth-O-Meter*.)[4]

+ "Qassem Soleimani assisted in the clandestine travel to Afghanistan of 10 of the 12 terrorists who carried out the September 11 terrorist attacks in the United States."— Vice President Mike Pence, in a tweet on January 7, 2020. (This statement deemed "false" by the *Truth-O-Meter*, for lack of supporting evidence.)[5]

+ "I am very proud that I am the only candidate in the Democratic primary to have voted against all of Trump's defense budgets." — Senator Bernie Sanders on December 20, 2019. (This statement deemed "false" by the *Truth-O-Meter*.)[6]

+ The U.S. pays "57 cents on the dollar on defense." — Congresswoman Ilhan Omar on December 13, 2019. (This statement deemed "false" by the *Truth-O-Meter*.)[7]

+ "Ukraine blatantly interfered in our election." — Senator Ted Cruz on December 12, 2019. (This statement deemed "false" by the *Truth-O-Meter*.)[8]

+ "The president had to confess in writing, in court to illegally diverting charitable contributions that were supposed to go to veterans." — Presidential Candidate, Mayor Pete Buttigieg on November 21, 2019. (This statement deemed "false" by the *Truth-O-Meter*.)[9]

+ "The fact is that right now the vast majority of Democrats do not support Medicare for All."

— Former Vice President Joe Biden during a Democratic presidential primary debate held on November 20, 2019. (This statement deemed "mostly false" by the *Truth-O-Meter*.)[10]

+ Voter roll purge would mean "more than 200,000 registered Wisconsin voters will be prohibited from voting." — House Speaker Nancy Pelosi on December 18, 2019. (This statement deemed "pants on fire" by the *Truth-O-Meter*.)[11]

+ "Between 27,000 and 200,000 Wisconsinites were 'turned away' from the polls in 2016 due to lack of proper identification." — Hillary Clinton on September 19, 2019. (This statement deemed "pants on fire" by the *Truth-O-Meter*.)[12]

+ "I was the person who saved Pre-Existing Conditions in your healthcare." — President Trump on January 14, 2020. (This statement deemed "pants on fire" by the *Truth-O-Meter*.)[13]

+ "Today in America—a new study came out—20 years out, whites who borrowed money, 94% of them have paid off their student loan debt; 5% of African-Americans have paid it off." — Senator Elizabeth Warren in a Democratic presidential primary debate held on November 20, 2019. (This statement deemed "mostly false" by the *Truth-O-Meter*.)[14]

Reading these statements reminds me of something Stewart Stafford said: "There is nothing as pitiful as a politician who is deficient in relaying untruths."[15]

GOVERNMENTAL FALSEHOODS

It is bad enough that politicians lie to lure voters to themselves, but what is worse than that is that they bring their pattern of deception into office. There is a long history of lies propagated by governmental leaders over the course of American history. In his book, *Lies the Government Told You*, Judge Andrew Napolitano, exposes seventeen major lies that the American government has told the U.S. population over the past two centuries. However, this propensity to falsify facts has steadily proliferated during the past century and is especially true of presidents.

Teddy Roosevelt wanted to build a canal across Panama to save American shipping from having to make the long journey around South America to reach the other side of the U.S. At that time, Panama was actually a region of Colombia. Roosevelt offered to purchase or lease the needed corridor from Colombia, but they refused his offers. For some time, Panamanian rebels had been attempting to throw their Colombian overlords out, so Roosevelt quietly supported their efforts, while denying to the public he had anything to do with the rebellion. Once the revolution was complete, the president was able to push through the construction of the Panama Canal.

Woodrow Wilson, his successor, hid the fact that he had suffered two strokes before running for president. He eventually had a devastating stroke that incapacitated him. This was hidden from the public, as well as the fact that his wife essentially ran the country during his last year in office.

Then there was Franklin Roosevelt's promise to the war-weary American people: "I have said this before, but I shall say it again and again and again: Your boys are not going to be sent into any foreign wars." This was spoken while, unbeknownst to the public, he was regularly ordering the U.S. Navy to take provocative measures against Germany and

Japan. He repeatedly told the nation that he did not want the U.S. in the war, but actually the exact opposite was the truth.

Twenty years later, Dwight Eisenhower denied that the U-2 plane the Russians shot down over their country was spying on them. This was an outright lie, which he was eventually forced to acknowledge. Not much better was John Kennedy's lie that the U.S. lagged far behind the U.S.S.R. in missile capabilities.

And who could forget all the lies Richard Nixon told during his Watergate cover-up? Or Ronald Reagan's denial of any involvement in the Iran-Contra affair? Or Bill Clinton's nationally televised statement, "I did not have sexual relations with that woman"? Or Barack Obama's statement, "If you like your health care plan, you can keep it"? (This was such a blatant falsehood that it won him Politifact's "Lie of the Year" award in 2013.)

I will not even begin to talk about President Trump's constant use of hyperbole or the downright whoppers he regularly tells the American people. In his 1987 bestseller *The Art of the Deal*, Donald Trump justified his lack of truthfulness in everyday speech: "People want to believe that something is the biggest and the greatest and the most spectacular. I call it truthful hyperbole. It's an innocent form of exaggeration—and a very effective form of promotion."[16]

Perhaps this is a good time for me to mention that my point in bringing awareness to all of this presidential deception is not meant as criticism toward these men. There were many factors that played into these decisions at the time and, of course, hindsight is always 20/20. I am only bringing these situations up to show how governmental officials can and regularly do fabricate the truth to the American public.

This has only been a quick scan of presidential falsehoods over the past century, but there are two that stand out to me as the most egregious lies that presidents have ever told.

LBJ AND VIETNAM

Once in office it did not take Lyndon Johnson long to establish for himself a dubious reputation of lying, (e.g., claiming an ancestor fought in the Alamo). Such was his propensity for falsehood that the term "credibility gap" was apparently coined in response to his regular distortion of truth. However, the most serious lie he ever told led to a terrible breach of the trust that U.S. citizens have in their government, a major blow to America's global prestige, and the loss of tens of thousands of American lives.

It was JFK who got the U.S. involved in Vietnam. He withheld the truth about the extent of our involvement in the tiny Asian nation. President Johnson felt obligated to continue Kennedy's agenda after his death. He was also greatly concerned that all Southeast Asia would come under communist control so he was anxious to escalate American presence in Vietnam. He found his opportunity in the Tonkin Gulf in August, 1964.

Johnson had quietly authorized support of a South Vietnamese commando attack on North Vietnam's Hon Me Island. At the same time, two U.S. destroyers left international waters to draw within a few miles of the isle. The North Vietnamese rightly connected these two incidents and sent three PT boats to confront the destroyers. One of the American ships fired on the patrol boats causing them to retreat. Not satisfied, American fighter jets were scrambled and attacked the vessels as they were heading back to port.

Three nights later, a twenty-three year old sonarman reported hearing torpedoes heading toward the ship. Later, it was determined that the young sailor was actually hearing the ship's propeller. Nevertheless, for the next four hours, the *Maddox* launched a withering cannon attack into the dark sea. As this was going on, the captain sent off a panicked report to Washington about the "attack." He began to suspect that something was amiss when the ship neither sustained a torpedo hit nor saw any evidence of another vessel on radar. He quickly passed along his misgivings to Washington: "Review of action makes recorded contacts and torpedoes fired appear doubtful. Freak weather effects and overeager sonarman may have accounted for many reports. No actual visual sightings by Maddox. Suggest complete evaluation before any further action."

President Johnson, anxious to take advantage of the opportunity, reported only the most damning elements of these reports to Congress. Hearing his account of what happened, Congress overwhelmingly passed the Gulf of Tonkin Resolution authorizing him to take "all necessary steps."[17] That evening, LBJ went on national television to describe the unprovoked attack by North Vietnam against two Navy warships, inferring that this occurred in international waters when, in fact, the incident happened in the coastal waters of North Vietnam. Less than two hours later, Johnson ordered the bombing of four Vietnamese patrol boat bases and an oil-storage facility.

On October 21st, LBJ once again went before the American people, explaining: "But we are not about to send American boys nine or ten thousand miles away from home to do what Asian boys ought to be doing themselves."[18] Of course, this was not true. He was already moving forward with plans for a massive infusion of American troops into the region.

Over the coming war years, Defense Secretary Robert McNamara and his commanders, continued to mislead the nation about what was really occurring in Southeast Asia. He and the president continued to issue the most optimistic reports while hiding the truth about the fact that we were losing the war. Not only was the South Vietnamese government completely corrupt and unsustainable, but the

Viet Cong controlled the jungles with their miles of tunnels and secret camps. Nevertheless, the president was resolute in his determination to win the war and American soldiers were sent by the thousands into southeast Asia. Years later, LBJ admitted that he was determined that no one would ever be able to accuse him of being "the first president to lose a war."[19]

Before it was over, nearly three million troops served in Vietnam. Of that number, 150,000 were wounded, nearly 60,000 killed in action and another 1,500 went missing. It was a terrible price for our country to pay and perhaps the worst part of it was that it was a decision the American people were not allowed to make for themselves.

GEORGE W. BUSH AND IRAQ

Fast forward nearly 40 years and perhaps hundreds of presidential lies later. Al Qaeda's attack on the World Trade Center had just occurred two years before. American troops had essentially overthrown the Taliban in Afghanistan and had Al Qaeda on the run. Meanwhile, a murderous butcher named Saddam Hussein was in power in Iraq.

On March 19, 2003, President George W. Bush ordered a full-scale strike against the nation of Iraq. However, the events running up to the president's declaration of war actually began two years prior to 9/11.

In November 1999, a low-level Iraqi chemical engineer entered Munich, Germany seeking asylum. The Defense Intelligence Agency, a department of the Pentagon, was on location to handle Iraqi refugees coming into Germany. Investigators for DIA debriefed this man and gave him the pseudonym Curveball—a name which turned out to be prophetic. For the next two years, the DIA funneled reports from him indicating that Saddam Hussein had constructed lethal germ factories in trucks and on trains. But when the CIA sought to interview Curveball, German intelligence officials rebuffed them. By the time 9/11 happened, nearly a hundred of these reports had arrived in Washington. Meanwhile, professionals aware of the situation began sharing their doubts about his allegations.

As the war in Afghanistan wound down, the Bush Administration began setting their sights on Iraq. On August 2, 2002 General Tommy Franks gave President Bush the war plan he had constructed for attacking Iraq. Less than a month later, Vice President Dick Cheney assured the nation that, "There is no doubt that Saddam Hussein now has weapons of mass destruction. There is no doubt he is amassing them to use against our friends, against our allies, and against us."[20]

Shortly after the Vice President made these comments, John McLaughlin, Deputy Director of the CIA, told Congress that the likelihood of Saddam launching some sort of attack using weapons of mass destruction "would be low."[21] Another official of the agency would later remark that people at CIA headquarters were questioning where Cheney was "getting this stuff from."[22]

Meanwhile, Tyler Drumheller, chief of the CIA European Division, met with a German intelligence officer who told him, "Don't even ask to see [Curveball] because he's a fabricator and he's crazy."[23] Drumheller alleges that he passed this information up to the highest levels of the CIA.

By January 2003, Dick Cheney, Condoleezza Rice, Donald Rumsfeld and other key administration figures were making regular appearances on various news outlets building a case for war against Saddam Hussein.

The clincher for the nation occurred on February 4th when Secretary of State Colin Powell gave a major speech at the United Nations. The day before he gave that pivotal speech, he had asked CIA Director George Tenet to personally affirm that the intelligence he would share the following day was legitimate. Tenet read the manuscript of his speech and assured him that his information was correct.

"Let me share with you what we know from eyewitness accounts," Powell told the world body. "We have firsthand descriptions of biological weapons factories on wheels and on rail." He did his utmost to lay out the administration's convictions about the situation in Iraq. Many of the diplomats in attendance that day remained unconvinced by the Secretary of State.

Of course, we now know that much of what we were told was based on misinformation and an exaggerated perspective of the situation in Iraq. It is unclear how much, if any, of the actual truth about Curveball made it to President Bush. Some people involved at the time believed that by that point, the truth no longer mattered. The president was dead set on war.

The whole situation is very reminiscent of the way LBJ was lured deeper and deeper into a falsehood about Vietnam because he *wanted* to believe it to be true. Undoubtedly, Bush had some good reasons for desiring the overthrow of Saddam. He had heard the reports and seen the grisly pictures of the victims of his cruelty. Perhaps he also wanted to finish what his father had begun in Operation Desert Storm. Others have suggested it was all about gaining control over Iraqi oil. Someone else conjectured that he wanted to send a clear message to unruly regimes that America was not afraid to confront exporters of terrorism. One Al Jazeera reporter believes that Bush was anxious to reestablish the U.S. as the world's leading power. Whatever was going on in the mind of George W. Bush, it is clear that those motives left him wide open to accept without question the spurious intelligence he had received. These actions led him down a dark path from which, he found, it was very difficult to be extricated.

DISCONCERTING FALSEHOODS REGARDING THE FUTURE

While it is true that deception has been a part of our political system from its earliest days, none of it can compare to the level of falsehood that is being propagated by our government today. In fact, it has gotten so bad that we now have a term to describe it: post-truth politics. Wikipedia defines this as, "a political culture in which debate is framed largely by appeals to emotion disconnected from the details of policy, and by the repeated assertion of talking points to which factual rebuttals are ignored."[24]

In one of his more honest moments, one famous press secretary put it this way:

> If you tell a lie big enough and keep repeating it, people will eventually come to believe it. The lie can be maintained only for such time as the State can shield the people from the political, economic and/or military consequences of the lie. It thus becomes vitally important for the State to use all of its powers to repress dissent, for the truth is the mortal enemy of the lie, and thus by extension, the truth is the greatest enemy of the State.[25]

Sad to say, but the overriding principle that framed the Nazi agenda Joseph Goebbels promoted is often at work in our own government.

This sort of truth-masking is typically unknown to the public except on rare occasions when the lid is temporarily lifted and we are allowed a glimpse into the reality of what is happening in our government.

One such occasion occurred a few years back when Edward Snowden released several thousand pages of highly classified information to several journalists who wrote stories based on it. What motivated this idealistic young man to take such drastic measures, knowing it meant giving up his dream job and American comfort? Apparently, as part of his work for the National Security Agency (NSA), he was privy to the massive collection of the private data of American citizens. Over a period of months, he grew increasingly more upset about this—to the point of being prepared to tell the public what was really happening.

His "breaking point" occurred in March, 2013 when he saw James Clapper, Director of the CIA, lie to Congress about what the NSA was doing. During a Congressional hearing, Senator Ron Wyden, asked the director, "Does the NSA collect any type of data at all on millions or hundreds of millions of Americans?" "No sir," Clapper lied. Wyden, a member of the Senate Intelligence Committee and fully aware of the untruth of this statement, wanted clarification. He asked, "It does not?" Without hesitation, Clapper responded, "Not wittingly. There are cases where they could, inadvertently perhaps, collect—but not wittingly."

This outright falsehood sent Snowden over the edge. Three days later he quit his $200,000 job with one NSA contractor to begin work for another, where he could gain better access to information about NSA's data collection programs. Within two months, he was on a plane to Hong Kong, where he shared the data he had accumulated with journalists Glenn Greenwald, Laura Poitras, and Ewen MacAskill.‡

Over the following months, James Clapper issued five different explanations over why he lied to Congress. First he said that he thought that Senator Wyden was only referring to emails. Since nothing was said about emails, he quickly must have thought better of that excuse so in an NBC interview a week later he said that his statement was "the least untruthful" answer he could offer. A month later he claimed that the whole

---

‡ Poitras produced and directed the Academy Award winning documentary, Citizenfour chronicling Snowden's time in Hong Kong with the journalists.

thing was "an honest mistake" on his part. His next explanation came in front of a security summit held in Washington D.C. where he argued that he was caught unaware by the question (in spite of the fact that the previous day his office had been told what to expect during the upcoming questioning). He said, "When I got accused of lying to Congress because of a mistake... I had to answer on the spot about a specific classified program in a general, unsecure setting."

His fifth excuse was offered through his general counsel, Robert Litt who suggested that he was thinking about the 702 [email] program. "When he is talking about not wittingly collecting," Litt added, "he is talking about incidental collection."§

Senator Wyden later clarified the situation: "So that he would be prepared to answer, I sent the question to Director Clapper's office a day in advance. After the hearing was over my staff and I gave his office a chance to amend his answer." Senator Wyden was not altogether happy with Clapper's handling of this incident. "Now public hearings are needed to address the recent disclosures," he stated. "The American people have the right to expect straight answers from the intelligence leadership to the questions asked by their representatives."[26]

Perhaps what former Florida governor Bob Graham said regarding a different potential government cover-up would be a fitting conclusion to this chapter. "The American government is founded on the consent of the governed. To give that consent, the people must know what the government is doing in its name. Distrust in government is reflected in the speeches of today's presidential candidates. The public's sometimes angry response is fueled by a sense of betrayal and deceit."[27]

---

§ My point in bringing all this up is not to justify Snowden's actions, which very well may have been treasonous. Again, I offer it simply to show how we are not being told the truth.

HAS THE POLITICAL SYSTEM BEEN LYING TO YOU?

We expect politicians to exaggerate, yes, but what does it say about our nation when we accept downright lies as if truth no longer matters? Where is the deceptive culture that has been bred within the political realm taking us? Right into the hands of the most convincing and prolific liar the world has ever seen—the antichrist.

But before we tackle the spiritual dimension of deception, I am compelled to address one more realm of lies, a source of deceit that has influenced millions and left them ripe for the coming period of delusion that will be unleashed in the world.

"Sex-packed porn films featuring freshly-dyed blondes whose evocative eyes say 'I want you' is quite possibly one of the greatest deceptions of all time. Trust me, I know. I did it all the time... none of us freshly-dyed blondes like doing porn. In fact, we hate it. We hate being touched by strangers who care nothing about us. We hate being degraded with their foul smells and sweaty bodies. But the porn industry wants YOU to think we porn actresses love sex."

-SHELLY LUBBENS[1]

SEVEN:
HAS THE PORNOGRAPHY INDUSTRY BEEN LYING TO YOU?

If I did not have so much to say on this subject, I could easily have made it an addendum to Chapter Four because, truly, pornography is just another form of the world's entertainment. An insincere Christian could feasibly respond to that statement with this sentiment: "Yeah, I don't think porn is that bad either. I don't know why people make such a big deal about it!" By contrast, the first thought that would come to the mind of an earnest believer would be something more like, "If our society has come to think of pornography as just another form of entertainment, then what is portrayed on television surely reflects this corrupt standard. I need to exercise real caution with it." The fact of the matter is that the gap between mainstream entertainment and obscenity is becoming narrower and narrower as time goes on— and it is not because pornography is becoming "softer."

I was one of those Baby Boomers who lived through the sexual revolution of the Sixties and was eagerly receptive to the X-rated movies that became available in the Seventies. At that point, mainstream America still considered porn to be abhorrent. They rightly saw us porn addicts as perverts. But the enemy has effectively transformed the moral landscape of our nation. The fact of the matter is that the adult entertainment industry has been accepted into the fold, even if most Americans do not personally view it.

The advent of the internet was a game-changer. As I discussed in Chapter Five, Millennials and subsequent generations have been raised in a whole new environment. In my day, young males occasionally encountered the comparatively tame fare offered by *Playboy* magazine. But in the screen-filled, device-oriented world we live in, viewing pornography is no longer considered shameful. Even young women, by the thousands, are engaging in it. Gone are the days that X-rated movies were confined to seedy bookstores. They can now be accessed quickly and easily with a tap of the finger. Sadly, the world of today contains electronic "adult bookstores" by the thousands—all of which can be entered in the privacy of one's own bedroom. Should we be surprised that thousands of texts each day often feature the sender starring in a self-made porn production, an X-rated "selfie"?

It is there, in this virtual world, that unclean spirits ply their trade and corrupt the minds of innocent children and teens. It is a furtive realm where everything imaginable can be seen; a world that seems to grow darker by the day. One can only imagine the kind of aberrant activities future generations will consider normal.

THE HISTORY OF OBSCENITY

Before we go any further, let's establish a working definition of pornography: it is any kind of writing, photographs, videos, figurines, etc. that have been created or are used for the purpose of inciting sexual arousal.

Of course, when we think of pornography, the triple X websites that abound on the internet come to mind, but actually porn has been around for thousands of years. The word "pornography" is derived from the Greek words *porni* (prostitute) and *graphein* (writing). It encompassed "any work of art or literature depicting the life of prostitutes."[2]

In Scripture, the Greek word *pornos* is used to describe someone who is given over to sexual sin. For instance, in 1 Corinthians 5:9-11 Paul tells believers not to associate with "*pornos* people" who claim to be Christians. In the following chapter, he says that "*pornos* people" and homosexuals will not inherit the kingdom of God. (1 Corinthians 6:9-11) The writer of Hebrews reminds its readers that, "Marriage is to be held in honor among all, and the marriage bed is to be undefiled; for "*pornos* people" and adulterers God will judge." (Hebrews 13:4) Finally, we are told twice in Revelation (21:8; 22:15) that "*pornos* people" will be excluded from heaven.*

It is clear that this lascivious thinking was very present throughout biblical times. Certainly, the Israelites constantly faced the temptation to give over to the fertility cults around them. And I would guess that erotic depictions were seen in the pagan temples of their day and perhaps eventually even in the Jewish Temple (cf. Ezekiel 8:10). In India, evidence of phallic worship can be traced back to the time of Abraham. Sexual figurines and pornographic images were pervasive throughout ancient Greece and Rome. In fact, around the time of the birth of Christ, Roman poet Ovid wrote *Ars amatoria* (*Art of Love*), which was basically an ancient sex manual.

Pagan cultures continued to provide a ready audience for anything erotic. Giovanni Boccaccio, an Italian writer who lived during the 13th century, wrote numerous stories of a licentious nature. In Japan, the new technology of color woodblock printing made it possible to "mass produce" erotic art in the 1600s. In England, John Cleland wrote the classic *Fanny Hill* in 1749, while French postcards featuring nudity were popular in Paris.

---

* The way pornos is translated into English depends on the Bible one uses, of course. The NASB typically uses the word "fornicators"; the NIV reads, "sexually immoral people," King James, "whoremongers," Amplified, "impure and immoral," and the New Living Translation, "those who indulge in sexual sin."

The inventions of photography and moving pictures allowed pornography to flourish in the West during the early part of the 20th century. Both supply and demand of obscenity continued to grow during the following decades. Hugh Hefner once boasted that *Playboy Magazine* helped launch the sexual revolution, which is certainly true. But it was the emergence of the adult entertainment industry of the early Seventies that really took it to new heights.

The grainy 8-mm films of the Fifties and Sixties were replaced with high quality, full-length motion pictures complete with story lines and scripts. This new branch of the entertainment world had its own producers, directors, camera crews, stars, and starlets. Nearly every imaginable fantasy was portrayed in vivid scenes. This new industry also had its own culture and values, impudently conveyed in every movie. It has also helped to foster an entire new tradecraft that includes thousands of massage parlors, strip clubs, escort services, and homosexual bars throughout the West.

These well-made films—later featured on the internet—communicated powerful messages that have impacted our culture. And these messages are laden with deception. So, let's take a look at a few falsehoods that are entrenched in the porn industry.

LIE NUMBER ONE: SEXUAL PLEASURE IS THE MOST IMPORTANT THING IN LIFE

This statement reflects a belief system that is subliminally communicated through erotica. Of course, it goes without saying that sex is a wonderful part of a healthy marriage. When two people love each other, sex is enjoyed and appreciated and yet, is also kept in its proper place.

The adult entertainment industry knows full well that its continued success depends on people buying into the mindset that illicit sex is of enormous importance. From their perspective, only religious prudes and frigid women think of it as anything less. They believe and promote the premise that every sexual fantasy should be encouraged and acted upon. Nothing should be considered taboo. Every sexual story, film and photograph has embedded in it the lie that sexual pleasure is what life is all about.

And in our licentious culture, the porn industry has perpetuated tremendous success by creating and catering to its own target market. By making sexual activity a national idol, they have drawn millions of men and women into sexual idolatry.

Elsewhere, I have used the analogy of a neighborhood drug pusher who will entice a young person with free marijuana with the hope of eventually leading him into hardcore drug addiction. In all honesty, I do not believe pornographers are that intentional in their thinking. They are just producing material in the hopes of making money. But there is an unseen enemy deeply involved in their efforts who is *very* intentional. Those unclean spirits use erotic material to entice people (especially youth) into viewing it, knowing full well that becoming addicted to it will probably be the end result. The deeper the addiction, the more X-rated material the person will consume in the future. This helps to explain why the adult entertainment industry has been so profitable year after year in their endeavors.

LIE NUMBER TWO: VIEWING PORNOGRAPHY WILL BE DEEPLY SATISFYING

The first time a teenager views an X-rated video, the experience is likely going to be overwhelming and exhilarating. Many are addicted from that moment on. And, of course, those first few experiences *are* tremendous. Mercifully, God built into sin the law of diminishing returns. Each time the new viewer engages in it, the thrill becomes a little less exciting. This is certainly true in a spiritual sense, but this dynamic has also been built into a person's physiological makeup. I will briefly explain.

The human brain contains a vast system of nerves. Every action a person commits sends an electric pulse through that complex of nerves. When he starts repeating that behavior, those nerves become connected to each other through a brain chemical known as a neuro-transmitter. In essence, the brain develops pathways that these chemical signals travel on.

One of the most important neuro-transmitters the brain produces is a chemical called dopamine. It has been called the "feel-good hormone" because it is associated with the motivation to repeat pleasurable experiences. This is how God established within us the desire to eat and to procreate.

When a person enjoys some small pleasure in life—such as eating a piece of chocolate or watching a favorite baseball player hit a home run—a small amount of dopamine is released in his brain. Like other neuro-transmitters, dopamine moves through those nerve pathways, creating a shortcut highway through the brain system as a person repeats a pleasurable experience.

However, dopamine is different from other neuro-transmitters, because the amount that is released into the brain's nerve center is dependent on the level of pleasure that was just experienced. Extreme examples of this would be the first time a person snorts cocaine or ejaculates; that level of intense pleasure causes a powerful surge of dopamine to flood the brain. This is why it can take a young person weeks to get in the habit of brushing his teeth but only days to establish a powerful habit of masturbation.

We were created to experience sexual pleasure in the confines of marriage and in godly proportions, but we were never meant to compulsively overindulge the behavior repeatedly. The problem for a sex addict is that the brain receptors become overwhelmed. So, the brain compensates for this by producing less dopamine as these chemical surges continue. Over time, every new sexual experience brings about a decrease in the euphoric sensation that dopamine produces. It is the scientific reality of what lies behind the principle of the diminishing returns of sin—what began as exhilarating experiences eventually lose their luster.

This cycle of the high of pleasure and the subsequent emotional crash deepens the brain pathways even more. Over time, the person goes from repeating these behaviors because they are pleasurable to doing it because he feels as though he needs it. When the craving for it intensifies, while the anticipated sense of pleasure lessens, the habit has crossed the line into an addiction.

Does viewing pornography and engaging in illicit sexual activity satisfy? I can only say that it can be extremely pleasurable at first, but that level of enjoyment will not last. (Hebrews 11:25) Nevertheless, it is a powerful illusion that a person can spend a lifetime chasing.

LIE NUMBER THREE: VIEWING PORNOGRAPHY WITH MY HUSBAND WILL KEEP HIM HOME

The enemy has used this lie to corrupt thousands of otherwise decent women. Typically what happens is that a young woman marries the man with whom she has fallen in love. Before long she discovers, to her unspeakable grief, that he is addicted to pornography. Once the initial shock wears off, they have a conversation in which he convinces her that if they could view adult movies together, he would not feel the need to maintain a secret life.

This is exactly how I convinced Kathy to join me in watching X-rated movies. There are simply no words to describe the effect this would have on her life. She wrote about it in a letter to a woman considering becoming involved in her husband's pornography. She shared it in her book, *When His Secret Sin Breaks Your Heart*:

> Many years ago I was, like you, very confused and hurt. At the time, viewing pornography with Steve seemed to be the only way to keep him from being unfaithful to me. His argument that it was something we could enjoy together and, at the same time, end any further sneaking around was very persuasive. I was so emotionally beaten down that I acquiesced to his wishes. I had no inkling then how untrue his arguments were. I was so short-sighted and shallow. I paid a heavy price spiritually and emotionally.
>
> Initially things went well. Steve was genuinely grateful that he wouldn't have to sneak around anymore. In his sin-sick mind, I think he sincerely believed what he told me. At the beginning of this period, he treated me better than he had in years. But before long, the thrill of it began to dissipate—as sin always does—and he began sneaking out to massage parlors again. Then, Steve suggested that we invite other people into our sex life. Again, in my obsessive desire to keep him, I reluctantly agreed. We both began to spiral downward. After just a few months of it, I became numb to this new fetish as well. My conscience was being seared. My sense of moral conviction was almost on empty. It was then that I finally realized I would have to leave him. I could not handle it anymore! I finally came to the place where I would rather be single than live like this. This was where I needed to be.
>
> Had I only known what it would cost me, I never would have gotten involved in the first place. In my great determination to win my husband's love, no matter what, I was willing to sacrifice my self-respect, the morals I was raised with and most importantly, my walk with God. For

years, I was riddled with guilt and shame over the things I had seen and done.

But that wasn't all. It took years for those images and unpleasant memories to go away. For some time, I had to deal with unnatural desires I had never experienced before. Pornographic movies create the illusion that every person alive is highly sexed and perverted. They warp a person's perspectives of other people. For a long time, I saw every woman as someone who wanted to seduce my husband and every man as a pervert.

Having said all this, allow me to ask you some penetrating questions. Do you think it is right to be so needy for a man that you would consider degrading yourself with pornography just to keep the relationship together? What kind of a person will you have to become to keep him happy? Are you really willing to involve yourself with, and consent to, your husband's secret perversions? Do you realize that becoming involved with pornography will only give your husband the license to openly lust over girls in your presence? Are you sure you are willing to subject yourself to that? Are you willing to involve yourself with something as evil and dark as pornography? Are you willing to walk away from God for the sake of appeasing your husband? Don't you realize that this will not cause him to love you more? Once you have hardened your heart against the Lord and filled your mind with perversion, what is going to stop you from taking the next step and the one after that? These are questions you better carefully consider before venturing one inch further down this path.[3]

The lie that pornography will fix my marriage is one more scheme of the enemy to draw people deeper and deeper into spiritual darkness.

LIE NUMBER FOUR: AFTER VIEWING IT, YOU CAN JUST REPENT AND MOVE ON

Many who pursue a course of sin convince themselves that they can simply "repent" and return to God afterwards. While it is true that genuine repentance does bring instantaneous forgiveness, also true is the fact that every sin committed bears a price. One of the great consequences of backsliding is that the further a person moves away from the Lord, the more difficult will be the return.

For instance, my wife and I once devoted quite a bit of time counseling a couple who were addicted to spending money. In spite of the fact that they both had well-paying jobs, they had racked up $40,000 in debt. In our counseling with them we carefully laid out a reasonable budget which would provide a limited amount of cash for "fun" and yet would enable them to pay off all of their financial obligations within two years. Unfortunately, they soon wearied of the plan. By coincidence, we ran into them two years later. How sad to discover that instead of being freed from that mountain of debt, they were now $80,000 in the hole!

A person can quickly get themselves in trouble through a habit of overspending. And obviously, it is much easier to climb out of $40,000 of debt than $80,000. Although it may not be as visible, the same fact holds true for those who give over to sexual sin. It is much easier to overcome a two-year masturbation habit than one that has been going on over the course of years.

Every time a person views an adult movie or gives over to some other form of sexual sin, his mind becomes more polluted, his heart more blackened, and his perspectives more distorted. Sin corrupts the soul and its vile touch does not simply disappear when a person makes a resolution to quit. Every act of sin leaves its nasty stain upon the heart and takes the person further away from God. That is why it is so important to stop the slide immediately. "Today is the day of salvation!" (2 Corinthians 6:2)

The old adage is painfully true: sin will take you further than you ever wanted to go, keep you longer than you ever wanted to stay, and cost you more than you can ever pay.

The fact is that no man ever became completely wicked all at once. It happens over time, little by little, and that is the deception of it. What young person would take that first hit of speed if he could fast-forward five years and see himself malnourished, with rotting teeth, and sores all over his body? What man would take that first drink if he could look into the future and see himself after he has lost his family, his career, and his self-respect, lying in some alley, with urine all over him? And, so it follows, what young man would look at that first pornographic image if he could see what his life would become when he would be constantly driven by lust, his mind filled with perverted thoughts, committing disgusting acts of deviancy? But the person being tempted that first time cannot see into the future; he can only see the intoxicating experience that is luring him at that moment.

Yes, it is true, that if a person truly repents, the Lord will forgive him. But this too can be deceptive because when a person becomes hardened by sin, repentance does not come easily. Tragically, I fear that most who go down that path never do come into true repentance. Most of them end up in a hopeless merry-go-round of sinning, making resolutions to quit but always returning for more. Endless, hopeless misery becomes their eternal lot.

LIE NUMBER FIVE: VIEWING PORNOGRAPHY HAS NO HARMFUL EFFECTS

The images of delicious smiles and thrilling moments of

ecstasy betray the truth of what comes with erotica. I will briefly mention a few.

First, pornography warps a person's perspectives on sexuality. A young believer who stays away from porn and eventually marries his childhood sweetheart is probably going to think of sex in a healthy way. He thoroughly enjoys his wife, and he is able to keep his interest focused there.

How different it is for a guy who becomes addicted to X-rated movies! He may not realize it, but his perspectives are undergoing a subtle, yet very real, transformation. If he is subjecting his mind and heart to pornography, his attitudes about women are going to become dark. He will come to see them as sex toys to be, at the very least, mentally enjoyed. At worst, he will enter into a promiscuous lifestyle of going from one girl to the next. He will also become increasingly more open to becoming involved in aberrant and even bizarre sex.

Another unavoidable consequence to carrying on a secret life of viewing porn will be a strong tendency to isolate himself from others. There is a huge part of his life unknown to anyone else. He may be able to interact with others at work, but there is always a part of him people do not know about. If he is married, these problems become even worse. He loses interest in his wife and children. He keeps himself aloof and distant. They cannot understand why he seems so emotionally disconnected. This causes friction in the marriage and a sense of rejection in his children.

I will deal with this more in Chapter Four of Book Two, but I should mention that sexual sin also sears the conscience and hardens the heart. The more a person gives over to sin, the farther he moves away from God.

Also true is that pornography and sexual sin engenders selfishness. As a man continues to cater to his pet sin, his world becomes increasingly smaller. Before long, there is very little room for anyone or anything else but his beloved object of adoration. He becomes increasingly self-centered, self-focused and self-indulgent in every aspect of life.

Yes, pornography promises enormous returns but leaves its user in utter misery. That is the truth that the pornographers will never tell those who succumb to its enticements. No wonder Solomon warned: "Keep your way far from [the prostitute] and do not go near the door of her house, or you will give your vigor to others and your years to the cruel one." (Proverbs 5:8-9) The X-rated website, like the house of the adulteress, is nothing more than a den of writhing vipers. It would be wise to avoid such a place!

And thus concludes *Book One: Deception in Western Culture*. I trust that getting a clearer sight of the proliferation of deception you are encountering in life will build within you a deeper discernment of the wiles of the devil and a greater determination to resist those lies at any cost!

It is now time to utilize that discernment to better understand how deception is at work in the evangelical community and within our own bosoms.

BOOK TWO
DECEPTION IN THE SPIRITUAL REALM

"You've got to deceive yourself
before you can be deceived."

-ANONYMOUS[1]

"Self-love cannot abide to see itself, the sight
would overwhelm it with shame and vexation;
and if it catches an accidental glimpse, it seeks
some false light which may soften and condone
what is so hideous. Thus we always keep up some
illusion so long as we retain any self-love."

-FENELON[2]

INTRODUCTION TO BOOK TWO:
FACING THE TRUTH
ABOUT MYSELF

When Deception came knocking, it found a receptive ear with Steve Gallagher. While it is true that I have been lied to by many sources since my earliest days, there is no getting around the fact that the door to my heart was wide open to being deceived.*

Actually, in my natural state, I was a fairly truthful person. To a large degree, this all changed when I gave myself over to the serious pursuit of sin. After that, deception became an integral part of my daily life. When I was single, most of my sexual sin was too shameful to allow others to know about it. As a married man, covering up and deceiving became a major aspect of my daily life.

This book is about truth and deception. One thing I hope will be accomplished in your life through reading it will be a strengthened determination to rid yourself of any pretense or deception that might be at work in your heart. But before I address any issues with deception you might be experiencing, I must first be willing to be thoroughly open about my own life.

---

* Solomon said, "The prudent sees the evil and hides himself, but the naïve go on, and are punished for it." (Proverbs 22:3) The Hebraic term for "naïve" here literally means "open," as in being open to suggestions and temptations. That perfectly describes me as a teenager and young man.

I suppose you already know that I was a sex addict for about a decade of my life. I had been obsessed with women from my earliest days. However, to be thought of as a womanizer is not such a bad thing, so I want to be a little more forthright with you about my sexual sin and what kind of person it made me.

In a sermon I gave some years ago, I described what I was like during that period when I had fully given myself over to sin:

> I want to talk about what it means to be a man of honor. I looked up this word 'honor' in a thesaurus. Listen to some of its synonyms: respectable, virtuous, of high standards and high-caliber, decent, having integrity, honest, solid, principled, upright, noble... in short, a man of character.
>
> I had been around men of character in my earlier years and somehow being around them helped me see the depth of debauchery I had given myself over to. Being around those men helped me to find my way into freedom.
>
> But I want to share a few words that somewhat portray my past life and what God has brought me out of. Here are some terms that would describe what I became during that time of my life: shifty, selfish, cowardly, deceitful, self-centered, disgraceful, self-absorbed, sleazy, despicable. I suppose there is one term that really described what I was like: I was what you would call a creep.

Yes, it is all true and actually does not tell the half of it. If I had been arrested for half of the crimes I committed during my younger years, I would probably still be in prison to this day. It is absolutely vital to my spiritual survival that I acknowledge my lack of character during that period of my life—and what I would be today if I ever backslid to the point of no longer walking in the Spirit. The Lord has forced me to look at the ugliness of my fallen nature many times over the years, and every time I acknowledged what He was showing me and committed myself to change, I was set free a little bit more.[†]

The transformation that occurred in my life happened because I heard the truth and I responded to the truth—not just once, but over and over again. For, you see, iniquitous poison had spread throughout my inner being and it needed to be purged out. That process required time along with many painful, humiliating breakings.

When my wife Kathy shared her testimony in her book, *When His Secret Sin Breaks Your Heart*, (and also in a recent video series, *Sacred Things: Hope for Struggling Marriages*), I insisted that she tell every bit of the ugly story. She told how I cheated on her from the very beginning, how I led her into pornography and the swinging lifestyle, how verbally abusive I had been to her, how I treated her like she was lucky to have me—all of it. From the earliest days of our relationship, Kathy absolutely adored me and was utterly devoted to me, but I repaid her love by devastating her life with my selfishness.

I take no pleasure in exposing my ugly past in this way. In fact, it is very painful to do so, but I discovered early on that utter transparency about my past would be a necessary part of my calling so others could see that there is no pit so deep that God cannot rescue, transform, and save the one mired in its depths.

Now, I should add that it was a lifetime ago that those things occurred, and they were lived by someone that neither I nor my wife would even recognize. And since I am being so honest about myself, I should hasten to mention the most meaningful compliment I have ever received. It came from my mother-in-law, Shirley Irwin, who was very acquainted with

---

† One of the sayings I often express to the students in our residential program is, "We initiate, God empowers." It is the balance taught in Scripture about how change comes about. Only God can change my character, but that change does not come about until I commit to doing my part in the process.

the Steve Gallagher of yesteryear. She watched me corrupt her baby girl and did her utmost to convince Kathy to divorce me. The Lord had other ideas, of course, and Kathy felt compelled to stick it out with me. Anyway, a few years ago, Shirley told Kathy, "I have never seen anyone change as much as Steve has." Those words are very meaningful to me because she fully understood what a creep I had been and how amazing grace truly has been in my life.

There is a beautiful old hymn that perfectly articulates what every believer should feel. The fourth stanza of *Beneath the Cross of Jesus* goes like this:

> Upon that cross of Jesus
> Mine eye at times can see
> The very dying form of One,
> Who suffered there for me;
> And from my smitten heart, with tears,
> Two wonders I confess,
> The wonders of His glorious love,
> And my unworthiness.

Yes, I was a real snake, but God has marvelously saved and transformed me. A huge part of that change has come about because I started recognizing the many falsehoods I had accepted and also because I was willing to be honest with myself, God and others. My hope is that as you go through this book, you, too will become more aware of the age of deception in which we live and become ever more willing to be honest about yourself. It really is true that honesty is the best policy. And for Christians, it should be the only policy.

FACING THE TRUTH ABOUT MYSELF

"The devil is the top hidden persuader—
the master of subliminal motivation."
-JESS C. MOODY[1]

"The devil is to be avoided as a lion, but he
is most to be feared as an angel of light."
-ANONYMOUS[2]

"Satan deals with confusion and lies. Put
the truth in front of him and he is gone."
-PAUL MATLOCK[3]

ONE:
SATAN IS A LIAR

All of the lies and half-truths people have told you; all of the falsehood that has been presented to you through the academic realm; all of the fabrications and doublespeak that have been choreographed by smooth-talking marketers; all of the misrepresentations communicated to you through the media; all of the underhanded dealings you have encountered through your internet journeys; all of the disinformation and distortions of truth politicians have propagated; and all of the embedded lies of the pornography industry find their inspiration from the master spirit who deceives the whole world. (Revelation 12:9) In fact, every form of deceit from Cain's cover-up to the antichrist's massive deception can be traced back to "the father of lies."

Satan is viler than the foulest child molester; a greater deceiver than the smoothest conman; and more brutal than the evilest serial killer. Scripture has assigned him at least seven names:

- ◆ Lucifer
- ◆ Satan
- ◆ Beelzebub
- ◆ Belial
- ◆ Leviathan

+ Abaddon
+ Apollyon

The Bible also labels him with thirteen designations:
+ the devil
+ the adversary
+ the enemy
+ the tempter
+ the old serpent
+ the dragon
+ the father of lies
+ the evil (or wicked) one
+ the accuser of the brethren
+ the prince of the power of the air
+ the prince of this world
+ the prince of demons
+ the angel of the bottomless pit

Finally, Scripture describes Satan with five appellatives:
+ a roaring lion
+ an angel of light
+ a murderer
+ a liar
+ a tempter

He is the ruler of an organized kingdom, apparently made up of various grades and types of fallen angels identified in Scripture as: "principalities," "powers," "unclean spirits," "lying spirits," "spirits of infirmity," "world forces of this darkness," and "spiritual forces of wickedness in the heavenly places."

The Voice translation of the Bible interprets Paul's description of the devil's kingdom as follows:

"We're not waging war against enemies of flesh and blood alone. No, this fight is against tyrants, against authorities, against supernatural powers and demon princes that slither in the darkness of this world, and against wicked spiritual armies that lurk about in heavenly places." (Ephesians 6:12)

Whatever terms you choose to use, Satan reigns over a vast domain of evil spirits.

It was not always this way. There was a time that Lucifer was a beautiful archangel of light attending the throne of God. However, the Lord had to permit the possibility of evil to enter that pure region as a test of loyalty. Lucifer allowed an ugly, overweening pride to rise up within him and take possession of him. Once evil took up residence in his heart, he was transformed into an angel of darkness whose name was changed to Satan. "Multitudes of the angels fell," comments Matthew Henry; "but this... was surely [the work of] the prince of the devils, the ring-leader in the rebellion: no sooner was he a sinner than he was a Satan, no sooner a traitor than a tempter, as one enraged against God and his glory and envious of man and his happiness."[4]

Satan became enraged when Michael and other angels loyal to the Lord threw him and his treacherous followers out of heaven. Jesus is quoted in Luke 10:18 as saying that He saw "Satan fall from heaven like lightning." If this occurred when Michael conquered him, then it is likely that he fell to Earth, where Adam and Eve were living contentedly.* In spite of the fact that he was full of rage and vengeance, he bided his time and, using great subtlety, made his devastating presentation to Eve.†

---

* Of course, we cannot know the order of these events with any degree of certainty. It is also possible that the insurrection in heaven occurred before Adam and Eve were created. For an in-depth discussion of what happened that day, please refer to Chapter Two in my book, i—The Root of Sin Exposed.

† See Chapter Three, "The First Seduction."

BOOK TWO: DECEPTION IN THE SPIRITUAL REALM

Since that fateful day, the devil has effectively turned most of mankind against Yahweh. A quick run through Scriptures shows what he has attempted or been able to accomplish during the 6,000 years of relative freedom he has enjoyed:

+ He launched a devastating assault on Job and his family. (Job 1-2)
+ He tried to steal the body of Moses to use it for some foul purpose. (Jude 9)
+ He stimulated King David into the prideful idea of numbering the people of Israel. (1 Chronicles 21:1)
+ He brought ugly accusations against Joshua the high priest. (Zechariah 3:1-2)
+ He had the audacity to tempt the Son of God— shamelessly exploiting the Word of God at one point, and later trying to bribe Jesus to fall at his feet and worship him. (Matthew 4:9)
+ He inspired Peter to rebuke Jesus when He announced His upcoming sufferings. (Matthew 16:22-23)
+ He entered the heart of Judas and led him through the steps to betray Christ. (Luke 22:3)
+ He demanded the right to "sift Peter" on the night Jesus was betrayed. (Luke 22:31)
+ He "filled the heart" of Ananias to lie to the Holy Spirit—a brazen attempt to cause division and suspicion in the Early Church. (Acts 5:3)
+ He caused "false apostles" and "deceitful workers" to disguise themselves as "apostles of Christ," "angels of light" and "apostles of righteousness." (2 Corinthians 11:13-15)
+ Numerous times he thwarted the Apostle Paul's attempts to return to Thessalonica to encourage the persecuted saints there. (1 Thessalonians 2:18)

These are only the directly referenced instances of his personal involvement in the lives of various biblical characters. His unseen and unmentioned involvement is woven through the entire narrative of Scripture.

Notice also that nearly every situation I mentioned in this group involves some leading spiritual figure of the day: Adam and Eve, David, Jesus, Peter and so on. But even when he filled the hearts of Judas and Ananias, he was instigating momentous treacheries.

Even still, Satan's primary functions over these many centuries have covered a much broader scale than individual lives. Consider the following:

- He is charged with planting unbelievers in the house of God. (Matthew 13:38-39)
- He is responsible for stealing the Word of God away from those in the process of conversion. (Luke 8:12)
- He is charged with oppressing many with numerous physical ailments. (Acts 10:38)
- He is said to have the "power of death" which all mankind must face. (Hebrews 2:14)
- He is said to prowl "around like a roaring lion, seeking someone to devour." (1 Peter 5:8)
- He is credited with building devilish "works" inside people. (1 John 3:8)
- He is said to have offspring who imitate his wicked behavior. (John 8:44; Acts 13:10; 1 John 3:10)
- He provokes and attempts to capitalize on people's anger. (Ephesians 4:26-27)
- He "schemes" against believers. (Ephesians 6:11)
- He "snares" people to do his will. (1 Timothy 3:7; 2 Timothy 2:26)
- He accuses and persecutes believers. (Job 1:11; Zechariah 3:1; Revelation 2:10; 12:10)

+ He devised "the deep things of Satan" to beguile men into gnostic heresy. (Revelation 2:24)
+ In the not-too-distant future, he will fully possess the antichrist, using him to perform false wonders. (2 Thessalonians 2:9)
+ He will be thrown into the pit for 1,000 years, at which time he will reemerge to seduce the nations one last time. (Revelation 20:2, 7)
+ And, of course, he "deceives the whole world"— which is the premise of this book. (Revelation 12:9)

Satan has spared no effort in his desire to hurt the Lord by ruining and destroying the lives of the humans He loves. He has tasted power and desires to rule all of creation. Of course, this is only the fantasy of someone who is deceived himself and has become deeply insane due to his pride and rebellion.

A MASTER INFLUENCER

Beyond all the designations and attributes we've already reviewed, Satan is also a communications expert. Anyone who can convince others to agree with his perspective could be considered an effective speaker. But someone who can appeal to people so that they dial into his frequency and accept his thoughts and motives as their own is truly a persuasive orator. Surely Satan must be considered the greatest communicator of all time—other than the Lord, of course.

Let's face it—when the devil speaks, people listen. Unquestionably, he boasts an extraordinary track record of successfully promoting his multifaceted agenda. One of the most powerful forms of deception he has spawned is religious conviction. Just think about how many billions of people he has deceived using false religion. Consider these noteworthy accomplishments:

SATAN IS A LIAR

. In Mesopotamia, he inspired the fertility cults,
the worship of "the host of heaven," polytheistic
idolatry, and the pseudo-science of astrology.
. He successfully promoted these cults across the known
world until every culture had their own "gods."
. In India, Satan concocted a religion called
Hinduism, which continues to thrive to this day.
. He seduced the Jewish people into serving
Baal, Molech, Chemosh, and Ashtoreth,
rather than the God of their forefathers.
. Once Israel returned from Babylon—cured
of their incessant devotion to idolatry—he
inspired religious men to adopt a dead formalism
rather than a heartfelt love for Yahweh.
. In the Far East, he crafted a new religion known as Buddhism.
. In the first century, he corrupted Christianity through
Judaisers, Gnostics, and various antinomian cults.
. The Dark Ages brought corruption of the Christian
Church in the rituals and formalities of Catholicism.
. In the seventh century, Satan appeared to a young
man named Muhammad in the guise of Gabriel,
giving him a mandate to conquer the known world.
. In more recent times, he has introduced cults into the
Church such as Mormonism and the Jehovah's Witnesses.

All of these false religious systems come from the mind of
Satan. He deceives in many ways, but his primary motivation
is to lead people into anything that will keep them from a
genuine relationship with Yahweh.

A PATHOLOGICAL LIAR

Earlier, I briefly mentioned pathological liars. These
are not people who occasionally tell lies or even those

who habitually lie. These people have, at some level, slipped over the edge of insanity and no longer have a grasp on reality. This surely describes Satan. Centuries of living in utter falsehood have left him emotionally and (obviously) spiritually ruined. Yes, he propagates deception, but more than that, he no longer even has the capacity to comprehend Truth.

When Lucifer went about convincing other angelic beings to join him in his insurrection, Jesus was there, watching the entire event unfold. In fact, He has witnessed all of the great deceptions that Satan has hatched. He knows the makeup of Satan's character like no one else.

Jesus said that the devil "...does not stand in the truth because there is no truth in him..." (John 8:44) I will offer this statement in a few other Bible versions because Greek terms do not always fit neatly with their English counterparts. My hope is that by looking at the verse in different translations, we can gain a fuller appreciation of what Jesus wanted to communicate to us.

+ Satan "...has never been truthful. He doesn't know what the truth is." (God's Word)
+ Satan "...has never dealt with the truth, since the truth will have nothing to do with him." (Philips)
+ Satan "...cannot tolerate truth because he is void of anything true." (Voice)
+ Satan "...has never been on the side of truth, because there is no truth in him." (AMP)
+ Satan "...abode not in the truth, because there is no truth in him." (KJV)
+ Satan is "...a hater of truth—there is not an iota of truth in him." (LB)

While the NASB reads in the present tense, the King James Version (KJV) reads past tense (reflecting the grammatical variations of different biblical manuscripts). I am uncertain as to which is true to the original Greek, but if the KJV is correct, Jesus was referring to the fall of the devil. In other words, the devil deserted the truth. He truly was the first backslider.

The word for "stand" (*steko*) in John 8:44 is typically translated as "persevere." There are occasions when Satan happens to find himself standing in the truth simply because he often misapplies it to accomplish his deceptive objectives with people. However, you can be sure that truth is never in his heart for long. As I mentioned earlier, he no longer has the capacity to differentiate between truth and falsehood because he is so permeated with all that is false.

Jesus also said that "Whenever he speaks a lie, he speaks from his own nature, for he is a liar and the father of lies." (John 8:44) Again, let's refer to other translations to round out this concept more fully:

+ "...When he speaks a lie, he speaks from his own resources, for he is a liar and the father of it." (NKJV)
+ "...At the core of his character, he is a liar; everything he speaks originates in these lies because he is the father of lies." (Voice)
+ "...When he utters falsehood, he is only uttering what is natural to him; he is all false, and it was he who gave falsehood its birth." (Knox)
+ "...he's full of nothing but lies—lying is his native tongue..." (Passion)
+ "...When he lies, it is consistent with his character..." (NLT)
+ "...When he lies, he speaks his native language..." (NIV)

- "...When he lies, he speaks out of his own character..." (ESV)
- "...when he tells a lie, he is expressing
his own nature..." (Moffitt)

Satan has spent 6,000 years basking in deceit. Everywhere he goes, he brings with him a powerful spiritual atmosphere of deception. (Ephesians 2:2) In the same way that a man in a rage will provoke fear in others when he enters a room, Satan's presence casts a false light on everything when he shows up. People's thinking becomes confused and slanted away from the Truth.

Satan taught himself to lie, taught his minions to lie, and has taught humans to lie. As Jesus said, he is the progenitor of all deception. As the master deceiver, he inspires his followers in the best way to convey false impressions; he teaches them the arts of disinformation, doublespeak, and half-truths; he coaches the most convincing actors in playing the part of sincere Christianity; and, he instructs the most effective subterfuge to cover up the very sins into which he himself entices. There simply is no escaping the truth of what Albert Barnes wrote: "...all liars possess his spirit and are under his influence."[5]

Unquestionably, Satan is at the root of all falsehood, but, at the end of the day, all of the devil's power to deceive notwithstanding, each human has a free will, along with the ability and responsibility to resist him. Yet he is so masterful at deceiving people that he has learned how to use their most basic desires to accomplish his great objective: to ruin their souls and take them to hell.

SATAN IS A LIAR

"An unmortified desire which a man allows in, will effectually drive and keep Christ out of the heart."

-CHARLES WESLEY[1]

"One of the best results of temptation is that it shows us what is in our hearts."

- A. B. SIMPSON[2]

TWO:
THE POWER BEHIND
SATAN'S LIES

Gladys Decker tried to calm herself, but it was useless. She was facing one of the most important decisions of her life and was well aware of its implications. What seemed like an opportunity of a lifetime lay before her. On the one hand, she was filled with a gnawing sense of dread if things backfired. On the other hand, the possibilities of such a lucrative return left her in a state of breathless exhilaration and fixed anticipation.

Her late husband, Wilbur, had left her a modest savings of $55,000. It was not a great fortune, even in 1920, but it was enough for her to live out her remaining years in relative comfort. At any rate, if the claims being made by Charles Ponzi proved to be true, an investment in his Securities Exchange Company would bring a 50% return within 45 days: a quick profit of $27,500! She could afford a brand new Model T Ford! She could even buy one of those grand houses on the north side of Boston! All this would be in addition to her retirement funds.

When Gladys first heard the claims coming from Ponzi, she wrote them off as the exaggerations of some kind of professional huckster. However, her neighbor Mildred was one of the first to invest in the new company—her entire savings of $1,500. Now, a month and a half later, Mildred received a check for $2,250, just as Ponzi had promised.

"What more proof do you need, Gladys?" Mildred had chided her. Here was tangible evidence to support the fact that the man's claims were legitimate. The newspapers were full of stories of others whose investments had earned huge profits. Gladys' growing feeling that she would miss the opportunity of a lifetime drowned out the thoughts of concern that nagged her. "I'll go to the bank today!" she announced to herself.

Unfortunately, Gladys Decker would never see her life savings again. She, along with ten thousand other people, had been taken in by what became famously known as the Ponzi Scheme.*

Before 1920, Charles Ponzi was a typical, run-of-the-mill con artist. But one day he stumbled across a bit of information that would help to earn him a place in the annals of modern day crime. He discovered that by buying American postal reply coupons and cashing them in at foreign post offices he could quadruple his money. In reality, the enormous undertaking of buying and selling these coupons made the enterprise virtually unworkable. But Ponzi was a master at creating and maintaining the illusion of success and somehow managed to convince a number of people to invest in his plan.

"As Ponzi paid the matured notes held by early investors, word of enormous profits spread through the community, whipping greedy and credulous investors into a frenzy."[3] Within a few short months over nine million dollars poured into his bogus business, an incredible sum of money in those days. Ponzi made it big through patience. Rather than take the money and run, he used the fresh capital to pay back the promised returns. Word quickly got around that his investment plan really did pay off.

Charles Ponzi's success can be directly attributed to his genius at manipulating people. Exuding a quiet confidence,

* The story of Gladys Decker is a fictional story based on real-life events.

he understood that in order to get people to give him their money, he would have to expertly manipulate their conflicting emotions of fear and greed. He knew he would have to present a plausible, likely scenario of how the profits would be made. Ponzi had a way of using words to throw such a false light on the subject that people would lose their ability to perceive the inherent dangers in the investment which he so cleverly attempted to conceal.

While he soothed away their fears with charm, he fanned their insatiable lust for instant gain and profit. He understood that the best way to quiet a person's suspicions was to dangle the anticipated payoff before his eyes. The hidden inner workings of greed would do the rest.

PEOPLE ARE OFFERED WHAT THEY WANT

The story of Charles Ponzi illustrates why Satan's strategy so effectively captures souls. In the same way he inspired Ponzi to appeal to the greed in people, the devil appeals to the desires of the fallen nature to lure people away from the Truth. It goes without saying that every human—whether they are true believers, hypocrites, or pagans—has inherent lust for various forms of sin (i.e., they are tempted to commit certain sins but not others). It is part of the fallen nature that has come to us in birth.

Satan's greatest asset in his efforts to influence and deceive is that he understands what people want to hear; their ears are wide open to anything that supports, encourages, and helps them achieve their cherished desires. As I wrote in another book, *"People are only vulnerable to being deceived when they want what is being offered to them."*[4]

This dynamic can be clearly seen in the ploy of espionage called the "honey pot." A honey pot is typically a beautiful woman who subtly makes herself available to a man who has information her intelligence chief wants. She allows herself to be drawn into a sexual relationship to gain the crucial information she is after.

The classic biblical example of this is Samson and Delilah. To his demise, she was able to manipulate him into sharing the secret to his immense power. The consequences were horrible: both of his eyes were gouged out and he was chained to a grinding wheel which he pushed around a circle for endless hours every day.

This is a common ploy in spycraft, and this is the very tactic lying spirits use against Christians. I would not push this opinion, but I think that every human being has at least one demonic entity assigned to observe them and strategize how to ruin their lives. Apparently C.S. Lewis believed this idea because it lies behind the storyline of his immensely popular satire, *Screwtape Letters*.

Hear me out on this. Let's say that there has been some foul spirit following your life since childhood. This demon knows *everything* about you: your interests, your likes and dislikes, the things you do when no one is looking—*everything*. In fact, I would guess it knows more about you than you know about yourself! This devil knows how powerful idolatry can be, so it simply ascertains which form of sin to nurture in your life until it eventually develops into a full-blown obsession.

Scripture confirms that we each have the potential for evil within us when it says, "But each one is tempted when he is drawn away *by his own desires* and enticed. Then, when desire has conceived, it gives birth to sin; and sin, when it is full-grown, brings forth death." (James 1:14-15, emphasis added)

True believers understand that the Lord wants them to maintain a vigilant war with these desires. (Galatians 5:17) Paul told the Galatians that "those who belong to Christ Jesus have crucified the flesh with its passions and desires."

(Galatians 5:24) There was a time, he told the Ephesians, that "we too all formerly lived in the lusts of our flesh, indulging the desires of the flesh and of the mind, and were by nature children of wrath, even as the rest." (Ephesians 2:3) But now we are called to "walk in the Spirit" so we "will not carry out the desire of the flesh." (Galatians 5:16)

Peter came along later and exhorted his readers, "As obedient children, do not be conformed to the former lusts which were yours in your ignorance." (1 Peter 1:14) In the following chapter he added, "Beloved, I urge you as aliens and strangers to abstain from fleshly lusts which wage war against the soul." (1 Peter 2:11)

The Bible could not be clearer: the passions of our lower nature should be resisted and overcome.

SATAN'S END GAME

The devil's primary target in the Last Days is not the ranks of unbelievers whom he already controls but Bible-believing Christians who desire to please God. Satan understands full well that the tendency of the Church is to lag but a step behind the world. He is using technological advances to lead churchgoers into becoming so addicted to a pleasure-oriented lifestyle that they will never find their way out.

Paul the apostle saw this day coming. Not long before he was martyred, the Lord opened the eyes of his heart to see into the distant future. The sight he received that day must have been shocking and disconcerting to him. Christians by the millions would be characterized by extreme self-centeredness and carnality. He quickly wrote down all the Lord was revealing to him in his final letter to his faithful disciple Timothy.

"Men will be lovers of self, lovers of money," he began. They will be "lovers of pleasure rather than lovers of God, holding to a form of godliness, although they have denied its power…"

(2 Timothy 3:2, 4-5) As Paul continued describing the moral climate within the Church during this difficult period, he exhausted his list of negative traits. He then turned the conversation toward what he clearly saw as the solution: the Word of God! It is the one source of Truth that God's people can always turn to when in times of confusion and declension:

> All Scripture is inspired by God and profitable for teaching, for reproof, for correction, for training in righteousness; so that the man of God may be adequate, equipped for every good work.
>
> I solemnly charge you in the presence of God and of Christ Jesus, who is to judge the living and the dead, and by His appearing and His kingdom: preach the word; be ready in season and out of season; reprove, rebuke, exhort, with great patience and instruction.
>
> For the time will come when they will not endure sound doctrine; but wanting to have their ears tickled, they will accumulate for themselves teachers in accordance to their own desires, and will turn away their ears from the truth and will turn aside to myths. (2 Timothy 3:16-17; 4:1-4) †

Paul could see the day when carnality and worldliness would overrun the Church. Once that happened, people would contort the fundamental beliefs of the Church into a new collective mindset dictated by their emotions and desires. Perhaps if he saw the church now, he would have expressed his concerns in an outburst more along these lines:

> Listen carefully! Make sure you hear me and never forget what I'm telling you here, Timothy! The Word of God

---

† This is one of many unfortunate chapter breaks that were artificially introduced into the Bible during the Middle Ages.

is the only trustworthy standard that can be used as a guide to life's decisions. That's why it is so important to effectively utilize the Word of eternal Truth in people's lives. Ministers must use Scripture to reprove those who are straying from truth. Only the clear teachings of the Bible can correct those who are developing errant ideas about Christianity. Pastors must constantly teach and reinforce what the Word says about the spiritual life. They must disciple people into righteous living.

This is so important because the Lord has shown me that the time is coming when professing Christians will be controlled by their carnal passions rather than by a love for God. If they don't have a bulwark of truth built inside them through Scripture, they will simply repackage the gospel into something that seems to support the self-indulgent lifestyle their flesh desires to lead.

No wonder Paul was so upset. He clearly saw a time in the future when professing Christians would be so given over to their lust for the things of the world that they would demand that the teachings coming forth from the pulpit be force-fitted into what they wanted. The message was clear: end time churchgoers will "not endure sound doctrine" and "will turn away their ears from the truth." *They will find for themselves man-pleasing preachers who will flatter them and give them a distorted gospel that will allow them to pursue their worldly interests and carnal desires without conviction.* One old time preacher summed up the driving force in these people:

> They love their lusts above the law, and therefore they hate him that reproves in the gates. Errors they can tolerate, and superstition they can tolerate, but the truth they cannot bear...

Unsound persons cannot endure sound doctrine...
They cannot endure to have the law preached, their
consciences searched, nor their sins discovered... In the
last days there will be many false teachers. There will not
be one or two, but there will be heaps of them, the world
will swarm with them. Men will have variety of lusts, and
those call for variety of teachers to uphold them... If men
once set open their doors, they shall not lack deceivers.[5]

REINFORCING FALSE BELIEFS

The enemy uses the driving energy of lust to make
temptation so alluring, to entice people into sin and idolatry.
But he also uses people's desires to trap them in other ways.
Consider this little known historical anecdote.

Yuri Andropov, the chairman of the KGB in 1981, had
convinced himself that the U.S. was preparing serious plans
to launch a preemptive nuclear attack on the U.S.S.R. The
memory of Hitler's sudden and unexpected attack on Russia
in 1941 still lingered in his mind. Even closer to home was
the Hungarian revolt of 1956, which he witnessed firsthand,
when members of the secret police were hung on lampposts.
Andropov, and Soviet Premier Leonid Brezhnev, were certain
that America was preparing a preemptive strike against Russia.

The first rule of Intelligence is that *you never ask for
confirmation of something you already believe to be true.* And
yet this is exactly what Brezhnev and Andropov did with
their agents. It did not take long for the Soviet intelligence
community to realize that any report that conflicted with
Andropov's opinion would be rebuffed and might even
provoke a reprimand. So Soviet spies only brought intelligence
that supported his theory. Of course, launching a preemptive
nuclear strike on the U.S.S.R. was the furthest thing from the
minds of U.S. military and political leaders of that time. But

the Russians preferred to believe a lie and allowed their bias to blind them to the truth.

I mention this story because it perfectly illustrates how professing Christians often turn to false teachings that support what they want to believe. Woe to the preacher who attempts to tell such Christians the truth! They are determined to reshape God into the god they want Him to be, but the desire to believe something does not make it true. A person can force-fit Scripture to affirm what he wants to believe, but one day he will have to face the Truth.

THE NEED FOR TRUTH

There is a story in John 8 that illustrates the inner-workings of our post-truth world. Jesus had been teaching in the temple and people were responding to His words. In fact, in verse 30, John tells us that "many came to believe in Him." This must have encouraged His disciples as it seemed people were really responding to the Lord.

Nevertheless, this newfound commitment to God quickly began to unravel when Jesus proclaimed, "If you continue in My word, then you are truly disciples of Mine; and you will know the truth, and the truth will make you free." (John 8:31-32) This did not sit very well with the people. "We are Abraham's descendants and have never yet been enslaved to anyone," they retorted. "How is it that You say, 'You will become free'?" Jesus answered them, "Truly, truly, I say to you, everyone who commits sin is the slave of sin." (John 8:33-34) This represents a huge problem between God and man—do not miss this! These people were offended by Jesus' implication that they were not free because that meant there was something wrong with them. John said that this particular group of Jews "believed in Him." However, in their hearts they "believed" in the same way that many of today's professing Christians "believe"—they believe in the Lord's existence and accept the primary doctrines of the Bible, but refuse to acknowledge any implication of sin in their lives.

The dialogue continued as Jesus attempted to reveal spiritual truth to them. His efforts, however, were not bearing fruit. The Lord exposed what was in their hearts when He said, "But as it is, you are seeking to kill Me, a man who has told you the truth, which I heard from God; this Abraham did not do." (John 8:40) Later, He would cry out in the temple, "Jerusalem, Jerusalem, who kills the prophets and stones those who are sent to her! How often I wanted to gather your children together, the way a hen gathers her chicks under her wings, and you were unwilling." (Matthew 23:37) Man's reaction to God's dealings often follow this same pattern: All is well while God's blessings flow, but when the man of God begins to expose and confront sin, a killing spirit manifests within the people.

Finally, Jesus said to them, "If God were your Father, you would love Me, for I proceeded forth and have come from God, for I have not even come on My own initiative, but He sent Me. Why do you not understand what I am saying? It is because you cannot hear My word. You are of your father the devil, and you want to do the desires of your father..." (John 8:42-44a)

Jesus put His finger on the root of the issue here. Most professing followers—even those who "believe"—will not listen to Him or anyone He sends if they expose what is really in their hearts. This crowd did not want the truth He was bringing to them because it meant they would have to give up the things of the world they lived for, the things their carnal appetites craved, and the "desires of" the devil.

Jesus told the people that the devil was a liar and that they should not listen to his promptings. Why was it so difficult for them to discern this? They would not hear the Lord because the devil was giving them a form of religion that allowed them to keep their carnal lifestyle.

Earlier, Jesus made the same point to Nicodemus, one of Israel's religious leaders. He said, "This is the judgment, that the Light has come into the world, and men loved the darkness rather than the Light, for their deeds were evil. For everyone who does evil hates the Light, and does not come to the Light for fear that his deeds will be exposed. But he who practices the truth comes to the Light, so that his deeds may be manifested as having been wrought in God." (John 3:19-21)

Those who rewrite Scripture to suit their personal tastes are bringing judgment upon themselves. And they remain completely oblivious to the fact that the judgment is the lying preachers who tell them exactly what they want to hear.

"Satan gives Adam an apple, and takes away Paradise. Therefore in all temptations let us consider not what he offers, but what we shall lose."

-RICHARD SIBBES[1]

"Every moment of resistance to temptation is a victory."

-FREDERICK W. FABER[2]

THREE:
THE FIRST SEDUCTION

By the time Satan had his first encounter with Eve in the Garden of Eden, he had already seduced a third of the angelic population to follow him in a great insurrection against God's authority. Although we have not been allowed to see the inner workings of that rebellion, we have been shown his first attempt at deceiving human beings.

Ultimately, the predominant purpose the devil has in attempting to lead humans astray is to win their allegiance for himself. As we saw in the last chapter, he primarily appeals to the "lusts of the flesh" that are inherent in every human being. But in the case of Eve, he had to use a different tack because at that point she did not have a fallen nature. So his approach with Eve was to cast doubt on God's intentions.

What we believe about God is extremely important. In fact, it is the foundation of the believer's faith. Jesus said, "This is eternal life, that they may know You, the only true God, and Jesus Christ whom You have sent." (John 17:3) How can a person be involved in a relationship with someone whom he distrusts? How can he live the Christian life—with all its demands and sacrifices—if he is uncertain that the Lord is actually who He claims to be? It simply will not happen. And so, Satan is always attempting to create doubt in people's minds about God's good intentions.

WHEN LIFE WAS PERFECT

Undoubtedly, Earth must have been a lush and beautiful planet, with the Garden of Eden—probably located in the southernmost region of Mesopotamia—being particularly verdant. Genesis One depicts the wondrous story of creation, the highlight of which was when the Lord created a being in His image. Man was to be a thinking, reasoning being with which He could enjoy a love relationship.

Remember, Adam was created as a fully-grown man. This means that he had no history—no childhood, no experience of puberty and those awkward teen years—no lifetime of interactions with other humans. It is unclear how long Adam lived alone on earth before God created Eve. However, one thing is certain: during that time he enjoyed unhindered fellowship with the Lord.

In Genesis 3:8, we are told that Adam and Eve "heard the sound of the LORD God walking in the garden in the cool of the day." I personally believe this was an everyday occurrence prior to the fall. Perhaps Adam spent his daytime hours exploring the Garden, observing and naming its creatures, and simply enjoying his beautiful habitat. But I would imagine that the highlight of each day was the evening when he knew Yahweh would come to spend time with him.

As blessed as this fellowship must have been for Adam, it was also a wonderful thing for Yahweh. When you love someone, there is enjoyment just being with them. One can see the Lord's feelings about people hinted at in Scripture. Psalmists would later write that Yahweh "delights in" a man's way and "takes pleasure in His people." (Psalm 37:23; 149:4) In Jeremiah the Lord exclaims, "I will rejoice over them to do them good and will faithfully plant them in this land with all My heart and with all My soul." (Jeremiah 32:41) And Zephaniah wrote that "He will exult over you with joy, He will be quiet in

His love, He will rejoice over you with shouts of joy." (Zephaniah 3:17) This is a Being of tremendous love!

As much as Yahweh enjoyed having Adam to Himself, His utterly unselfish nature motivated Him to think about what would make Adam most happy. Apparently the Father, the Son, and the Holy Spirit got into a conversation* about the first human. The Father said to Jesus and the Holy Spirit, "It is not good for the man to be alone; I will make him a helper suitable for him." (Genesis 2:18) The Lord then put Adam under divine anesthesia, extracted a rib, and used it to create a woman.

The beautiful agape love he had enjoyed with the Lord could now also be shared with a fellow creature. From this time on, God would fellowship with both Adam and Eve.

However, for love to come into full maturity, it must first pass the test of fidelity.

THE INITIAL SUGGESTION

This amazing relationship with Yahweh must have been the predominant feature of the daily lives of Adam and Eve. It is into this glorious setting that an intruder enters the picture. "Now the serpent was more crafty than any beast of the field which the LORD God had made." (Genesis 3:1) "These words fall as a sudden intrusion into an otherwise glorious account of God's majestic work of creation," comments R.C. Sproul. "With the words 'Now the serpent,' the whole atmosphere of the biblical record changes dramatically. A sudden and ominous sense of foreboding enters the narrative."[3]

The first thing that stands out to me about the unfolding of this drama is when and where it occurs. It is clear that Satan waited until Eve was by herself—out from the covering of her husband. He found her alone and unfortified by Adam's

---

* In some inexplicable way that is beyond our comprehension, the members of the blessed Trinity speak to each other. One example of this is found in Psalm 2.

authority and counsel. Though sinless, she was still vulnerable to temptation and seduction.

He also waited until she was near the tree of the knowledge of good and evil so he could draw her attention to it. No wonder Paul the apostle would later warn the Corinthians: "But I am afraid that, as the serpent deceived Eve by his craftiness, your minds will be led astray from the simplicity and purity of devotion to Christ." (2 Corinthians 11:3) The Apostle of Grace perfectly described what happened in the Garden. It was through a subtle, underhanded conversation that he seduced Eve. People may think he came up to her hissing out his statements, but I think he came across as an angel of light; i.e., a friendly being with a warm smile.

Notice also how he began his assault with an innocent sounding question. He casually asked her, "Indeed, has God said, 'You shall not eat from any tree of the garden'?" (Genesis 3:1)

His approach is something one would expect from a concerned friend. I have long believed that this was not actually the first conversation Satan had with her. There seems to be no surprise from Eve that a snake was talking to her. If there is one thing that stands out about the devil it is his impeccable timing when presenting temptation. He will gladly wait for a long time to catch a person in the perfect moment of vulnerability to make his presentation.

Notice secondly how he misquoted what the Lord had told her husband. He deemphasized the lavish bounty God had bestowed on this couple in the Garden. The Lord had told them to "eat freely," denoting a tremendous bounty of pleasure. Eden probably offered dozens of different kinds of exotic fruit. The Lord had essentially told them, "You can have any of it and as much as you want, you just can't eat from this one tree."

Satan masterfully understated what they were allowed and quickly led her to focus on the one thing that was forbidden to them. The unspoken (or maybe it was spoken, just not recorded) implication was, "Why was this tree withheld?" Perhaps the devil even asked her, "Eve, doesn't it strike you as strange that God has put restrictions on you? Why would He do that?"[4]

One other thing I should point out about his suggestion is how he put her into the position of questioning God's word. The insinuation was that she had every right to express doubts as to His intentions. In Satan's thinking, it would only be right for the Lord to prove His trustworthiness to her.

Satan's tactic was designed to start Eve on a path that would lead her to doubt God, to distrust God and finally, to disobey God. All temptation begins with the idea that we have a right to evaluate what God has said or required. And the process of every sin follows this same pattern of temptation and indulgence.

Perhaps he suggested other questions as well: "You've been assuming God has your best interests in mind, but what if He's holding out on you? Don't you think God is being needlessly narrow and restrictive? Don't you think it's time you start thinking for yourself? Don't you think it's time for you to enjoy a little freedom?"

The enemy especially brings such suggestions to us when we are going through a difficult time in life. In fact, once God meted out their punishment, I could imagine Satan coming back to Eve saying, "See! I told you God isn't good! Look at what He's done to ruin your life!"

The enemy has an arsenal of arrows at his disposal. If things are going well in our lives, it is used as proof that the Lord only wants to lavish us with material blessings and overlook all of our sins. It is the faulty reasoning that exaggerates God's love and grace at the expense of His righteousness and justice. On the other hand, if we are experiencing trials and facing difficult circumstances, the enemy will introduce thoughts that cast doubt on God's goodness and tell us He's not being fair. Satan is perfectly content to lead people off into either error.

THE TEMPTATION

Eve had never had any reason to question the Lord about anything before this day. At this point, she was still completely innocent, as can be seen by her response to the snake's suggestion: "From the fruit of the trees of the garden we may eat; but from the fruit of the tree which is in the middle of the garden, God has said, 'You shall not eat from it or touch it, or you will die.'"

At this point, Eve has put herself in an extremely vulnerable position. For the first time in her life she began considering the desirability of the forbidden fruit—a thought she had not even entertained before this conversation. Like the decision to commit any sin, she was choosing to go her own way rather than staying within the confines of God's will. For the first time in her life, mistrust of the Lord had entered her thinking.

THE LIE

Satan's first open attack on God's word was to call into question the reality that sin has consequences. "You surely will not die!"

By this point, Satan had established himself as Eve's friend and benefactor. He had led her to mistrust God's intentions and motives. He had gotten her to consider the possibility that the Lord was being overly restrictive and even unfair. Now he introduces the idea that there are no consequences for sin.

He has successfully introduced this same lie into the Church of our day. He has spun a theological system that convinces people that they can sin willfully, continuously, and indefinitely without consequence.

The enemy has successfully used this tactic for the entire history of man. Satan is continually attempting to discredit God and His messengers. The greater the purity of truth a messenger brings, the more the enemy casts suspicion about him in the minds of his sheep; demons do their utmost to drive wedges between Christians and faithful ministers.

As Matthew Henry once said, "Satan teaches men first to doubt and then to deny. It is but a short step from questioning God's Word to denying it."

After introducing doubt, Satan offered Eve an exciting alternative: "For God knows that in the day you eat from it your eyes will be opened, and you will be like God, knowing good and evil."

In other words, the day, the very moment you eat of the fruit, your eyes will be opened to marvels you could never imagine. This is clearly an attempt at creating a sense of dissatisfaction with the many blessings God had already bestowed upon them.

This situation is very reminiscent of the Ponzi scheme where the conman skillfully soothed away people's fears while, at the same time, excited their greed. This scheme has been practiced from time immemorial. Temptation always offers itself as win-win: there are fantastic pleasures to be had and there will be no consequences. Deception contains within it all of this intricate and slimy trickery.

THE RESPONSE

Up until this time, Eve had probably not even noticed the fruit on that tree. God had told her she could not partake of it, so there was no reason to pay any attention to it. Now she allowed her mind to dwell upon it; she savored the thought of what she might experience. "When the woman saw..." (Genesis 3:6) Here again, we see how this fiend works. Satan does his utmost to get our eyes off the things of God and onto the temporal pleasures of this world. *Then,* he presents the temptation.

In this one exchange, lust entered the human race. For the first time ever, Eve was driven by the desire for something she did not have. Even though God had supplied an entire paradise full of delights, it was not enough. Now she wanted not only more, but also what was forbidden.

"When the woman saw that the tree was good for food, and that it was a delight to the eyes, and that the tree was desirable to make one wise..." (Genesis 3:6) Her mind had become opened to an entirely new realm. She became so fixated on these exciting new possibilities that God and His commandment were completely lost to view.

Lust within the human heart takes on a life of its own. It lies dormant in the human breast, but once its desires are stirred, it comes to life. If lust is fed, it grows—if fed continually, it becomes an insatiable monster.

In Eve's case, we see all three forms of lust coming alive: lust of the flesh ("the tree was good for food"), lust of the eyes ("it was a delight to the eyes"), and the lust of pride ("the tree was desirable to make one wise"). Satan will always appeal to one of these lusts which lie dormant within every human.

The *good* knowledge God wanted His people to have was to be brought about by seeking Him, loving Him, and learning from Him what was good and right and true. But "the tree which is in the middle of the garden" offered a mixture of good *and* evil. If it were simply a tree of evil, it still would have been tempting, but how much more powerful is the enticement when good is mixed in with it. Such disobedience is easily justified.

The realm of evil can be very inviting. There is something in our fallen nature that is drawn to its darkness. This horrible domain includes sexual perversion, idolatry, hatred, self-will, envy, and every other form of evil imaginable. These enticements are fascinating to the one who has not been bitten by the snake enough times to understand the cost that comes with them.

Once Eve allowed herself to focus on the fruit, the fall was inevitable. Her eyes and her mind *were* opened, just like Satan had promised. The best illustration I can think of what Eve experienced was the first time I walked into an adult bookstore in 1972. An entire world of evil knowledge opened up to me. Every wall was covered with images I had never before seen. What was represented in those pictures was delicious, exhilarating and powerfully captivating.

Once a person opens his mind to the images of pornography, it takes a long time of abstinence before any semblance of innocence can be regained. But even then, the person's mind has been stretched with forbidden knowledge that can never be completely forgotten.

For Eve, there was no going back at this point. In her attempt to create a paradise of her own—a paradise of carnal delights—she lost the true paradise and would never be able to regain it.

When Eve bit into that fruit, her taste buds must have become electrified. Her senses were probably lit up by the fires of hell. In one instant, she went from being one with Christ to being one with Satan; from loving to taking; from having a beautiful spirit to having ugly desires growing within her; from having a sound mind to being estranged and disconnected from the kingdom of God; from being a sweet and innocent girl to being a seductive pleasure-seeker.

The first thing Adam and Eve did after biting into that fruit was to cover themselves with fig leaves. What does that tell us about what was going on inside them? I believe we cannot fathom how dramatically their sexuality was transformed. When they bit into the fruit it was as if they took a tab of LSD or smoked a joint of PCP. It must have seemed like a horrible acid trip and it was one from which they never recovered.

Of course, once she sinned, Eve's first order of business was to act as Satan's advocate and the promoter of his interests. She immediately found her husband and convinced him to join in her rebellion. And it is often the case that when one person gets seduced into sin, they immediately find someone else to join them. This can especially be true of husbands and wives who can so easily lead each other astray. So, in effect, Eve had unwittingly signed on to advance Satan's objective—to derail God's plan to create mankind in His spiritual image.

So often temptations fall short of what was promised, but in this case Adam and Eve got exactly what they so badly wanted — the knowledge of good and evil. Was it worth it? Now there was nothing left but the penalty of sin—and it was an overwhelming penalty. Their lives were turned upside down by this one act of rebellion.

When they *dis*-obeyed God's commandment, the process of death was set into motion—in their souls, in their bodies, and in the world in which they lived.

THE JUDGMENT

Of course, God was aware of the temptation and their sin, but how sad it is to think about the Lord coming down into the Garden to fellowship with His beloved people, only to find them hiding in the bushes in stark terror, desperately wanting to avoid Him.

"They heard the sound of the LORD God walking in the garden in the cool of the day, and the man and his wife hid themselves from the presence of the LORD God among the trees of the garden." (Genesis 3:8)

What a pathetic sight: Adam and Eve hiding from that marvelous Presence that you and I fight and struggle to find.

Yet, we unwittingly do the same thing when we give over to sin. A wedge is thrust between ourselves and God every time we purpose within ourselves to commit some flagrant act of defiance.

"Then the LORD God called to the man, and said to him, 'Where are you?'" This was a call of tremendous pathos. It was divine sorrow grieving over the plight of the sinner.

It reminds me of David mourning over the death of Absalom. "The king covered his face and cried out with a loud voice, 'O my son Absalom, O Absalom, my son, my son!'" (2 Samuel 19:4) I could just imagine the Lord crying over Adam in the same way, "O my son Adam, O Adam, my son, my son! What have you done? What's to become of you now?"

Of course, we are all familiar with the consequences of their actions. They were driven out of Eden and forbidden to ever return. From that moment on, life became exceedingly difficult. Yes, Satan truthfully promised that their eyes would be opened to a new realm they had never experienced. But as is so often the case with him, he shields people from the reality of the terrible price that comes along with that sin.

THE GREAT QUESTION

There was a reason God put that tree in the garden and told them not to eat of it. The whole point was to create a situation where they would have the choice to obey or disobey. How could they truly love God if they did not have the choice *not* to love Him?

In his sermon entitled, *How to Escape Deception*, Zac Poonen raises the question as to why God allows His people to be tempted: "I wouldn't allow some deceiver to come into my home and sit with my children," he remonstrates. "Why does God allow it with His children? He allows it to test them to see if they are truly devoted to Christ. The Apostle Paul shared this same thought when he said to the Corinthians, 'For there must also be factions among you, so that those who are approved may become evident among you.'" (1 Corinthians 11:19)[5]

The bottom line is that this universe has been established as a testing ground whereby angels and humans have had the right to choose to love and obey God or to turn away in self-love and rebellion. This choice does not vanish when we say "the sinner's prayer." It remains before us the rest of our lives. As Jesus warned, "But the one who endures to the end, he will be saved." (Matthew 24:13)

As I said, the Lord created man so that He might have a thinking, reasoning being with which He could enjoy a love relationship. But the only way that man's love would have any meaning or value would be for him to have the option not to love and obey God. People cannot choose to love unless they have an alternative.

The great deception Satan executed on Adam and Eve succeeded by getting them to forget about God and to lose sight of the promised consequences if they disobeyed. Yet this is only one of the lies that play a part in the enemy's attempts at seducing people into sin.

THE FIRST SEDUCTION

"Sin has many tools, but a lie is the handle which fits them all."

-OLIVER WENDELL HOLMES, SR.[1]

"One great power of sin is that it blinds men so that they do not recognize its true character."

-ANDREW MURRAY[2]

FOUR:
THE TEMPTER'S LIES ABOUT SIN

When Satan enticed Eve into that first sin, his intentions were simply to get her to rebel against God's command. I doubt that he had any idea how devastating Adam and Eve's first transgressions would be to the human race.

Nevertheless, what occurred in the Garden that day was certainly a game-changer for mankind. The disease of sin had wormed its way into the hearts of people and they now had a propensity to repeat their folly again and again and again. From that moment on, there was an inherent desire within them to pursue that which God had forbidden. The latent "lusts of the flesh" in the bosom of every human could easily be stirred to life.

That first allurement into sin was so momentous, that Satan felt disposed to handle the temptation himself. But once the sin principle became established within the human heart, he could let loose his army of demons to go to work on people. This great resolve to lead people into sin became the unifying purpose of the kingdom of darkness.

The foul spirits Satan dispatches find the human heart is now entirely open to their suggestions. Once they succeed in tempting a person into some particular sin, that individual quickly discovers and relishes its pleasures. The dark spirit working on his heart returns time and again with the reminder of that pleasure. And it seldom takes long before habitual sin has taken hold in the person's heart.

As John the aged apostle said, "To lead a sinful life is to belong to the devil since the devil was a sinner from the beginning..." (1 John 3:8a JB) And that is the great prize that motivates the work of demons among mankind: to capture the hearts of people so that they might become the possession of the devil. However, Jesus Christ also has a mission, as the rest of the verse shows: "It was to undo all that the devil has done that the Son of God appeared." (1 John 3:8b JB)

When a person engages in some sort of sinful practice, the enemy is able to build a structure of wickedness and deception within him. The NASB calls it "the works of the devil," which represents all of the different sorts of evil things one would expect from the enemy: fetishes, phobias, hang-ups, addictions, and perhaps above all else, deception.

The writer of Hebrews also addressed the issue of sin for people. He made an urgent call to avoid entering that path:

> Take care, brethren, that there not be in any one of you an evil, unbelieving heart that falls away from the living God. But encourage one another day after day, as long as it is still called "Today," so that none of you will be hardened by the deceitfulness of sin. (Hebrews 3:12-13)

"Today" shows that sin must be dealt with immediately. "Day after day" reveals that this would be an ongoing battle. In the relaxed atmosphere of Latin countries, the term "mañana"—which literally means "tomorrow"—has also come to mean, "Look, there's no reason to get overly excited about stuff. Things take care of themselves. Just take it easy. You'll see!"—Mañana! This is not necessarily a bad philosophy to incorporate into one's life, as can be seen in the natural joyfulness found in the people of that culture compared to the stressful lives of most Americans.

However, when it comes to dealing with habitual sin, "mañana" is most definitely not the approach to take! Sin must be dealt with now, and it must continue to be confronted and dealt with until victory is achieved. As one old-time commentary suggests, "Tomorrow is the day when idle men work, and fools repent. Tomorrow is Satan's today; he cares not what good resolutions you form, if only you fix them for tomorrow."[3]

Over time, every act of sin deepens the subtle deception and imperceptibly diminishes the person's ability to discern truth. This is typically how the enemy devastates, desolates and destroys a human soul. Webs of deception are spun that diminish the person's ability to discern truth. Over time, layers of falsehood bury him so deeply that his only hope of finding his way back into the truth is through the work of the Spirit of Truth.

Of course, Satan and his minions will do their utmost to keep a person locked into the darkness and confusion of habitual sin. They will not allow him to find his way into the Truth uncontested. Their purpose, from the opening temptation, is to forever lock him into a prison house of sin and deception.

Every temptation builds upon the false foundation of satisfaction and fulfillment. We must remember that these enemies of the human race are spiritual beings and, as such, have the capability to create spiritual atmospheres that are conducive to sin. While such an atmosphere makes sinning easier, perhaps the more serious impact is that it also obscures sin's inevitable consequences.

It is good to keep it in the forefront of the mind that every transgression brings with it varying consequences. When the voices of passion are screaming to be fed, the believer needs to know that there is a massive system of deception that comes along with every sin. J.C. Ryle marvelously captured the sense of this in the following passage:

> You may see this deceitfulness in the wonderful proneness of men to regard sin as less sinful and dangerous than it is in the sight of God and in their readiness to extenuate it, make excuses for it and minimize its guilt. "It is but a little one! God is merciful!"…
>
> Men try to cheat themselves into the belief that sin is not quite so sinful as God says it is, and that they are not so bad as they really are… We are too apt to forget that temptation to sin will rarely present itself to us in its true colors, saying, "I am your deadly enemy and I want to ruin you forever in hell." Oh, no! Sin comes to us, like Judas, with a kiss, and like Joab, with an outstretched hand and flattering words."

Sin is a liar. It reminds me of the proverbial used car salesman who does his utmost to keep the buyer's attention focused on the highlights of the car, while ignoring or downplaying the car's problems that should cause alarm. A person cannot expect agents of temptation, or even his own flesh nature, to be honest with him when the enticement presents itself. But if he will keep Truth ever-present in his mind, the lure will be seen for what it is when it appears.

THE TERRIBLE JOURNEY OF THE PRODIGAL

One can see the lure, the process, the price, and the solution to sin in the parable of the Prodigal Son. The story begins in the Father's house, a place of childhood innocence. This environment undoubtedly provided a simple yet joyful upbringing. True, there were no momentary thrills of sin, but also true is that his childhood years were free from sin's painful consequences.

Be that as it may, one day the young man began hearing voices telling him of a place called the Far Country where unspeakable pleasures are available for the taking. Dissatisfaction and discontentment began settling within his soul as he contemplated that thrilling place. Day after day, he daydreamed about what it would be like to go to such a place. And as he continued to dwell on it, his fantasy carried his heart further away from his Father's house.[*]

One day he announced to his Father that he wanted his inheritance so he could leave. "I'm tired of living in this boring place!" he exclaimed. "I want to go somewhere exciting—like the Far Country!"

Now that he had set his heart on sin, the young man could not get away from his Father's house quickly enough. Perhaps his Father considered attempting to stop him but thought better of it when he considered the wise words of Solomon: "Better to meet a bear robbed of its cubs than a fool carried away with his stupidity." (Proverbs 17:12 GW)

No, the Prodigal was bent on his sin and would not be swayed until he had tasted its delights. Now he couldn't get away quickly enough. Every step away from the family farm increased his sense of freedom. He felt as if obedience and discipline had been an enormous weight on his shoulders. Now he felt free from their constraints.

Unbeknownst to him, his first step out the door set his feet on the path to ever-growing darkness. Gradually a change came about within him, but it was so imperceptible that he did not realize what was happening to him.

---

[*] Fantasies have a way of gaining strength and momentum, which is why it is always best to stop them when they first appear.

Along the way he encountered stop signs emerging from the voice of his conscience warning him not to go any further down this road. Had he been more familiar with the Holy Scriptures, he might have remembered Solomon's warning: "The wise are cautious and avoid danger; fools plunge ahead with reckless confidence." (Proverbs 14:16 NLT) At this point though, he was so bent on his sin that he blew past every warning.

What he did not realize is that every time he bypassed those internal misgivings, he was silencing the voice of his conscience just a little bit more. Before long he had built up a nearly unstoppable momentum propelling him further toward the Far Country. Is not this momentum properly called backsliding?

One day, he finally arrived. And, just as he had been promised, the Far Country truly was a place where all restraints were removed. His pockets bulging with inheritance cash, the Prodigal threw himself into the party life. In the midst of all of the excitement though, he failed to notice that every party and sexual escapade took him deeper into the Far Country and ever farther from his Father's home.

Eventually, of course, his money ran out, illustrating the fact that "the pleasures of sin last [only] for a season." (Hebrews 11:25) Poverty soon overtook him and he ended up in the pigpen where he eventually "came to his senses."

In his case, the story ended well because he experienced true, life-changing, life-giving repentance. He made his way back home where he was greeted with his Father's love and acceptance.†

It would do us all good to consider this story and the fact that when the Tempter comes with his enticements, he does not tell us where that sin is taking us. So let's take a few minutes to consider seven different consequences of sin that the Tempter hides from his intended victim.

---

† It has been my experience that the percentage of people who have traveled this path and come to repentance is fairly small.

1. SIN DEADENS THE CONSCIENCE

The ability to perceive sin's presence in a person's heart and life comes from the conviction of the Holy Spirit through a person's conscience. It operates as an inward monitor of the rightness and wrongness of a person's thoughts, words and behavior.

Unfortunately, sin has affected the spiritual hearing of many people, so it seems that *conscience is loudest when it is least needed and most silent when most required.* An interesting phenomenon I have witnessed on countless occasions over my many years of dealing with people in habitual sin is that those who are most free from its grip are the ones who are most aware of its evil presence in their hearts. Conversely, those who are deeply involved in ongoing sin have the least amount of discernment to its existence in their lives.

The story of the Prodigal Son is an apt picture of how the conscience is defeated by one's infatuation with sin. Little by little, as he became increasingly involved in wickedness, the voice of conscience was becoming silenced; it was becoming seared and losing its ability to operate as the moral guardian of his soul. In fact, no one can persist in habitual sin *without* hardening his heart.

Over time, his perspectives become altered—imperceptibly at first—but a definite change begins to take place within him. Every step that took the Prodigal Son farther from his Father's house was changing him as a person: his values and attitudes about life and sin resembled his Father's less and less. When he had traveled only five miles from home, he had already undergone noticeable changes in his thinking. By the time he had arrived in the Far Country and had spent time splurging in sensuous pleasures, he was a different person; he saw right as wrong, wisdom as foolishness and good as evil.

One of the wages earned through giving oneself over to sin is the gradual loss of the ability to discern truth. As Charles

Spurgeon once remarked, "You can sin yourself into an utter deadness of conscience, and that is the first wage of your sin." Sin is a liar and the more it is engaged, the deeper the deception.

2. SIN CORRUPTS THE SOUL

Another unavoidable consequence to ongoing sin is the spiritual contamination of the soul that takes place. This is the very point Paul the apostle made when he told the Galatians, "Do not be deceived, God is not mocked; for whatever a man sows, this he will also reap. For the one who sows to his own flesh will from the flesh reap corruption." (Galatians 6:7-8a)

This is an unavoidable law of the kingdom of God—every time a person gives over to sin (no matter how trivial it may seem) a spiritual corruption is working its way through his constitution.

Not only was the Prodigal's conscience losing its voice in his heart, but his natural innocence and purity were dying with each new indulgence. It is true that every human is born with the germ of sin in his heart, but it is when he acts upon those impulses that he begins to forfeit his innocence.

Unfortunately, humans have a tendency to quickly forget their sin and move on, but this does not alter the fact that there will be consequences for one's actions. Ruth Copeland poignantly explains this process: "When you have finished committing sin, it is not finished with you. The first cost is high, but it is only the down payment. You keep paying in your conscience, in your body, in the suffering you produce for your family, your friends and your community."[4]

The sinner may forget all about what he has just done, but there is within the human being a recording mechanism that perfectly stores the memory of every thought, word, and action. It is as if we have an internal flight recorder that will be presented to God for His review on Judgment Day.

Recently I heard about a man who underwent brain surgery performed with only local anesthesia so that he could be awake during the operation. The surgeons were trying to determine which parts of the man's brain performed different functions. So they would press on one part and ask him what he experienced. As they began to manipulate the part of the brain that stores memories, he began to recall experiences so vividly that it was as if he were reliving them.

The memories of things we have done fade from view, but the effects of those deeds do not magically vanish. Whether we are aware of them or not, the effects of sin have been introduced inside our inner being, spoiling and rotting us within.

Each new transgression corrupts motives, attitudes, imaginations and values. A sinner's perspectives about God, other people, and life in general become more and more twisted. Over time, the person's perceptions change, his godly values become diminished, his desire for sin grows stronger, and his overall thinking becomes altered. Little by little he is becoming another person.

All these intricacies of sowing and reaping are present in Paul's urgent warning. When a person has finished with his sin, sin has not finished with him.

3. SIN DRAINS AWAY SPIRITUAL VITALITY

Yet another consequence of sin that the enemy hid from the Prodigal is the way it deadens spiritual life. Every step he took toward and into the Far Country took him one step farther away from the life-giving atmosphere of the Father's house.

It was for good reason that Paul reminded his readers that "the wages of sin is death, but the free gift of God is eternal life in Christ Jesus our Lord." (Romans 6:23) This is both a warning and a promise.

The warning is similar to what he told the Galatians that "the one who sows to his own flesh will from the flesh reap corruption." (Galatians 6:7-8a) The Greek word for "corruption" is often used as "destruction." From heaven's perspective, the two are synonymous. When a soul is being corrupted by sin it is, at the same time, being destroyed and put to death; i.e., losing the spiritual life that was once there.

However, just as true is the fact that "eternal life [is] in Christ Jesus our Lord." (Romans 6:23) He is the fountain and source of all spiritual life and the antidote to spiritual death. If a person loses his connection to Him, he has lost everything. As he experiences life *in* Christ Jesus, his spiritual life is going to become increasingly healthy and robust.

It is the life of God that can infuse a sinner with the spiritual energy to fight temptations. It also instills in him an enthusiasm for the things of God.

On the other hand, a life of giving over to the flesh produces death in the soul. How is it possible for a sinner to resist temptation without God's life in him? The only thing such a person can expect will be the sort of apathy, despair, and hopelessness that are the lot of all transgressors who have completely lost the presence of God.

4. SIN ENSLAVES THE SINNER

Those who pursue any form of sin soon experience a painful and tragic change. When the pursuit first began it was only pleasure that was evident. However, it does not take long before sin's chains of enslavement wrap around the person's soul.

The Prodigal would have been wise to consider what Jesus said: "Truly, truly, I say to you, everyone who commits sin is the slave of sin." (John 8:34) Truer words have never been spoken!

Paul the apostle later restated this truth in the form of a question: "Do you not know that when you present yourselves to someone as slaves for obedience, you are slaves of the one whom you obey, either of sin resulting in death, or of obedience resulting in righteousness?" (Romans 6:16) Any honest soul who has traversed the path of darkness intuitively knows the answer to this question.

In the seventh chapter of Book One, I showed how an addiction to a pleasure such as pornography has adverse physiological effects on the body. The soul is also vulnerable to the effects of sin. It may be exhilarating at first, but before long, those experiences lose their luster. And yet, in some inexplicable way, the burning passion for sin becomes more intense. In the end, the pleasure vanishes and all that remains is a cruel taskmaster driving the person on.

Whether it was the life of an African-American in the 19th century or a Greek slave during the Roman Empire, living under the tyranny of a human master is a miserable existence. How much worse is it to have some foul spirit as one's master? One can only imagine how demons toy with their prey, fanning the flames of lust inside the person until he gives in, and then tormenting him with feelings of condemnation and guilt.

Samuel Shaw gives the best advice possible to anyone considering the path of the Prodigal: "Sin, itself is hell, and death and misery to the soul. Avoid sin, therefore, as you would avoid being miserable."[5]

5. SIN LEADS THE SINNER INTO EVER GREATER DARKNESS

The Bible uses darkness as a metaphor that illustrates complete separation from God. Thus, the utter lack of Light presents an apt picture of the lost condition of unredeemed mankind. The prophet foretold the day when the Messiah would appear in Israel: "The people who were sitting in darkness saw a great light, and those who were sitting in the land and shadow of death, upon them a light dawned."

(Matthew 4:16) This image of people sitting contentedly in the domain of darkness is a frightening reality for billions of souls alive today. "Sitting" means they are totally at ease and do not perceive their frightening dilemma; there are no frantic efforts to find their way into the Light, as they remain serenely in the grasp of the Prince of Darkness.

However, this powerful metaphor is even more important to consider for those who had once been in the Light, but have pursued sin right back into the regions of darkness. The first chapter of Romans presents a terrible picture of people being given over to their sin. It is said that "their foolish heart was darkened." (Romans 1:21) This is the same sense that is presented by the psalmist: "There were those who dwelt in darkness and in the shadow of death, prisoners in misery and chains, because they had rebelled against the words of God and spurned the counsel of the Most High." (Psalm 107:10-11)

Sin is both the cause and the product of spiritual darkness. It is the love of sin that leads a person into darkness, and it is darkness that keeps a person in sin. In fact, Jesus said, "This is the judgment, that the Light has come into the world, and men loved the darkness rather than the Light, for their deeds were evil." (John 3:19) Jesus looked at mankind and saw that people had so fallen in love with darkness that they came to worship it. The "judgment" is that they would love it more and more while appreciating and loving the Light less and less. To "love darkness" means to love the things of darkness, thoughts of darkness, and the domain of darkness. Such a person can claim to love Christ, but the reality of his life shows that he loves the things and beings that make up Satan's kingdom.

Paul pleads with his readers to "lay aside the deeds of darkness and put on the armor of light." (Romans 13:12) He exclaims, "Do not participate in the unfruitful deeds of darkness" (Ephesians 5:8) for "what fellowship has light with darkness?"

(2 Corinthians 6:14) In Ephesians 4:18 he mentioned those whose minds have been darkened. Paul is showing darkness to be a spiritual disease that quietly and systematically takes over a person's entire inward life.

6. SIN WILL LEAD A PERSON INTO DANGER

The commander of a military unit that is setting out on a mission into enemy territory knows that he has the latitude to quit the operation if circumstances seem unfavorable. However, he also knows that when he gets to a certain spot in this trek, he can no longer abort the mission. He has crossed the point of no return. Whatever the situation may be, there comes a time when he must go through with the plan, regardless of what he encounters.

Likewise, the person who is bent on having his sin will eventually come to the place where he must make a decision. Will he continue to plunge ahead, regardless of the obvious dangers? Or will he fall to his knees like the Prodigal and return home?

It is one thing to backslide; a Prodigal can still repent and find his way back to the Father's house. But it is also possible for a sinner to reach a point where he has moved beyond the influences of the Holy Spirit. He has become so hardened that he cannot—will not—listen. I believe this phenomenon is what the Bible refers to as apostasy.

Only God knows where that line of rebellion is—when "the cup of iniquity is full." Paul urgently warned against grieving and quenching the Spirit. (Ephesians 4:30; 1 Thessalonians 5:19) Stephen warned about resisting the Spirit (Acts 7:51); the Lord warned that the Spirit will not strive with man forever. (Genesis 6:3) The first chapter of Proverbs tells of those who go so far in their rejection of God that even when they cry out, He will not listen. The biblical story of King Saul is just one example of a man who lost God's presence when he rejected God's authority.

7. SIN EVENTUALLY BRINGS ETERNAL CONSEQUENCES

In spite of all these biblical warnings, many professing Christians will lie themselves right into hell. They are so in love with their sin that they will find any biblical pretense that seems to support their desire to hold onto it.

Albert Barnes lamented sin's power:

Sin is a stubborn and an amazing evil, where it can resist all the appeals of God's mercy; where the sinner can make his way down to hell through all the proofs of God's goodness; where he can refuse to hear God speaking to him each day, and each hour, it shows an amazing extent of depravity to resist all this, and still remain a sinner.[6]

As is so often the case, Scripture presents to us a stark contrast between two paths for every human: Will you be the slave of righteousness or the slave of sin? Will you labor under sin and receive the wages of sin or will you accept the free gift of God?

As we saw earlier, Paul said very clearly that "the wages of sin is death." This connection Paul makes with sin and death is actually a pretty common theme throughout the book of Romans (cf. Romans 5:12; 6:16; 7:5, 24; 8:2, 6, 13). So in Romans 6:23, when he tells his readers that "the wages of sin is death," he is not just making a passing remark. It is something he has been saying all along. How is it that so many are willing to deceive themselves into thinking this Kingdom law is not applicable to them?

Part of the deceptive nature of sin is that people convince themselves that the eternal consequences of it do not apply to them. Most seem to simply shrug and avoid personally wrestling with the question of what their fate will actually be in eternity, as if somehow God's goodness and mercy obligates Him to work things out in their favor. Others have been so inoculated to truth that they have believed the world's opinion that there is no hereafter: when a person dies, he simply ceases to exist.

Oh, how a glimpse out of the realm of Time would change such a flippant attitude! Consider what would happen to the cynic if he could spend but a moment on the outer fringes of hell: if he could smell the stench of sulfur, sense the despair of outer darkness, catch a glimpse of the lake of fire, or hear the screams of its inhabitants. Perhaps then he wouldn't treat such a great salvation with such contempt.

When people stand before God, their self-serving opinions on such matters will be swallowed up in Reality. Then they will know the truth, but it will be too late to enter the freedom it had once offered.

"A divided heart loses both worlds."

"Truth is the life of reality; my outer life corresponds with my inner life. If you love the life of inner reality you will never be deceived. But many Christians are satisfied with a life of pretense. They are external Christians who only emulate the outward life of Christ."

-ZAC POONEN[2]

FIVE:
HYPOCRISY AND
PLAYING THE PART

Each February, the Academy of Motion Picture Arts and Sciences hands out Oscars for various positions in the film industry; e.g., director, cinematography, original screenplay, etc. However, movie connoisseurs most look forward to seeing the winners for Best Picture, Best Actor in a Leading Role, and Best Actress in a Leading Role. Down through the years, actors and actresses have been handed the golden statue for various reasons: sentimental preference for a beloved performer, the best performance in a year of mediocre selections, or a role that was written so well it would make even an average performer look great. Back in the day when I was a movie buff, the performances that always stood out to me were those requiring the actor or actress to get completely out of character.

A quality movie typically has a number of actors that bring life to the storyline. Each artist provides his own brand of impersonation. One such actor who plied his trade during the Fifties and Sixties was Ernest Borgnine. For instance, in *From Here to Eternity* he played mean-spirited Sergeant "Fatso" Judson who pulled a switchblade on Frank Sinatra's character. Yet, in *Jesus of Nazareth* he played a warm-hearted centurion who appealed to Jesus to heal his servant. He was a true character actor in that he could play a variety of different parts. Yet it was his title role in the 1955 movie *Marty* that won him the coveted award for Best Actor. He won the Oscar that year because he magnificently brought to life the role of an Italian-American butcher who, despite being a socially awkward, 30-something bachelor, finds the love of his life. Borgnine made *Marty* a box office success and a somewhat surprising pick as Best Picture because his performance was so compelling and believable.

It was Jesus who first employed the Greek noun "hypocrite" (previously only used in the Greco world to describe actors in a play) as a descriptor of someone who acted as though he had a piety which he did not actually possess. Jesus regularly observed a competition between religious leaders of that time to see who could best play the part of a God-fearing, God-loving man before the audience of his peers. There was an unspoken understanding that the religious leader was not really expected to be the person in his private life whom he depicted on the stage of temple activity—it was his performance that was important. The man who could best execute that part was elected to one of the coveted seventy seats of the Sanhedrin. Jesus labeled these men hypocrites because their private lives did not match their public lives.

INCONSISTENT BEHAVIOR

The main criticism John Wayne received during his years of filmmaking was that he never learned the art of acting. You could say that he was a "what you see is what you get" sort of guy. Wayne did not typically adapt himself to the character written into a script. If anything, scripts were built around his persona. Of course, people flocked to see his movies because they admired the way he carried himself.

No professional in the business would have compared John Wayne's acting abilities with actors like Marlon Brando or Ingrid Bergman.* These were people who became so absorbed in their roles that they would actually become their characters while the cameras were rolling.

The Pharisees' religious performance was the sort of acting which caused Jesus to censure them as hypocrites. "Hypocrite" is a Greek term that was transliterated into English. Strong's Bible Dictionary defines *hupokrisis* as, "acting under a feigned part; that is, (figuratively) deceit ('hypocrisy')."[3] In other words, hypocrisy is simply another way to deceive other people.

This was the sort of religious playacting Jesus could not tolerate. At one point, He said, "You hypocrites, rightly did Isaiah prophesy of you, saying, 'This people honors Me with their lips, but their heart is far away from Me. But in vain do they worship Me, teaching as doctrines the precepts of men.'" (Matthew 15:7-9) In spite of all of their religious activities, they did not possess a viable relationship with God or a sincere desire to please Him.

Some people imagine that claiming to be godly is all that is necessary. They have deceived themselves into believing that because they have the ability to effectively communicate to others that they truly walk with God means they do. In their delusion, they are oblivious to the fact that a discerning person can see that there is no substance behind the façade. They lack credibility in spite of the fact that they have become adept at saying all the right things.

In speaking of the Pharisees, Jesus would later tell His audience to, "be careful to do everything they tell you. But do not do what they do, for they do not practice what they preach." (Matthew 23:3 NIV) Or, as one fanciful paraphrase has

---

* Marlon Brando was nominated for eight Oscars, winning twice. Ingrid Bergman won three Oscars out of her seven nominations.

it, "They don't take it into their hearts and live it out in their behavior. It's all spit-and-polish veneer." (MSG)[†]

At issue is the fact that such people, unlike John Wayne, have two personas—one for other people to see, and the real person who is not for public consumption. This is the meaning of the word duplicitous, isn't it?

Paul had this type of concern over the professing Christians of Corinth. He said to them, "But I am afraid that, as the serpent deceived Eve by his craftiness, your minds will be led astray from the simplicity and purity of devotion to Christ." (2 Corinthians 11:3) The Greek term he used here for "simplicity" was *haplotes*, which literally means singleness or wholeness. In other words, Paul wanted their lives to be consistent; their outward lives should have been consistent with their inward lives. He did not want them to be led by Satan into a duplicitous or double-minded lifestyle. When it comes right down to it, hypocrisy is just another form of deception.

The most comprehensive book I have read on the subject of hypocrisy is *Pile of Masks*, written by Dustin Renz, an evangelist (and a graduate of the Pure Life Ministries Residential Program). He addressed this very subject in his book:

> Double-mindedness is a term that the Bible uses to describe hypocrisy. James uses this term when he talks about a man who prays for something but does not believe that anything will happen. (James 1:6-8) The Greek word for double-minded is di (twice) psychos (mind/soul). It means to be, "inclined toward antithetical ideologies, having conflicting disposition." One lexical aid explains it this way: "It is not merely weak in faith,

---

† I do occasionally glance at The Message translation, but I am certainly not a proponent of it. Someone once said, and I concur, "The Shack is the Pilgrim's Progress of the Emergent Church and the Message is their Bible."

but being disposed to embrace the way of righteousness in faith (believing God's commands and ethical dictates to be good and following them, and believing His promises to be true and relying upon them) while being equally disposed to embrace the way of unrighteousness (disbelieving God's commands and ethical dictates to be good and disbelieving His promises and relying upon one's own means). Such a person is spiritually unstable and prone to duplicity."[4]

Dustin went on to talk about Jesus' statement, "No one can serve two masters; for either he will hate the one and love the other, or he will be devoted to one and despise the other. You cannot serve God and wealth." (Matthew 6:24) He pointed out that hypocrites are actually attempting to live "two lifestyles that are diametrically opposed to each other... the hypocrite tries to force two lives to fit together that simply cannot and will not co-exist. This can be seen when we to try to live for both God and ourselves. If we do this, we will begin to resent God for standing in between us and what we want."[5]

LOVE OF APPROVAL AND THE FEAR OF MAN

Why do people act as though they are living at a certain spiritual level when they clearly are not? The motivating factor of hypocrisy really boils down to the two-sided motivation of wanting to receive the approval of others and/or fearing their disapproval. If a person acts in such a way that he "loses face," he knows he will be treated with little respect. On the other hand, if he acts in such a way that he gains the approval of others, he will be praised. The human ego constantly strives to avoid losing face and to gain approbation.

This compulsion to receive the approval of others is a lust that is every bit as impossible to satisfy as sexual lust. No matter how much admiration a person gains from others, it will never bring true satisfaction. One cannot help but think of the Pharisees who squandered a tremendous opportunity to really know the Lord when He appeared on earth. John the apostle said, "many even of the rulers believed in Him, but because of the Pharisees they were not confessing Him, lest they should be put out of the synagogue; for they loved the approval of men rather than the approval of God." (John 12:42-43)

The word "love" [Gk. *agapao*) here should not be overlooked, because it describes the ruling passion of a person's heart. Hypocrites are those obsessed with their image; therefore, what people think of them is their greatest concern in life. The thoughts of others define their character and expose the chief incentive that compels them in life.

Jesus touched on this motivation on another occasion when He said that, "Hypocrites... love to stand and pray in the synagogues and on the street corners, in order to be seen by men." (Matthew 6:5) It was obvious to Him that these religious actors derived a great deal of pleasure in people thinking of them as being close to God. On yet another occasion, He said that the religious leaders "love the place of honor at banquets... [they love] the chief seats in the synagogues; [they love] respectful greetings in the market places; [they love] being called by men, Rabbi." (Matthew 23:6-7)‡ These men lived to receive the applause of others, as do many in the Church today. For instance, how many pastors use manipulative methods of attracting crowds to their churches because they lust after the respect that comes with having a big church? How many laypeople present themselves as godly, simply so they might gain the approval of other churchgoers?

---

‡ Jesus actually used the word phileo in these passages. Both terms, agapao and phileo, capture the sense of extreme affection for something.

While many are primarily moved to play the part of godliness for the sake of winning approval, others exaggerate their piety from the worry of not receiving respect. Solomon addressed the negative side to hypocrisy when he wrote, "The fear of man brings a snare, but he who trusts in the LORD will be exalted." (Proverbs 29:25) The snare the wise king referred to is a trap the enemy uses extremely effectively to lead people down the path of pride. It is the fear of man that causes many Christians to go along with the world's peer pressure rather than standing for Christ, isn't it?

The converse of this fear, according to Solomon, was to live with real trust for the Lord. He equated having faith with putting one's reputation into the hands of Yahweh: he believed that if he entrusted his ego to the Lord, one day he would ultimately be highly praised by God and man.

CONSIDERING THE ISSUE FROM THE ETERNAL STANDPOINT

Jesus was well aware of the fact that His disciples had been raised in a religious culture that greatly deferred to these religious actors. On numerous occasions He exposed the false-heartedness of the Pharisees. While He was still with them, He wanted to be certain that there was no misconception about God's perspective on what kind of person truly gains His approval. So one day He offered the following life and death advice to His disciples:

Beware of the leaven of the Pharisees, which is hypocrisy. But there is nothing covered up that will not be revealed, and hidden that will not be known. Accordingly, whatever you have said in the dark will be heard in the light, and what you have whispered in the inner rooms will be proclaimed upon the housetops. I say to you, My friends, do not be afraid of those who kill the body and after that have no more that they can do. But I will warn you whom to fear: fear the One who, after He has killed, has authority to cast into hell; yes, I tell you, fear Him!" (Luke 12:1-5)

Jesus made four basic points about the person who is overly concerned with what others think. First, he likened hypocrisy to leaven, which works its way through the entire lump of dough. This illustrates how spiritual acting can become entrenched within a Christian community. Once people begin competing with each other, striving to be highly thought of, it becomes very difficult for them to adopt the humble mindset of the kingdom of God. Hypocrisy has a way of becoming entrenched within a culture.

Second, He wanted His disciples to understand that a day was coming when the truth will come out about every human being. The Final Judgment is a constant reality to genuine believers. At some level, their daily behavior is dictated by the knowledge that one day they will give an accounting for the way they lived. In some inexplicable way that we cannot fathom, our lives will be displayed on a mega-screen in heaven for all to see. "There is nothing covered up that will not be revealed," Jesus assured them.

Third, what Solomon said in the form of advice, Jesus said in the form of command: "do not be afraid of" people. (Matthew 10:26) He did not refute the idea that people can hurt us; they can. We live in a fallen world and being rejected, insulted, or even physically harmed are all possibilities. But, as painful as those things can be, there are limits as to how much people can hurt us. The worst they can do would be to end our time on earth.§ Jesus used the extreme example of death, but the reality is that most people do not live in a

---

§ Trials are a part of the Christian life, but they can only happen to a true believer with God's sanction.

daily fear of being murdered; much more common for people is to live in fear of what others think.

Lastly, Jesus reminded the Twelve of the primary purpose of Judgment Day: that our lives will be evaluated on the issue of obedience.⦗ Elsewhere He said, "...an hour is coming, in which all who are in the tombs will hear His voice, and will come forth; those who did the good deeds to a resurrection of life, those who committed the evil deeds to a resurrection of judgment." (John 5:28-29) No wonder He told His people that it would behoove them to live with a very real fear of God!

SINCERITY IN THE CHRISTIAN FAITH

There is a word that is not used much in Scripture but is huge in separating genuine believers from those who are only playing the part; it is the word sincerity. There are two primary Greek words used to convey the sense of sincerity in the NT.

The first word group stems from the term *eilikrinēs*, which Paul used only a handful of times. However, these verses furnish an important look into the true spirit of Christianity. He told the Corinthians that "...in holiness and godly sincerity [Gk. *eilikrineia*]... we have conducted ourselves in the world, and especially toward you." (2 Corinthians 1:12) He also said, "For we are not like many, peddling the word of God, but as from sincerity [Gk. *eilikrineia*]..." (2 Corinthians 2:17) To the Philippian believers he wrote, "And this I pray, that your love may abound still more and more in real knowledge and all discernment... in order to be sincere [Gk. *eilikrinēs*] and blameless until the day of Christ." (Philippians 1:9-10) Peter would later tell his readers that his purpose for writing to them was to stir "up your sincere mind [Gk. *eilikrinēs*]..." (2 Peter 3:1)

The second Greek term that should be mentioned is *anupokritos*. Dustin Renz writes, "This term is the exact

---

⦗ In Scripture, obedience equates to saving faith (cf. James 2, et al).

opposite of the word for hypocrisy. Its original meaning is, 'inexperienced in the art of acting.' Basically, *anupokritos* describes a bad actor." He went on to add, "*Anypokritos* is the idea of wholeness. If hypocrisy is a divided heart, *anupokritos* is a heart that is put back together."[6]

What most interests me about this term is that it is used antithetically about hypocrisy. Paul told the Romans to let their love be "without hypocrisy [Gk. *anupokritos*]." (Romans 12:9) James would later say that wisdom from God was "without hypocrisy [Gk. *anupokritos*]." (James 3:17)

This was one of the qualities about Charles Spurgeon that won him so much respect and admiration in the late 1800s. On one occasion, he contrasted a hypocrite with a true believer who "will at times begin to be terribly alarmed, lest, after all, his godliness should be but seeming, and his profession an empty vanity. He who is true will sometimes suspect himself of falsehood, while he who is false will wrap himself up in a constant confidence of his own sincerity... Often do I fall on my knees in an agony of doubt, and cry, 'Lord, make me sincere; if I be deceived, undeceive me.' I do not think that any Christian will live long without some such seasons of anguishing self-examination."[7]

Scripture clearly offers two paths a professing Christian might take: He can live a false life of pretense, motivated by the twin desires of gaining undue approval and avoiding legitimate disapprobation; or, he can live a sincere life of godliness and be concerned about pleasing only one Person.

Any sincere believer immerses himself in the one source he can trust to give him the Truth: the Holy Bible.

HYPOCRISY AND PLAYING THE PART

"Ignorance of Scripture is the root of all error, and makes a person helpless in the hand of the devil."
-J.C. RYLE[1]

"Christ's words must abide in us. We must day by day increase our reserve of Bible knowledge —this is like gathering the grain in a barn."
-ANDREW MURRAY[2]

SIX:
ETERNAL WORD OF TRUTH

When the Lord formed the nation of Israel, the very first thing He did was to convey a written communication that future generations would be able to turn to in their quest to know and understand the truth about God.

This record began with the giving of the Ten Commandments, but afterwards, a steady stream of divine inspiration, and even audible communication, came to Moses to add to those ten "sayings," eventually involving some six hundred distinct laws contained in the Torah. Later, the great narrative portion of the OT was added; then the Wisdom books were introduced; finally, the inspired writings of the Prophets rounded out the Old Covenant. The Jewish Messiah appeared after 400 years of silence. After His death and resurrection, the Spirit of Truth inspired godly men with a fresh word from heaven which they faithfully recorded. The first century closed with the great Revelation granted to John.

Whatever else it might be or contain, Scripture is the history of God's revelation of Himself to mankind. Through various modes of instruction (stories, commandments, general teachings, wise sayings, prophecies, etc.) the Bible claims to contain and offer to man an utterly reliable presentation of the revealed will of God for the human race.

However, familiarity with the "Word of Truth" (cf. Psalm 119:43; John 17:17; 2 Corinthians 6:7; Colossians 1:5; 2 Timothy 2:15; James 1:18) does not necessarily constitute possessing the "knowledge of the truth." One comes to that spiritual understanding through a process of steps.

WE MUST BELIEVE THE BIBLE

An immoveable conviction that the Bible is the inerrant Word of God written by various men under the inspiration of the Holy Spirit is the only the starting place to discovering Truth. How can one hope to find Truth if there is no credible source in which to turn? Truth must have a firm foundation; otherwise, it is entirely subjective to one man's opinion against that of another.

Of course, you likely would not be reading this book if you did not believe the Bible. You and I accept its creeds, claims, and stories. We believe that God parted the Red Sea; that Elijah called fire down from heaven; that David killed the beastly giant Goliath with a slingshot; that Jonah was swallowed by a great fish and so on. We believe in the virgin birth of Christ; that He was the Son of God, indeed, God incarnate. We believe that He made a way for our redemption by His atoning death on the cross. We believe He will return for His people one day. These are truths and tenets of the faith we all hold dear.

However, it is one thing to deem the Bible to be true and something altogether different to have such certainty in it that one's life is radically changed by the things it says. If we *really* had complete and wholehearted trust in Scripture, we would fall to our knees in convulsive tears of contrition over our lack of love for God and our callousness to the lost condition of our loved ones. A deep yearning for the presence of God would grip our souls, compelling us to spend hours every day seeking His face. I think you get the point: our belief in God's Word is not as strong as we may have imagined.

The virtual onslaught of lies directed against believers undermines our faith in God and His Word. These lies primarily come from two sources: the secular culture and the church culture.

Most people have been raised in a scholastic system that holds in derision the claims of Scripture—especially Creation. Product marketers have convinced us to live for the temporary pleasures of the world. The media offers sitcoms, dramas, "reality" and news shows that present life without God. The internet is a handy gateway whereby we can tap into vast resources of worldly information. Politicians tell voters what they want to hear for the sole purpose of getting elected to office. All of these elements of our culture provide a fatal, relentless message that we should live for the temporal life this world affords.

The second source that assaults the believability of Scripture has actually come from elements within the Church. There is a long history of heresies in Christianity, all the way from the Gnosticism of the first century to the higher criticism of more recent days. One of the latest brands of falsehood at work in the Christian community has come through the Emergent Church. Men such as Donald Miller, Rob Bell, Tony Campolo, William Young, and Brian McLaren have attempted to connect with church kids who have become disillusioned with the hypocrisy and lifelessness they have sensed in much of today's evangelical world.

These modern teachers have enjoyed wildly successful careers by challenging orthodoxy. They have correctly pointed out the lack of life and power in much of the modern Church but, rather than calling Christians back to the ancient paths where the true life in God is always found, they have joined forces with our godless culture in questioning the very foundational truths of Scripture.

The common denominator among false teachers of all ages has been the desire for acceptance from the world. "Woe to you when all men speak well of you," Jesus exclaimed; "for their fathers used to treat the false prophets in the same way." (Luke 6:26) Outright falsehoods are bad enough, but even more dangerous are teachings that contain a mixture of truth and falsehood.

It has been said that bank tellers are taught to spot counterfeit money not by studying counterfeit bills, but by doing a thorough examination of authentic bills. This is a trustworthy method to finding biblical truth as well. The personal quest for truth must begin through a regular, systematic study of Scripture.

THE ATTITUDE TOWARD SCRIPTURE

A sincere seeker will not discover truth until he has disengaged from deception. There is a reason why "many" end up on the broad way that "leads to destruction" and "few" live on the "narrow way that leads to life." One path takes no effort to tread, while the other requires great diligence and effort.

One passage of Scripture that offers these opposing roads is Psalm One. In six short verses, it exposes the folly of listening to the voice of the world, contrasts it with the wisdom of Scripture, and concludes by showing the ultimate end of each of these paths.

Keil and Delitzsch, considered to be the classic expositional commentary on the OT, offers this profound translation of verse one: "Blessed is he who does not walk in the state of mind which the ungodly cherish, much less that he should associate with the vicious life of sinners [i.e., the lifestyle of godless people], or even delight in the company of those who scoff at religion."

I offer their paraphrase of this verse because it really

captures the sense of what David* was communicating. He wanted the readers of the book of Psalms to be aware of the powerful effects godless influences can have on the heart. We all have a worldview that exists in a state of flux because it is constantly being biased by outside influences. Satan is unceasingly communicating his message through the spirit of this world. He may speak his message very subtly, but make no mistake about it, he is whispering his lies through every streaming movie, sports site, and news program. Lying, lying, lying; always distorting the truth; always advertising the "benefits" of life without God.

People who regularly subject themselves to "the state of mind which the ungodly cherish," have little interest in the Word of God. Such people are immediately contrasted with those who long for the fulfilling life that only Scripture can provide: "But his delight is in the law of the LORD, and in His law he meditates day and night. And he will be like a tree firmly planted by streams of water, which yields its fruit in its season, and its leaf does not wither; and in whatever he does, he prospers." (Psalm 1:2-3)

The word "delight" rules out those who open their Bibles reluctantly and think that a sermon on Sunday morning should suffice. No, such people are invariably those referred to in verse one and who will share the fate of those who "are like chaff which the wind drives away." (Psalm 1:4) Churchgoers who spend hours every day subjecting themselves to sinners and scoffers rather than God's Word will one day be "put to shame" and "dismayed," because they have essentially "rejected the word of the LORD." (Jeremiah 8:9)

The reason I typically spend anywhere from one to four hours in Scripture every morning is because I greatly need

---

* Most scholars attribute this psalm to David even though its author is not named.

God's influence in my heart and life. Yes, I need to study it because I am a minister, but much more importantly, I am in the Word every day because my life depends on it.

I am amazed at how little interest God's people show for Scripture. I can assure you His Word is not ignored or arrogantly dismissed in the eternal realm; the Lord puts an incredible degree of value on His Word. In fact, David claimed that God magnified His Word even above His own name! (Psalm 138:2) The Psalmist exclaimed, "The law of Your mouth is better to me than thousands of gold and silver pieces." (Psalm 119:72) Jesus said, "For truly I say to you, until heaven and earth pass away, not the smallest letter or stroke shall pass from the Law until all is accomplished." (Matthew 5:18) Only earthly minded humans feel that they need not be bothered with Scripture, and such haughtiness has no place in God's kingdom. "This is the Lord's declaration," we are told in the book of Isaiah, "I will look favorably on this kind of person: one who is humble, submissive in spirit, and trembles at my word." (Isaiah 66:2 CSB)

Paul said, "Let the word of Christ richly dwell within you." (Colossians 3:16) "Retain the standard of sound words which you have heard from me... Guard, through the Holy Spirit who dwells in us, the treasure which has been entrusted to you." (2 Timothy 1:13-14) The writer of Hebrews admonishes us to "...pay much closer attention to what we have heard, so that we do not drift away from it." (Hebrews 2:1) Peter posited, "like newborn babies, long for the pure milk of the word, so that by it you may grow in respect to salvation," (1 Peter 2:2) John Wesley later added:

> I have thought, "I am a creature of a day, passing through life as an arrow through the air. I am a spirit come from God, and returning to God: just hovering over the great gulf; till, a few moments hence, I am no more seen; I drop

into an unchangeable eternity!" I want to know one thing: the way to heaven; how to land safe on that happy shore. God Himself has condescended to teach the way; for this very end He came from heaven. He hath written it down in a book. O give me that book! At any price, give me the book of God! I have it: here is knowledge enough for me.[3]

The necessity of a daily infusion of truth from God's Word cannot be overstated—our need is tremendous. We are being bombarded with falsehood from our culture, and to make matters worse, our fallen nature wants to hear and believe those lies!

To derive any real benefit from Scripture requires a balanced approach to the Bible: i.e., we must not only grasp what the Bible writer was actually saying mentally, but we must also absorb it as the living Word with the power to transform one's heart.

WE MUST SPEND TIME IN GOD'S WORD

It has been my experience that those Christians who do spend time in the Bible usually just read it. There is value in reading it with purpose, but many are content to put forth the least amount of effort as possible. Vance Havner once compared those who only superficially skim through the Bible with window shoppers, who move from store to store but never actually purchase anything:

The Bible window-shopper moves along through the Book reading its precious promises, hearing its high challenges, looking at its deep messages of peace and power and victory. But he never makes them his own. He appreciates but does not appropriate. He respects his Bible, argues for it, counts it dear, but its rich treasures never become living realities in his own experience. He is a window-shopper amongst the storehouses of God's revealed truth.[4]

To *study* the Bible means to utilize trustworthy resources to gain a better understanding of what the original text was communicating. There are various ways to accomplish this. A believer who wants to understand the Bible no longer needs to be fluent in biblical languages because of the quality study materials available. Some materials offer analysis on the Hebrew and Greek terms employed by the original writers.[†] One of my favorite ways to study biblical terms is to do word searches with a quality Bible study program to see how those words are used elsewhere.[‡] I find this immensely helpful in acquiring a well-rounded understanding of the word as it was actually being used by its author.

Also helpful in this regard are modern commentators who can be very adept at breaking down the Hebrew and Greek grammatically. They also have the latest discoveries available through archeology and other scientific disciplines enabling them to offer important background information to their readers. This is especially true when reading eschatological passages. For instance, Matthew Henry could not imagine the technology of our day or the Jewish people in possession of the Holy Land. So there are definite benefits to referring to current writers.

However, my experience has been that modern commentators tend to be spiritually limited. One thing I have noticed about scholars who approach the Bible academically is that their examination lies outside of and is not dependent upon their personal walk with God. While such men can offer

---

† Two resources I use regularly are the *Theological Wordbook of the Old Testament* and the *Theological Dictionary of the New Testament*.

‡ I use e-Sword. Please see appendices for examples of this kind of study.

helpful historical and textual material, I rarely walk away from their writings feeling as though I have been challenged or fed spiritually. Most simply do not seem to have experienced the life of God spoken of in the Bible.

It is entirely possible, in fact rather commonplace, to be instructed in the essentials of Christianity and still have no real comprehension of their profound significance. There are scholars who know the Bible from cover to cover yet do not understand what it means to be instructed by the Holy Spirit. They have never undergone the internal revolution that is a vital part of personally knowing the Lord.

Personally, I prefer the writings of old-time commentators who really walked with God. In my book, *A Biblical Guide to Counseling the Sexual Addict*, I referred the reader to Galatians 6:1 where Paul described the type of person who would possess the wherewithal to help a person caught in habitual sin. He said, "Brethren, even if anyone is caught in any trespass, you who are spiritual, restore such a one…" In my book, I went on to describe what I understood "spiritual" to mean, based on what is laid out in Galatians 5:

> A "spiritual" person is one who manifests the fruit of the Spirit in his daily life. Love—whole-hearted devotion to God—is the life force that permeates the being of those who are full of the Holy Spirit. The secret of their indescribable joy lies in the fact that their hearts are perpetually turned toward the One they love. Nothing can disturb the peace—the tranquility of soul—of the saint who regularly communes with God. Out of this rich life in God comes the loveliness of character described in the following terms: patience, kindness, goodness, faithfulness, gentleness, self-control.

With all of this in mind, let us briefly review what some commentators say about those whom Paul calls "spiritual." Robertson's *Word Pictures in the New Testament* concisely defined this term as, "The spiritually led (Gal 5:18), the spiritual experts in mending souls."[5] Dr. John Gill described them as those "such as live and walk in the Spirit, and are strong, and stand by the power and grace of the Spirit of God..."[6] Adam Clarke said that they "have wisdom and experience in Divine things..."[7] Albert Barnes wrote that they are those "Who are under the influences of the Holy Spirit... holy persons..."[8] Finally, Dr. George Findlay remarked that they have "a knowledge of the human heart, a self-restraint and patient skill..."[9]

The inescapable fact is that mere dissemination of facts on sexual addiction will not touch a heart that is hardened by years of sin. Frankly, if the counselor is not walking in the Spirit, he will not be much help to the man coming to him in deep need. Indeed, he will discover that a Christian leader can only take someone to the same depths he himself has gone. Only God has the power to transform a person's heart and only the godly have the spiritual expertise to offer any real help.

In the introduction, we discussed the great depravity of the sexual addict. Men in this spiritual condition need a counselor who is connected to God. Book knowledge about the problem has its place, but that alone is not sufficient to help another. The man actively indulging in the "deeds of the flesh" desperately needs help from someone whose life is exhibiting "the fruit of the Spirit." He needs personal ministry from someone who is feasting daily on the riches of God. "The teaching of the wise is a fountain of life, to turn aside from the snares of death." (Proverbs 13:14)

I realize that the subject of this instruction was the ability to minister to those in sexual sin, but the same principles apply to ministering to any hungry soul. As I said, "a Christian leader can only take someone to the same depths he himself has gone." If we are to sit under the teachings of a minister, we need someone who knows what it means to meet with God, to sit in His presence, to receive from the Spirit of Truth.

The reason that these commentators—A.T. Robertson (c. 1863-1934, Southern Baptist minister), John Gill (c. 1697-1771, Baptist minister), Adam Clarke (c. 1762-1832, Methodist minister), Albert Barnes (c. 1798-1870, Presbyterian minister), and Dr. George Findlay (c. 1849-1920, Wesleyan minister)—could speak with authority on the subject of being spiritually-minded is that they clearly walked in the Spirit themselves. It is obvious reading their commentaries that their writings were inspired—not by "book knowledge about the problem"—but from their personal life in God.

It is not enough to have an academic understanding of what the Bible teaches. We must be in the Spirit who originally inspired it. R.A. Torrey rightly said, "Trying to comprehend a spiritual revelation with the natural understanding is a great mistake."[10] A.W. Tozer expressed the same sentiments in his own way: "The Bible was written in tears and to tears it will yield its best treasures. God has nothing to say to the frivolous man."[11]

"They say the truth hurts. It does at times, but the alternative to the truth is deception— something no right-thinking believer would want, no matter how easy its path might seem."

-THE AUTHOR

"Have I therefore become your enemy because I tell you the truth?"

-PAUL THE APOSTLE[1]

SEVEN:
WHEN THE TRUTH
SEEMS TOO PAINFUL

O ne would expect unbelievers to reject and avoid the truth about themselves. Why should they want to hear something that stings their egos when they feel they have nothing to gain by hearing it? As someone said, "The truth only hurts when you want to believe a lie."[2] Personally, I would prefer to be told a painful truth about myself than to have my ego pampered with lying flatteries. "Listen," I might say to someone close to me. "Give it to me straight. Don't lie to me. There is too much at stake in this lifetime to allow some form of deception to ruin my life."

There was a time when, however fearfully or hesitantly, David prayed, "Search me, O God, and know my heart; try me and know my anxious thoughts; and see if there be any hurtful way in me, and lead me in the everlasting way." (Psalm 139:23-24) The day would come when the Lord would abundantly answer that prayer.

From the time he was a young boy tending sheep in the wilderness, David hungered for the Lord in a unique way. His spiritual appetite intensified as he spent time with Samuel, and deepened during his years of running for his life from Saul. Undoubtedly, David was hitting his spiritual peak when he became king at the age of 30. Yet, within 20 years, he had committed the unthinkable: he had lured

Bathsheba into adultery and had her husband killed to cover up his deeds. How did such a godly man become an adulterer, deceiver, and murderer?

No situation like this is an isolated incident in a person's life. There are circumstances that lead up to a person committing such sin. The story of David and Bathsheba's affair shows how deception gradually took hold of the heart of one of God's mightiest warriors. To really grasp what happened, we must begin in David's early years.

As the youngest of eight sons, David was forced out into the wilderness with the sheep. In those days, shepherds would lead their flocks deep into the wilderness in search of grass. It was not uncommon for them to be out there completely alone for days at a time, with no distractions and nothing to do. While hundreds of other young Israelis would while away their hours throwing rocks and fooling around, a deep longing to know God compelled David to instead spend that time in prayer and worship—God was building something rare and beautiful in this young teenager.

The time came when Saul, king of Israel, was rejected by the Lord. God told Samuel to go "to Jesse the Bethlehemite, for I have selected a king for Myself among his sons." (1 Samuel 16:1) So the old prophet went to the home of Jesse and asked to see his sons. Setting his eyes on Eliab, the oldest son, Samuel said to himself, "'Surely the Lord's anointed is before Him.' But the Lord said to Samuel, 'Do not look at his appearance or at the height of his stature, because I have rejected him; for God sees not as man sees, for man looks at the outward appearance, but the Lord looks at the heart.'" (1 Samuel 16:6-7)

One by one the sons were passed before him and each one was rejected by the Lord. Finally, he was told that the youngest son was out in the wilderness with the sheep. Samuel found him and anointed him to be the next king.

In the ensuing years, David was exalted in ways that were unbelievable. First, he was summoned to the king's tent to play the harp for him as he was being plagued by a tormenting demon. This was followed by his incredible defeat of the nine foot giant. That tremendous exploit opened the door for him to lead his men in victory after victory over the Philistines.

Yet God was not all that interested in raising up another Joshua or Gideon. He saw a rare and priceless hunger for the Lord deep within David that He wanted to foster and encourage. So what did He do? Just when everything looked so promising for this sincere young man, God orchestrated a series of events that forced David to flee for his life. For the next 13 years, he and the men who followed him lived in the wilderness, separated from their loved ones, hiding from Saul.

Most people of Israel wanted to see David immediately inaugurated as king. Think of the heartache they could have been spared had Saul been removed from the throne. He was a terrible king, ruling the country as a cruel dictator. It would have been so easy for God to remove Saul from the picture so that David could have his rightful place on the throne. But no, God allowed this ungodly, degenerate man to run the country right into the ground. Why? Because what He planned to accomplish in the inner life of young David was even more important to Him than the smooth running of His earthly kingdom.

The fact that God dealt with His anointed this way is very difficult for many modern Christians to accept, especially those who emphasize the outward signs of ministry success rather than the character of the man who runs it. However, we should all take note of the fact that the Lord is not awed with the size of a ministry's budget. The number of radio stations a preacher is heard on does not impress Him, or even how many people are supposedly being "saved." God is interested in people entering into a love relationship with Him. He is concerned about the cultivation of true disciples. He is looking for people who know what it means to walk with Him. The work that God accomplishes within a person's heart means everything to Him.

To the sincere believers alive during David's time, it must have seemed like such a disaster when he was run out of the country. However, what was accomplished inside David during those extremely difficult years allowed him to build Israel into a mighty nation. For 3,000 years since then, believers sincerely striving to develop an intimacy with God find much-needed help in the profound psalms David wrote as a result of what God accomplished within him.

The Lord's ways are not our ways. Achieving great exploits for the kingdom of God has its place, but an individual's personal battles are what yield eternal results.

THE BLESSINGS FLOW

Only a handful of men have been able to enjoy the level of fellowship with the Lord that David enjoyed during those years he was running for his life. But the truth is when a believer shows a willingness to suffer for the Lord like David did, God almost cannot help Himself. Goodness is such a part of His nature that He must find a way to bless the person.

After Saul's horrible days on earth came to an end, David was anointed king over Judah, and then, seven years later, over all Israel. Later, when the Lord confronted David through Nathan, He revealed just how great His willingness is to bless the one who obeys Him from the heart. He said, "It is I who anointed you king over Israel and it is I who delivered you from the hand of Saul. I also gave you your master's house and your master's wives into your care, and I gave you the house of Israel and Judah; and if that had been too little, I would have added to you many more things like these!" (2 Samuel 12:7-8) For twenty years wonderful blessings flowed into David's life and his kingdom.

However, during those years a worm began to quietly eat away David's love for the Lord. The palace life with all of its luxuries and power was doing a silent and insidious work on his soul. First, he began multiplying wives. He was king and told himself he could have whatever he wanted. So when he saw some young beauty, he added her to his growing harem. Little did he understand that enjoying the bodies of these girls would not satisfy his sexual passions. In fact, they only served to further inflame them.

When David first became king, what the Lord told Saul could have just as easily been said to him: "Is it not true, though you were little in your own eyes, you were made the head of the tribes of Israel?" (1 Samuel 15:17) But David also became increasingly prideful over those years. It seemed that everything he touched turned to gold. Yes, God was blessing, but was it not because he was such a great man? As his power grew, so did his ego. Hundreds of years later it would be said of King Uzziah what could have been said of David at this point: "But when he became strong, his heart was so proud that he acted corruptly, and he was unfaithful to the LORD his God…" (2 Chronicles 26:16) *The Pulpit Commentary* captures this terrible tendency to be ruined by success:

> If adversity has slain its thousands, prosperity has slain its tens of thousands. When his pillow was the rock and his curtain the cave; when his sword, under Providence, procured him his daily bread from the foes of his country, and the means of existence formed the object and pursuit of life—he was pious and immovable; he must have been active or he must have resigned his life. But now the case

was widely different. He had not only all the necessaries, but all the luxuries which the most refined voluptuousness could devise, attending in rich profusion around him.[3]

THE FALL

Once a man is used in a tremendous way such as David was, it becomes easy to forget what it was like to walk humbly with God. An attitude can creep in that he could do no wrong. From there it is but a short step into the mindset that he is so special that the laws of the Kingdom do not apply to him. "God understands that I carry a huge burden," goes the reasoning. "He understands that I need outlets for my passions. He appreciates the great price I have paid to bring Israel to where it is now." And so goes the fatal thinking that leads to disaster.

David was about 50-years-old when he walked on his roof that fateful day. By this point, his complacent and sloppy spiritual life had drained away the resolve to live uprightly. So when he looked down upon a beautiful woman bathing herself, he found that he had no spiritual strength inside him to resist temptation.

There was a time when David exclaimed, "I will give heed to the blameless way. When will You come to me? I will walk within my house in the integrity of my heart. I will set no worthless thing before my eyes; I hate the work of those who fall away; it shall not fasten its grip on me. A perverse heart shall depart from me; I will know no evil." (Psalm 101:2-4) But he wrote those words when he was pressed in with the Lord. Like the Prodigal, he was now a different man than the one who had penned those words. Now, rather than turning away in shame, as he would have done when he was upright, he allowed his lust to drive him to do the unthinkable.

He sent for Bathsheba and committed adultery with her. This was only the beginning of his troubles. Now David, the sweet psalmist of Israel, the one who all Israel looked on as their spiritual guide, the one they loved not just for the victories he had won for them, but for his life with God—this David—would now be exposed as the man who took the wife of one of his most committed and decorated soldiers.

Had he turned to God right then and humbly repented, things would not have gone so badly for him. Perhaps his son remembered hearing about this situation when he would later write, "He who conceals his transgressions will not prosper, but he who confesses and forsakes them will find compassion." (Proverbs 28:13) Unfortunately, the Lord was not in David's thoughts. Only one thought occupied his mind: how could he get out of this situation with the least amount of damage.

So, rather than turn to God as he had always done in the past when in trouble, he began to scheme his way out of his dilemma. In an effort to cover up his sin, he sent for Uriah and contrived a plot to get his faithful soldier to go home to sleep with his wife, but Uriah refused to do it. Now David's only recourse was to arrange to have him killed. "So hardened does the heart become by dalliance with sin and indulgence in it," wrote a saint from yesteryear; "that even the character and souls of others are to be ruined in order to gratify self and hide iniquity for a few years from human view."[4]

THE AFTERMATH

Once the dust settled, David quickly married Bathsheba and attempted to get back into his normal routine of running the kingdom. But he was in deep spiritual trouble and the worst part of it was that he was oblivious to his condition.

For at least ten months David languished spiritually.* If his carnal pursuits had created distance with the Lord before his

---

* The fact that there was at least a ten month period between committing adultery and being confronted by Nathan is evidenced by the fact that Bathsheba carried the child through an entire pregnancy before its birth.

crime, now he was completely disconnected from God. When he eventually repented, one of his cries was, "Do not cast me away from Your presence and do not take Your Holy Spirit from me." (Psalm 51:11) He had witnessed firsthand the torment that Saul had endured when the Lord withdrew His presence and instead, sent an evil spirit. David did not fall away from God in the same way Saul had so the Lord did not see fit to send a tormenting spirit to him, but he did experience the horrible emptiness of the Lord's departure.

"When I kept silent about my sin, my body wasted away through my groaning all day long," he would later write. "For day and night Your hand was heavy upon me; my vitality was drained away as with the fever heat of summer. Selah." (Psalm 32:3-4)

It is true that David was miserable because God's presence was absent, but it was also because he was bearing an enormous burden of guilt over the things he had done. However, the ugliness of his crimes was too much to acknowledge, so he just kept stifling his sense of guilt. It is exactly this attitude that Paul would later refer to when he spoke of those "who suppress the truth in unrighteousness." (Romans 1:18)

It is an interesting side note that God did not confront David immediately. As is so typical of His dealings with people, He bided His time until the right moment. God understands that to accomplish the most good in a person's heart, timing is everything.

The last statement in 1 Samuel 11 is, "But the thing that David had done was evil in the sight of the LORD." (2 Samuel 11:27) Yahweh was there watching all of this unfold; a quiet presence which David, in his pitiful condition, could not sense.

CONFRONTATION

Finally, when the Lord saw that David was sufficiently spiritually, emotionally, and physically exhausted, He sent

Nathan to confront him. The prophet understood David's fallen condition. He knew that in order to reach his heart with truth, he must present it in such a way that his listener would not stiffen into a defensive posture. Rather than walking up to the king and blasting him with truth, Nathan presented a somewhat plausible tale of a rich man who abused a less fortunate neighbor. But David was so "out of it" spiritually that he was completely oblivious to whom Nathan was actually referring. Surely Nathan's approach was divinely inspired because once he presented the situation, out of the king's own lips came the proper sentence on himself: "As the LORD lives, surely the man who has done this deserves to die." (2 Samuel 12:5)

It was then that the fiery prophet pointed his finger at David and said in the most heart piercing words, "You are the man!" We turn once again to *The Pulpit Commentary*:

> The guilty king sat in silence till the prophet had delivered his charge. The time was brief, but the power accompanying the words was Divine. Swifter than lightning the spell of hypocritical concealment was broken. The bonds in which the unholy passion had long held the soul were snapped asunder. The eye of conscience, turning in upon self, gave fresh life to the old suppressed loyalty to righteousness and God, and, as a consequence, the confession came, "I have sinned against the Lord."[5]

REPENTANCE

After months of misery and delusion, David would later write of this momentous occasion: "I acknowledged my sin to You, and my iniquity I did not hide; I said, 'I will confess my transgressions to the LORD'; and You forgave the guilt of my sin." (Psalm 32:5) Truth penetrated his hardened heart in the same way it did for the Prodigal who "came to his senses" in the pigpen and cried out, "Father, I have sinned against heaven, and in your sight; I am no longer worthy to be called your son..." (Luke 15:18) It is the willingness to humbly respond to truth—no matter how painful it might be—that reveals that a person is a genuine believer.

In the prayer he recorded in Psalm 51, David wrote, "Behold, You desire truth in the innermost being, and in the hidden part You will make me know wisdom." (Psalm 51:6) He had not allowed Truth to reign in his mind and heart for quite some time, but Nathan's confrontation was like the lancing of a painful boil. Yes, it hurt terribly, but, at the same time, it set in motion his path into inward freedom. He had to become absolutely honest with himself and to allow truth to once again have its sway over his innermost being. Until that occurred, there could be no freedom.

This is exactly what Peter was referring to when he would later confront the Jewish people with the truth that they had murdered the long-awaited Messiah. But, at the same time, he wanted them to know that they were not without hope! He said, "Therefore repent and return, so that your sins may be wiped away, in order that times of refreshing may come from the presence of the Lord." (Acts 3:19)

God is gracious and willing to forgive when a person acknowledges wrong, sincerely seeks forgiveness, and turns away from his sin. What a sad comparison are those who demand that God forgives them of sin which they think lightly of and only reluctantly acknowledge.

What a glorious thing about the Lord that He is so willing to receive the penitent sinner. "How blessed is he whose transgression is forgiven, whose sin is covered!" David exclaimed as God's presence returned to him. "How joyful is the one whose transgression is forgiven, whose sin is covered! How joyful is a person whom the LORD does not charge with iniquity and in whose spirit is no deceit!" (Psalm 32:1-2 CSB) The man whose guilt is expunged is the one who completely faces the truth about himself.

Yes, David was now forgiven and his relationship with God restored. But, as we know, he committed awful crimes worthy of death and so was forced to undergo severe discipline from the Lord that continued to unfold throughout the rest of his life. "You acted in secret, but I will do this before all Israel and in broad daylight." (2 Samuel 12:12)

SAUL'S SELF-DECEPTION AND REBELLION

What a contrast was Saul's response when Samuel confronted him for his disobedience some forty years earlier. A brief overview of the story should suffice. The Lord had instructed him, through the prophet, to destroy the Amalekites and everything they owned. God's justice is usually slow and is always sure. The "cup of iniquity" was full for that wicked nation and it was time to execute judgment on them.

Rather than explicitly obeying the Lord though, Saul spared the king, who would serve as a trophy of sorts. He also spared the best of the cattle to feed his men. What happened next was a disgraceful debate that, at first glance, might seem to be no more than differing opinions over instructions the Lord had issued. Actually, this was a completely one-sided argument. Samuel was speaking, "the word of the LORD" to Saul, but the recalcitrant king was unwilling to humble himself and sincerely repent over his disobedience. Instead, what ensued was a back-and-forth exchange of pure truth with insincere excuses. "Woe to the one who quarrels with his Maker." (Isaiah 45:9)

The disagreement began when Samuel found Saul. Immediately Saul began his disingenuous campaign to avert any possible criticism. "Blessed are you of the LORD! I have carried out the command of the LORD." Samuel's response revealed his incredulity: "What then is this bleating of the sheep in my ears, and the lowing of the oxen which I hear?" (1 Samuel 15:13-14)

Undaunted, Saul immediately began to blame-shift: "The people spared the best of the sheep and oxen, to sacrifice to the LORD your God; but the rest we have utterly destroyed." (1 Samuel 15:15)

To this doublespeak Samuel replied, "Is it not true, though you were little in your own eyes, you were made the head of the tribes of Israel? And the LORD anointed you king over Israel, and the LORD sent you on a mission, and said, 'Go and utterly destroy the sinners, the Amalekites, and fight against them until they are exterminated.' Why then did you not obey the voice of the LORD, but rushed upon the spoil and did what was evil in the sight of the LORD?" (1 Samuel 15:17-19)

Saul's attempts to justify himself continued: "I did obey the voice of the LORD, and went on the mission on which the LORD sent me, and have brought back Agag the king of Amalek, and have utterly destroyed the Amalekites." He went on: "But the people took some of the spoil, sheep and oxen, the choicest of the things devoted to destruction, to sacrifice to the LORD your God at Gilgal." (1 Samuel 15:20-21)

A godly minister who has allowed the Holy Spirit to purge him of his own deception can see right through it in others. Samuel would have none of it. "Has the LORD as much delight in burnt offerings and sacrifices as in obeying the voice of the LORD? Behold, to obey is better than sacrifice, and to heed than the fat of rams. For rebellion is as the sin of divination, and insubordination is as iniquity and idolatry. Because you have rejected the word of the LORD, He has also rejected you from being king." (1 Samuel 15:22-23)

Now that it seemed as though there will be consequences for his sin, Saul became distraught. But because his heart was not right, and because he was still self-deceived, all he could offer was insincere repentance and more excuses. "I have sinned; I have indeed transgressed the command of the LORD and your words, because I feared the people and listened to their voice. Now therefore, please pardon my sin and return with me, that I may worship the LORD." (1 Samuel 15:24-25)

Samuel's response was devastating: "'I will not return with you; for you have rejected the word of the LORD, and the LORD has rejected you from being king over Israel.' As Samuel turned to go, Saul seized the edge of his robe, and it tore. So Samuel said to him, 'The LORD has torn the kingdom of Israel from you today and has given it to your neighbor, who is better than you.'" (1 Samuel 15:26-28)

Saul lost the kingdom and, much more importantly, forfeited the presence of God simply because he would not respond when the Lord confronted him with the truth about himself. He did what so many people do today: avoid the truth because they are unwilling to face it and unwilling to deal with it.

Yes, the truth can be painful, but the alternative is unthinkable.

"God uses broken things. It takes broken soil to produce a crop, broken clouds to give rain, broken grain to give bread, broken bread to give strength. It is the broken alabaster box that gives forth perfume. It is Peter, weeping bitterly, who returns to greater power than ever."

-VANCE HAVNER[1]

EIGHT:
GOD DESIRES TRUTH IN THE INNERMOST BEING

In Book One, I painstakingly laid out the case that Satan is using the world system to lie to us on a regular basis. He has filled this planet with falsehood and deception. Whatever segment of society you look in, you will find an enormous amount of untruth.

At some level we have been helpless victims of this onslaught of deception. However, if we are honest with ourselves, we will admit that the effects of this falsehood could have largely been avoided had we not been so plugged into the world's entertainment system. We have presented our hearts, so to speak, to the father of all lies and said, "Here is the core of my being. I put it in your hands—do your worst!"

This constant stream of lies can have a deep and powerful effect on a person's spiritual condition. It is like raw sewage that seeps into a clear stream, contaminating everything it touches. Deception has a way of permeating the deepest recesses of the human heart.

It is the Lord's desire to undeceive those who have come under the enemy's spell. He longs to unravel the falsehood that has become entrenched inside. And it is that desire that brings us back to David's psalm of repentance. Psalm 51 contains statements that are vital to the pursuit of truth.

THE NEED FOR INWARD TRUTH

As David poured out his heart in deep and sincere contrition, he cried, "Behold, You desire truth in the innermost being..." (Psalm 51:6) This statement not only touches on one of God's great desires regarding people, but it also speaks of an important Kingdom principle. Humans are very taken up with what they can *see* in people's lives: how nice they look, their accomplishments, their children, how well or poorly they speak and so on. But, as we saw in the previous chapter, "the LORD looks at the heart." (1 Samuel 16:7) It is the inward being that He is most concerned with because it is the seedbed of all our behavior.

There are a number of Hebraic terms that refer to a person's inner man. Those words are very similar in meaning and are often used interchangeably to designate the entirety of a person's inward life: heart, soul, spirit, and mind. However, *tuwchah*, the word translated by the NASB as "innermost being," seems to carry a slightly different meaning. The ESV translates it as "the secret heart" and the Voice speaks of it as the "unseen places deep within." These three versions of the Bible seem to best capture the overall sense of this word which represents the core of a person's being. It goes without saying that God longs to see truth reigning over our entire inward life, yet how much more concerned is He that it holds sway over the deepest part of our being.

The Hebrew word *châphêts* is translated as "desire" by the NASB, "long to" by the Voice and "delight in" by the ESV. As far as I can tell, all three translations are accurate and reflect different shades of meaning in this ancient word. The NASB alludes to the fact that it is God's will (equivalent to "desire" in Scripture) that His children are constrained by truth. The ESV reflects the fact that the Lord takes joy ("delights") in seeing truth reign in His children. While the Voice brings out the sense of God's yearning ("longs") to see truth held deeply within His people. No matter which rendition of the term one might use, it is clear how much it means to the Lord. I see three important reasons this means so much to Him.

First, we must remember that truth is a major attribute of His nature, characterizing all three members of the trinity. Yahweh is called the "God of truth." (Psalm 31:5; Isaiah 65:16) Jesus revealed Himself as "the Truth" (John 14:6) and also referred to the Holy Ghost as the "Spirit of truth." (John 15:26) MacArthur puts it this way: "Truth is that which is consistent with the mind, will, character, glory, and being of God. Even more to the point: Truth is the self-expression of God."[2] So the Lord continually and relentlessly works to establish and maintain that reality inside His children. *The Spirit of Truth will not feel at home in a temple that houses deception.*

The second thing we should keep in mind is that God hates everything that is false and deceptive. Many professing Christians have unwittingly allowed various falsehoods to take residence inside of them. They have believed lies about themselves, about God, and about the world. If we are going to overthrow any vestiges of deception in our hearts, we must begin by sincerely asking the Spirit of truth to search out our hearts and expose what is false in them. We need the Lord to deal with every inconsistency, every pretense, and every falsehood in the "unseen places deep within."

To grasp the third aspect of truth's importance to the Lord, we must briefly return to the "location" of truth. A person's "innermost being" surely must be synonymous with the substance of his character. In the Introduction to this section of the book, I offered two sets of terms to describe character. First, there were the adjectives describing what I should have been: an honorable man. The second group of words defined what I actually was: "shifty," "selfish," "deceitful," and so on.

Through the sanctifying work of the Holy Spirit, I long ago transitioned out of that second set of adjectives into the first. The truth that reigns within my "secret heart" is a reflection of who I am now. It has been God's will and delight to transform my character into being an upright, honest, and truthful man. In fact, for many years He longed to accomplish this spiritual metamorphosis within me.

CHANGE BEGINS WITH INWARD TRUTH

David's failure with Bathsheba was an enormous wake-up call for him. He was in real trouble. Yes, he had done wicked things, but worse than that, he had long since fallen away from the Lord in his heart. That inward apostasy was the reason he fell with Bathsheba in the first place.

David's prayer of repentance began with a complete and open acknowledgement of what he was like and what he had done.

> "Be gracious to me, O God, according to Your lovingkindness; according to the greatness of Your compassion blot out my transgressions. Wash me thoroughly from my iniquity and cleanse me from my sin. For I know my transgressions, and my sin is ever before me. Against You, You only, I have sinned and done what is evil in Your sight, so that You are justified when You speak and blameless when You judge." (Psalm 51:1-4)

These are the words of a true penitent and stand as a rebuke to those who do their utmost to avoid the truth about themselves. He looked inside and saw how he had allowed uncontrolled lust and pride to grow and fester within him. He saw how corrupted and twisted his perspectives had become. He had offended a holy God by his actions and was undone once he recognized it! He knew that tremendous change must take place inside of him if he was going to find his way back to right standing with the Lord.

This kind of change begins with a person being absolutely honest with himself. Those who gloss over their inward faults experience nothing more than shallow repentance and, at best, a superficial walk with God. This is why many professing Christians never really enter into a meaningful or even saving relationship with the Lord. They do not want to submit to that level of honesty. They have allowed their lives to be directed by their passions and emotions rather than by the Word of God. Elsewhere I wrote:

> The reason that unconverted churchgoers can sidestep the truth about themselves is that the human heart is an inveterate liar. It truly is "deceitful above all things." (Jeremiah 17:9) If a person were to catch an acquaintance in an outright lie once or twice, he would never again trust anything the person might tell him. How amazing then is the level of trust people have for their own hearts—in spite of the fact that they have repeatedly caught the wretch fabricating the truth. Nevertheless, those who want to be flattered will return to this polluted well for facts about themselves time and again. They return because they are told what they want to hear. Nothing hinders an honest self-evaluation like self-flattery.[3]

In the last chapter we took a fairly in-depth look at what happened in the lives of Saul and David. The great difference between these two men was how they responded to confrontation. It is true that David had been in a terrible state of delusion for nearly a year. The truth about what he had done was too painful to face. However, when he was finally confronted with it, he responded in true contrition. His response represents believers down through the centuries who have gotten off track or even sinned terribly, but truly repented to the Lord once confronted.

Saul epitomizes the multitudes that have been unwilling to own up to their sinful behavior. As soon as someone suggests that they need to acknowledge and repent of their sin, their walls go up and their ears go deaf. They might be willing to admit to being sinful in a general way, but they are not willing to get gut level honest with themselves about what is really going on inside.

This unwillingness to admit the sinfulness of one's actions has been a human tendency from the very beginning (e.g. Adam, "The woman you gave to be with me—she gave me some fruit from the tree, and I ate." [Genesis 3:12]) and will continue all the way to the end of time (i.e. "People gnawed their tongues because of their pain and blasphemed the God of heaven because of their pains and their sores, but they did not repent of their works." [Revelation 16:9-10]). It occurs every day from one end of the globe to the other. It occurs in the Church and it certainly occurs outside of it.

One of the most egregious examples of this unwillingness to acknowledge truth was the Lance Armstrong situation that occurred a number of years ago. He won the Tour de France cycling title an unprecedented seven times (1999-2005). As the victories mounted, people in the sport began suspecting that he was using performance enhancing drugs to give him an edge. Here is a quick overview of his responses to reporters over these allegations:

+ 2000—"I am appalled at the unfounded report containing baseless accusations against me."
+ 2002—"Now if that's not a witch hunt, I don't know what is!"
+ 2005—"I've always been open and honest."

+ 2006—"The recycled suggestion that I used steroids is categorically false and distorted sensationalism. My cycling victories are untainted."
+ 2010—"With regard to the specific allegations, I'm not going to waste my time. I think history speaks for itself here."

He refused to come clean with what he had done until he was absolutely painted into a corner. But how many others have done the same thing—even in the Church? As one example, Ted Haggard, former president of the National Association of Evangelicals, who emphatically insisted, "I did not have a homosexual relationship with a man in Denver."

How could these people be so brazen in their lies? This kind of blatant dishonesty is possible because they have been lying to themselves for a long time. These are men who did not want to face the truth about themselves. Although the truth ended up coming out and they eventually acknowledged it, they probably still have not really dealt with that truth in their innermost being.

Perhaps more disconcerting than public figures who feel it is necessary to lie their way out of some allegation are the millions of professing Christians who refuse to acknowledge the sinful attitudes inside them and the sinful practices they do when no one is watching. Such people are unwilling to get honest with themselves, let alone with their mates, spiritual leaders, or God. Therefore, the needed change of character that comes through real repentance never actually happens.

TEARING DOWN THE STRUCTURE OF FALSEHOOD

To understand how the Holy Spirit establishes "truth in the innermost being" and transforms a person's character, I must mention the "change formula" ("We initiate, God empowers.")

I came up with to describe how transformation occurs. It goes without saying that the Lord constantly beckons His people to draw near to Him and to allow Him to have His way in their hearts and lives. However, many Christians do not respond to this call. They prefer to blandly wait for God to do all the work. While it is true that we do not have the wherewithal to change ourselves, we must show the Lord that we are serious about change. As we do, the power of the Holy Spirit will step in and begin to bring about the needed transformation.

To begin this vital process, we must sincerely go to the Lord and acknowledge that we really do not possess a clear sense about what kind of sin and dishonesty resides in our hearts. Earnestly and continuously pray David's prayer until the Lord answers: "Scrutinize me, O God, as you will, and read my heart; put me to the test, and examine my restless thoughts. See if on any false paths my heart is set, and yourself lead me in the ways of old." (Psalm 139:23-24 KNOX)

This is a prayer that God will surely answer. If you will persist in it, He will begin to reveal to you your true condition. Once your eyes open to the reality about yourself, just acknowledge it, ask Him to forgive you and commit yourself to overcoming every vestige of sin and deception.

A commitment to living a truth-filled life requires intentional effort. We must also renounce every form of deceptive communication such as telling half-truths, lies, and any other embellishments of truth. All our social lies and misrepresentations of ourselves must come under God's light.

We must also limit the lying voice of the world in our lives—which most likely means a great deal less time watching television, viewing the internet, and being involved in things like social media. As long as we allow deception to have unhindered access to our hearts, we will never know what it means to live in the truth.

As in all repentance, it needs to be more than one simple act. True repentance is an ongoing and continual attitude. It is never enough to say, "I repented." You must be able to say, "I am repentant. Day in and day out, month after month, year after year, unceasingly, I live in the spirit and attitude of repentance. Furthermore, I live as a changed person."

To allow truth to reign in the inward life, we must determine within ourselves that complete honesty is going to lie at the heart of our new lifestyle. After all, if God really does desire truth in the inward parts, how can He bless someone who will not give up falsehood?

Okay, so that is our part of the formula. We can initiate, but we need God's power to really change us. Part of the reason for this is that the very part of us that needs to undertake this work—our mind—has been terribly corrupted with Satan's lies. Our perspectives of everything have become twisted over the years. This tangled web of deception cannot be undone by making a few resolutions—no matter how sincere they might be. It must be the work of the Holy Spirit in our innermost being. He establishes truth and overthrows deception in two primary ways.

First, He purges falsehood out of us. To understand how the Lord accomplishes this, we must momentarily return to our Hebrew noun, *tuwchah*. It is actually a derivative of the verb *tuah*, which simply means to cover one item over with something else. "It is employed to describe... the process of cleansing a house infected with a plague ("leprosy?") (Leviticus 14:42-48). The priests remove the infected plaster and stones which harbored the disease and repair the house with new stones and plaster."[4]

One gets the sense that this was what David had in mind because in the very next verse of his prayer he asked the Lord to, "Purify me with hyssop, and I shall be clean; wash me, and I shall be whiter than snow." (Psalm 51:7) Alexander MacLaren held that, "purging with hyssop alludes to sprinkling of lepers and unclean persons, and indicates both a consciousness of great impurity and a clear perception of the symbolic meaning of ritual cleansings."[5] David was asking the Lord to purge out of him every vestige of the plague of deception that had established itself in his "secret heart." It is reminiscent of Solomon's statement that, "Stripes that wound scour away evil, and strokes reach the innermost parts." (Proverbs 20:30)

The other significant work the Holy Spirit does to transform us is to tear down every structure of falsehood the enemy has built within us. In his first epistle, the Apostle John offered an amazing insight into how the Lord reverses the devil's work in a human soul. He wrote, "The one who practices sin is of the devil; for the devil has sinned from the beginning. The Son of God appeared for this purpose, to destroy the works of the devil." (1 John 3:8)

We have all had a lifetime of opening ourselves up to the enemy's lies. Other people have misrepresented God and His kingdom to us. We have entertained errant views about life. And, most of all, for many years we have puffed ourselves up with fawning and flattering views of our own goodness. The enemy has been at work in our inward lives, constantly building up a great structure of falsehood within us. Over the period of many years, the devil has buried us with layer after layer of falsehood. But praise God! If we will allow the Lord to work within us, He will break up and tear down that horrible structure of deception. Jesus came "for this purpose, to destroy the works of the devil." He will replace the false with His truth.

As David poured out his heart to the Lord in Psalm 51, he must have thought back to all of the times during that terrible year when he had sanctimoniously offered sacrifices at the Temple. The hypocrisy of it all must have stood out clearly to him. Maybe he remembered what Samuel had told his recalcitrant predecessor when he said, "Has the LORD as much delight in burnt offerings and sacrifices as in obeying the voice of the LORD? Behold, to obey is better than sacrifice, and to heed than the fat of rams." (1 Samuel 15:22)

He surely knew about this incident and yet he too allowed himself to sink into the pretension of hypocrisy. "For You do not delight in sacrifice, otherwise I would give it; You are not pleased with burnt offering," he acknowledged. "The sacrifices of God are a broken spirit; a broken and a contrite heart, O God, You will not despise." (Psalm 51:16-17)

God was doing a deep work inside David through this experience. He had allowed His son to wallow in delusion for nearly a year because He understood that his entire edifice of deception would come crashing down.

This tearing down of the deceitful Self-life is an integral part of the Christian life. As Solomon would later declare, "There is an appointed time for everything... A time to tear down and a time to build up." (Ecclesiastes 3:1, 3b) Before God can build a structure of godliness and truth inside of us, He must first dismantle the selfishness and deception the devil has constructed. God does not tear us down because He enjoys hurting us, or frustrating us, or making us miserable. He does it because He cannot build us up into Christlikeness until He has first torn down our Self-life. He cannot fill us with His Spirit until He has emptied us of ourselves.

"Come, let us return to the LORD," Hosea called out. "For He has torn us, but He will heal us; He has wounded us, but He will bandage us. He will revive us after two days; He will raise us up on the third day, that we may live before Him." (Hosea 6:1-2)

This concludes Book Two. It is now time to examine the roles that Truth and Deception play as the events of the Last Days unfold.

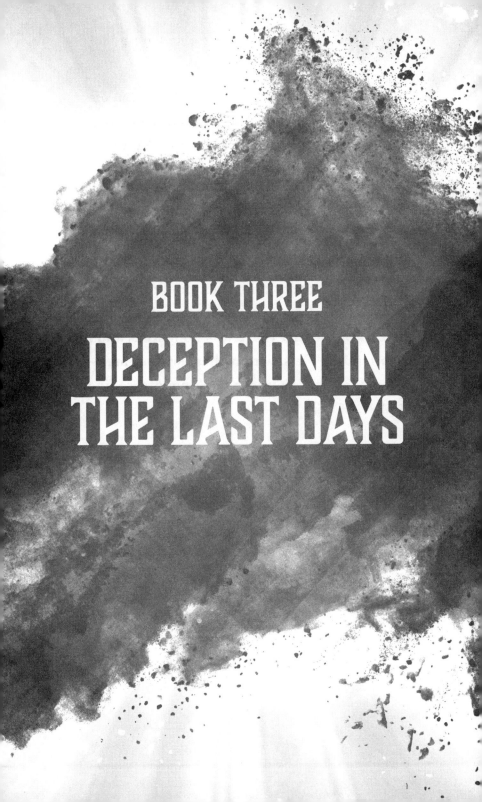

BOOK THREE
DECEPTION IN THE LAST DAYS

"Hear the word of the LORD, you children of Israel, for the LORD brings a charge against the inhabitants of the land: 'There is no truth or mercy or knowledge of God in the land.'"

-THE PROPHET HOSEA[1]

"Justice is turned back, and righteousness stands far off. For truth has stumbled in the public square, and honesty cannot enter. Truth is missing, and whoever turns from evil is plundered. The LORD saw that there was no justice, and he was offended. He saw that there was no man—he was amazed that there was no one interceding."

-THE PROPHET ISAIAH[2]

INTRODUCTION TO BOOK THREE:
BEFORE THE BAR OF GOD

Isaiah's passage quoted above sits in the middle of a national confession of sin by the prophet. This particular portion of Scripture has to do with the lack of truth in the Jewish judicial system of the time.

In all free societies, the administration of justice depends upon a responsible pursuit of truth. When a person has been accused of a crime, the court system is charged with discovering the truth of what actually happened. Did this person actually commit the crime with which he has been accused? This pursuit of truth should be the primary goal of every officer of the court whether it is the judge, the prosecutor, or the defense attorney. However, we know from our own court system that this is simply not what actually happens.

The United States employs what is called an adversarial system of justice. That simply means that the court proceedings are built around the efforts of two advocates who argue their parties' cases before a jury.

The district attorney speaks on behalf of the government and presents his case in such a way that it will prove beyond a reasonable doubt that the defendant is guilty. He does this by presenting direct evidence (e.g., a witness testifies that he saw the defendant commit the crime) and/or circumstantial evidence (e.g., DNA found at the scene of the crime that is explained through an expert witness). It should be noted that, in their determination to win their case, some prosecutors have suppressed evidence that could have cast doubt on the guilt of the defendant.

The defense attorney represents the accused and his job is to use every means allowable in a court proceeding to attack and cast doubt on the veracity of that evidence. For instance, these lawyers can ruthlessly cross examine witnesses produced by the prosecutor. A shrewd defense attorney will craft his questions in such a way as to create doubt either about what the person actually witnessed or about his personal character. Any attempt on the part of the eyewitness to explain himself (i.e., bring out the whole truth of the matter) is quickly stifled with a curt, "Just answer the question!" Even expert witnesses such as crime scene investigators can be personally attacked by a defense attorney in the hopes of casting doubt on their ability to produce accurate testimony.

In his book, *The Lincoln Lawyer*, novelist Michael Connelly brought to light the thinking of defense attorneys through his character Mickey Haller:

> "It didn't matter in terms of the strategy of the case whether the defendant 'did it' or not. What mattered was the evidence against him—the proof—and if and how it could be neutralized. My job was to bury the proof, to color the proof a shade of gray. Gray was the color of reasonable doubt."[3]

Having been a bailiff in the Los Angeles Superior Court Building, I can testify that an honest pursuit of truth about a matter rarely, if ever, occurs. What actually happens in our court system is really nothing more than a game of brinkmanship on the part of the attorneys. You see, the outcome of a case has more to do with who is the most talented and capable at playing the game than it does on discovering the truth. Prosecutors who are adept at winning cases tend to be promoted to prominent positions such as district attorney. Defense attorneys who have a track record of winning acquittals for their clients can command enormous fees for their services.*

The American judicial system is probably as fair as any in the world, but the sad fact remains that it is not established upon the pursuit of truth in the way originally intended. One story has been told that an English judge, frustrated by conflicting testimonies, exclaimed, "Am I never to hear the truth?" The response of one of the lawyers was, "No, my lord, merely the evidence."[4]

What I just presented is a modern version of what Isaiah witnessed in the Jewish courts of his day. However, his metaphor was only meant to be a microcosm of what the Lord was watching throughout the nation of Judah. He personified justice, righteousness, and truth as upright individuals who are not welcome in the court system. Justice attempts to enter the court but is denied admission. Righteousness seems to be so upset over the proceedings that she just keeps her distance. Truth somehow makes it into the court but is tripped up by all of the deception that is being propagated. She is like a reliable witness that has been so cruelly badgered by a relentless barrister that she runs out of the court weeping at the injustice of it all.

When I survey the church scene across America and throughout the western world, I see a similar picture. In our case, the Lord is the judge and He is overseeing the judicial proceedings

---

* While it is true that most people charged with crimes are, in fact, guilty, also true is the fact that defendants who cannot afford prominent attorneys must be represented by stressed out, overworked public defenders. As Clive Stafford Smith once quipped, "Capital punishment means, those without the capital get the punishment."

as they unfold. The Holy Spirit presents a seven point indictment against the apostate church, which is not dissimilar to what was issued by Hosea and Isaiah against the Jewish people mentioned above. The same basic elements are present:

+ Charge One: Many professing Christians have not repented and continue to indulge in corrupt behaviors (deceit, pride, worldliness, carnality, immorality, etc.).
+ Charge Two: In large part the house of the Lord has been defiled by rampant idolatry.
+ Charge Three: The Word of the Lord has been ignored and despised.
+ Charge Four: Many professing Christians have proven to be so unfaithful that they have, in effect, divorced themselves from the Lord.
+ Charge Five: Many ministers have failed to live up to the godly standards of their high calling and have brought reproach on the name of Christ.
+ Charge Six: Many ministers have twisted Scripture by deemphasizing its call for godly living and by exaggerating God's grace.
+ Charge Seven: God's faithful ministers have been ridiculed and verbally attacked by the people they have attempted to reach with the truth.

The defense attorney is Satan, who categorically denies each of the charges brought forth. In each case, his clients are provided every possible means to dispute and cast doubt on the allegations. They shift the blame off themselves by aiming it at others. They minimize the severity of the accusations through levity and denial. They justify themselves by presenting themselves as victims. They offer elaborate rationalizations of their behavior by offering extenuating evidence to explain away their guilt.

The Lord eventually throws up His hands, as it were, and exclaims, "Am I never to hear the truth?" Satan's response is, "No, my lord, merely the evidence. You see, I am devastatingly proficient at supplying every means at my disposal to keep professing Christians from facing the truth of their condition. I have used deception to bring so much confusion into the situation that those who claim to be Your followers no longer have the capacity to discern what is actually true and what is false."

Any sincere believer would acknowledge that we are guilty as charged. Rather than defending ourselves with elaborate excuses meant to diffuse the truth, we should confess our sins and acknowledge our national guilt in much the same way as Nehemiah and Daniel did in their day. Outside of divine intervention, I do not see this happening on any significant scale. I'm afraid that the only recourse is to watch as judgment after judgment pounds our nation until God's people finally fall to their knees, beat their breasts as the publican once did, and cry out, "God, be merciful to me, the sinner!" (Luke 18:13)

"It is difficult to conceive any situation more painful than that of a great man, condemned to watch the lingering agony of an exhausted country, to tend it during the alternate fits of stupefaction and raving which precede its dissolution, and to see the symptoms of vitality disappear one by one, till nothing is left but coldness, darkness, and corruption."

-J.C. MACAULAY[1]

ONE:
THE DEATH OF A NATION

There is no doubt in my mind that earth is experiencing her final gasps of Time. Scripture has much to say about the spiritual climate of the Last Days. We will examine many of these issues—especially deception—throughout this final section of the book. However, before we begin digging into our period of man's history, I would like first to look at life during the final years of the nation of Judah. The Jews were His chosen people and, in that sense, typify the Christian Church of our day. The growing separation from God that occurred in Judah during that period closely resembles what we are experiencing now. It is imperative that we consider how God dealt with the Jewish people, because it is certain that we can expect a similar treatment if we follow the same path.

LIFE IN JUDAH

Although there was the occasional godly king who led the people back to the Lord, for most of its existence, the Jewish nation was plagued with idolatry. The following statement from 2 Kings sums up that period in Canaan: "They worshiped the LORD, but they also served their own gods in accordance with the customs of the nations from which they had been brought." (2 Kings 17:33 NIV) In other words, their religious life contained mixture. By and large, the Jewish people continued to serve Yahweh outwardly, while, at the same time, giving their hearts to the fertility cults they allowed to thrive in their midst.

It could be said that the "last days" of Judah began when the northern tribes were exiled to Assyria in 722 B.C.* This should have been a major wake-up call to the southern tribes, a sign that the incredible patience of Yahweh would eventually exhaust itself with them as well if they did not repent of their waywardness. However, other than a couple of brief periods over the following years,† there is no evidence that the Jewish people took this threat seriously.

What is of primary concern to us in this story is the spiritual condition of the Jewish people during those final years. If there is one word that describes the atmosphere in Judah during that time it is deception. Jeremiah lived and ministered during the final generation of the nation and he mentioned different aspects of deceitfulness some 80 times in his book alone. By the time he began ministering, the Jewish people had become false in every aspect of life. With pinpoint accuracy the Lord identified the problem with the Jews when He told Jeremiah, "You live in a world of deception. In their deception they refuse to know me. This is the LORD's declaration." (Jeremiah 9:6 CSB)

A heavy cloud of dishonesty and duplicity hung over the nation. The spiritual atmosphere was teaming with lying spirits, infesting every edifice from the king's palace to the precincts of the very Temple itself; even "their houses [were] full of deceit." (Jeremiah 5:27) It had gotten so bad that people

---

* Please refer to timelines of approximate dates on page 247.

† The reforms of Hezekiah (2 Chronicles 29) and Josiah (2 Kings 23:1-25) were two such exceptions, though these reforms did not last long because they were superficial and never touched the hearts of the people.

THE DEATH OF A NATION

APPROXIMATE TIMELINE OF JUDEAN KINGS AND PROPHETS

KING	REFERENCE	DATE	PROPHET
Hezekiah	(2 Chronicles 29-32)	728-686	Isaiah, Micah
Manasseh	(2 Chronicles 33:1-20)	697-642	Isaiah, Nahum
Amon	(2 Chronicles 33:21-25)	642-640	Nahum
Josiah	(2 Chronicles 34-35)	640-609	Jeremiah, Nahum, Habakkuk, Zephaniah
Jehoahaz	(2 Chronicles 36:1-4)	609	Jeremiah
Jehoiakim	(2 Chronicles 36:5-8)	609-597	Jeremiah
Jehoiachin	(2 Chronicles 36:9)	597	Jeremiah
Zedekiah	(2 Chronicles 36:10-21)	597-586	Jeremiah

OTHER SIGNIFICANT DATES

Jeremiah & Nebuchadnezzar both born	644	
Daniel and Ezekiel born	622	
Nebuchadnezzar's 1st siege of Jerusalem	605	2 Kings 24:1-4
Nebuchadnezzar's first dream	601	Daniel 2
Nebuchadnezzar's 2nd siege of Jerusalem	597	2 Chronicles 36:5-7
Jeremiah tells Zedekiah to surrender	588	Jeremiah 37-38
Nebuchadnezzar's 3rd assault on Jerusalem	588	2 Kgs 25:1; Lam.
Destruction of Jerusalem and Temple	586	2 Kgs 25:8-21; Jer. 39

could no longer trust anyone to tell the truth. "Everyone deceives his neighbor and does not speak the truth, they have taught their tongue to speak lies." (Jeremiah 9:5)

It was in this wicked culture that Jeremiah was called to minister. From the very beginning the young priest faced a daunting challenge. It seemed that the people were so bent on satiating their lusts with the fertility cults of the day, that they no longer had the capacity to receive spiritual truth. "The prophets prophesy falsely," the Lord lamented. "And the priests rule on their own authority; and My people love it so!" (Jeremiah 5:31) Moral corruption prevailed over Judah from the palace to the Temple and flowed freely in the public streets.

Through all of the opposition he faced, Jeremiah never wavered in his message. In fact, his book speaks of repentance more than the writings of any other prophet. One great passion compelled him and that was that his people would turn back to the Lord in sincere contrition. It was only the sustenance and empowerment of the Holy Spirit that enabled Jeremiah to hold out hope for a people who had so given themselves over to sin.

One cannot spend quality time in the book bearing his name without the undeniable conviction that this was a man who maintained a deep and profound life of prayer. There is simply no other explanation for his indomitable spirit and his unwavering convictions. Dr. Michael Brown conveys his quandary:

Jeremiah was a man shut up to God, utterly trapped and with no way out. He could not run away, and his situation was not like that of Jonah, who tried to evade and avoid the divine call. Jeremiah would have had to try to evade and avoid reality itself! There were two things he could not deny, two things written on the depths of his soul: first, his beloved nation was incorrigibly wicked; second, horrific divine judgment was inevitable. How could he run away from this? With devastating, crushing certainty, Jeremiah knew he could not. Neither could he escape the divine call itself—not a specific mission, as in the book of Jonah, but a lifelong mandate for prophetic ministry. God was upon him; God was within him. God's word proclaimed brought reproach and rejection; God's word held back burned like fire in his bones. How does one escape from this?[2]

One can only imagine how difficult Jeremiah's long years of ministry were. He faced the rejection and even hatred of his nation to the point of physical abuse at times. And, other than a couple of associates, he faced all of this alone. It is clear in his writings that there were times when he felt like he could go on no longer; yet the call persisted and therefore he remained at his post.

In spite of the fact that Jeremiah, Zephaniah, Habakkuk, and others had been warning the people throughout these final years, the vast majority of the Jewish population paid no attention to them. God had been extremely longsuffering with them, but the cup of iniquity was nearly at capacity and the final curtain was about to fall on the nation of Judah.

Having no other recourse left to Him, the Lord finally sent Nebuchadnezzar and the Babylonians against Jerusalem twice—first in 605 B.C. (when Daniel and others were exiled to Babylon) and then again eight years later (when Ezekiel and 10,000 others were exiled as well). Unfortunately, neither of these national calamities brought the people to their knees. In the meantime, Zedekiah was installed as king, bringing with him a hope that the situation could be turned around. If he would obey the Lord, total disaster could still be averted.

ONE FINAL OPPORTUNITY

Jeremiah did his utmost to convince the new king and the people that it was God's will that they repent of their idolatry and submit themselves to the authority of Nebuchadnezzar. However, the prophet's efforts were constantly thwarted by the false teachers of his day. As we will see in ensuing chapters, one of the primary characteristics of false prophets is that their messages are conceived by determining the mood of the people, rather than by seeking to know and proclaim God's will.

"They have healed the brokenness of My people superficially," lamented the Lord; "saying, 'peace, peace,' but there is no peace." (Jeremiah 6:14)

Tragically, it was to these false prophets that Zedekiah chose to turn. His leadership must have been a terrible disappointment to Jeremiah. Just as it seemed that things could get no worse, they did. At the end of the book of Second Chronicles, Ezra described the spiritual condition of Judah in her final years and why the Lord was left with no choice but to send irrevocable judgment:

> Furthermore, all the officials of the priests and the people were very unfaithful following all the abominations of the nations; and they defiled the house of the LORD which He had sanctified in Jerusalem. The LORD, the God of their fathers, sent word to them again and again by His messengers, because He had compassion on His people and on His dwelling place; but they continually mocked the messengers of God, despised His words and scoffed at His prophets, until the wrath of the LORD arose against His people, until there was no remedy. (2 Chronicles 36:14-16)

This statement may be regarded as a formal and final indictment upon the people of Judah, and it warrants our careful consideration. Judgment begins at the house of the Lord (1 Peter 4:17), therefore crimes against the Temple are God's first concern. Ezra said, "The priests and the people… defiled the house of the LORD which He had sanctified in Jerusalem." (2 Chronicles 36:14)

The word "sanctified" [Heb. qadash] is an exceedingly important biblical term because it describes the very nature of God and establishes the basis for His interactions with mankind. He is holy [Heb. qadosh], altogether set apart from

THE DEATH OF A NATION

everything that is common and profane. "By those who come near Me I will be treated as *qadash*," He told Moses. "And before all the people I will be honored." (Leviticus 10:3)

Yahweh had established the House of God as the one place on earth where He could "dwell." It was a sacred place, hallowed by His presence. "While the realm of the holy was conceptually distinct from the world with its implications, it could nevertheless operate within the world as long as its integrity was strictly maintained."[3]

One need only think about what happened to Nadab and Abihu when they offered strange fire on the altar of the tabernacle to see that the Lord takes His place of earthly habitation very seriously. (Leviticus 10:1-2) Later, Uzzah was struck dead for daring to touch the Ark as it was being moved. (2 Samuel 6:7) Still later, King Uzziah was struck with leprosy in the Temple because he dared to take it upon himself to burn incense in it. (2 Chronicles 26:19) The Jewish people, much like American Christians today, had gotten too familiar with the sacred things of God and began to treat them very lightly.

We are told that "the priests and the people... defiled the house of the LORD." (2 Chronicles 36:14) This verb "defiled" is principally used to describe the corruption caused by touching a corpse or eating the flesh of animals considered unclean. It is then extended to describe anything that defiles spiritually.[‡] It is clear that the Jews had lost their fear of God. When people lose sight of God's holiness, they will no longer fear breaking His commandments. Once that occurs, judgment is seldom far behind.

Secondly, we are told that the people were "unfaithful." This word is typically used in the sense of people breaking covenant with God. The Lord saw Israel as His bride. So when they flouted

‡ It was also the word lepers were required to cry out when approaching others. (Leviticus 13:45)

His laws and treated Him with disdain, He saw it as spiritual adultery. Judah was in a full scale backslide into worldliness and idolatry. They were so united with the pagans around them that they had become one with the spirit of the world.

In spite of their condition, the Lord continued to send prophets to warn them that if they did not repent they would face certain doom. Their response was to mock these precious men of God. The people despised the Word of the Lord because it was not what they wanted to hear. They wanted the prophets to tell them that God would bless their plans and bless their lives—in spite of their sinful ways.

While it is true that there have been those who openly mock the things of God, it would be wrong to limit this term to such open and brazen attacks. More important is the underlying attitude of flippancy such men have toward sacred things. The word Ezra used to describe the prevailing attitude was "despise," which means to hold such a low opinion of something or someone that it is considered of little value. This is the same term used when Esau "despised his birthright" (Genesis 25:34) and when Goliath showed disdain for David and his slingshot. (1 Samuel 17:42) Matthew Henry shares how grievous it was that the people treated the prophets so shamefully:

> This brought wrath upon them without remedy, for it was sinning against the remedy. Nothing is more provoking to God than abuses given to his faithful ministers; for what is done against them he takes as done against himself... Those that mock at God's faithful ministers, and do all they can to render them despicable or odious, that vex and misuse them, to discourage them and to keep others from hearkening to them, should be reminded that a wrong done to an ambassador is construed as done to the prince that sends him.[4]

THE DEATH OF A NATION

The mocking of prophets who bring a warning from the Lord is the final step into apostasy. Once the situation deteriorates to that point, there is nothing left but terrifying judgment. It is here that two words are introduced into the passage: "until" and "therefore" both show that time had run out for this wayward people:

> But they continually mocked the messengers of God, despised His words and scoffed at His prophets, *until* the wrath of the LORD arose against His people, *until* there was no remedy. *Therefore* He brought up against them the king of the Chaldeans who slew their young men with the sword in the house of their sanctuary, and had no compassion on young man or virgin, old man or infirm; He gave them all into his hand. (2 Chronicles 36:16-17. Emphases added)

Ezra summarized the ensuing destruction of Jerusalem in one sentence, but one can see the appalling details describing the unspeakable suffering of the Jewish people in the book of Lamentations. The fact that women had to eat their children in order to survive should be enough to show how bad things got in the holy city. Alexander MacLaren offers these thoughts on God's judgment:

> A time arrives when even God can hope for no amendment and is driven to change His methods. His patience is not exhausted, but man's obstinacy makes another treatment inevitable. God lavished benefits and pleadings for long years in vain, till He saw that there was 'no remedy.' Only then did He, as if reluctantly forced, do 'His work, His strange work.' Behold, therefore, the 'goodness and severity' of God, goodness in His long delay, severity in the final blow, and learn that His purpose is the same though His methods are opposite.[5]

SPIRITUAL ATMOSPHERE OF THE WESTERN CHURCH

I believe America is facing a very similar situation. There seems to be no way around the fact that we are on the brink of disaster. We are suffering the same kind of internal corruption that Judah experienced, but I believe we will face greater judgment because our sin is greater.

We won't be destroyed by a marauding nation; we will simply be taken over from within. That is exactly what is happening. The United States is gradually falling in line with the socialism prevalent in Europe and much of the rest of the world. It will not be long before America is no longer recognizable as a truly free nation, as can be seen by the lockdown Americans have been forced to endure due to the Covid-19 pandemic. It is all part of the judgment that we have brought upon ourselves.

There are three reasons why we face greater and more severe judgment than Judah. First, our culpability is greater because our sin is more pervasive. People treat marriage as a temporary commitment which can be abandoned as soon as feelings change. Millions of Americans are addicted to both illicit and prescription drugs. Abortions abound by the millions. The homosexual lifestyle has become a mainstay of American life. Pornography use has become so rampant that even a large percentage of young girls are engaging in it. In fact, it has become fairly acceptable among teenagers to send illicit pictures of themselves to each other. Child pornography has become the new "high" for sex addicts, evidenced by the fact that there are over 100,000 searches for child porn every day.[6]

Not only have Christians failed to respond to this increasing darkness through fasting, prayer, and national repentance, but the darkness has become pervasive even within the Church. Every wicked item mentioned above is currently flourishing in the evangelical community. Can you imagine what Matthew

Henry or Charles Spurgeon would have thought if they could have foreseen the day when tens of thousands of Christian men and pastors would be addicted to watching people have sex on film? The spiritual epidemic of our day is pervasive both outside and inside the western Church.

Second, our blameworthiness is greater than that of Judah because our sin is much darker. With the technological advances we have seen, people are exploring depths of evil that people in past centuries could not have imagined. Every kind of filth a sin-sick human mind might conceive can be found somewhere on the internet. One of the newest online innovations is virtual reality, a concept that is quickly being utilized by pornographers. Before long, virtual sexual encounters will be prevalent. Human-like dolls possessing artificial intelligence are being conceived and produced. One can only imagine the depths of evil in which people will participate in the days ahead.

Third, our culpability is greater than that of Judah because we have sinned against tremendous light. Yes, Judah had the oracles of God, but they did not have the revelation of Jesus Christ and the power of the Cross. There weren't Bibles available by the millions. They did not have access to audio and video sermons of the greatest preachers of the day. They were not privy to the writings of centuries of godly men.

All of the spiritual light we have been given has only made us arrogant and hardened us to the Lord. Our tepid response to the knowledge of God will provoke more judgment on this nation than anything else. This was the very point Jesus made to the people of His day:

"And you, Capernaum, will not be exalted to heaven, will you? You will descend to Hades; for if the miracles had occurred in Sodom which occurred in you, it would have remained to this day. Nevertheless I say to you that it will be more tolerable for the land of Sodom in the day of judgment, than for you." (Matthew 11:23-24)

Jesus was grieved over what He witnessed in Sodom and Gomorrah, but He also saw what was in the hearts of the people of Capernaum. The wickedness that went on regularly in Sodom and Gomorrah was horrible, but from God's perspective, the rejection of the light the people of Galilee encountered was even worse.

The ongoing sin of our day has been confronted repeatedly, but most professing Christians involved in it will not repent. The truth has been offered to us, but we are not interested. How could we possibly expect anything other than overwhelming judgment to come upon our nation?

THE DEATH OF A NATION

"Truth is not the feeble thing which men often think they can afford to disparage."
-HORATIO BONAR[1]

"Truth is so obscure in these times and falsehood so established, that unless we love the truth, we cannot know it."
-BLAISE PASCAL[2]

"False teaching had attached itself to the true, used its language, and professed to be at one with it."
-RAWSON LUMBY[3]

"The chief danger of the 20th century will be religion without the Holy Spirit, Christianity without Christ, forgiveness without repentance, salvation without regeneration, politics without God and heaven without hell."
-WILLIAM BOOTH[4]

TWO:
A WHOLESALE
REJECTION OF TRUTH

There are thousands of articles, books, sermons, and movies available on the internet that address the Last Days. If some energetic soul were to read every book and article, listen to every sermon, and watch every movie, I think he would find two subjects dominating nearly all of this material: the rapture and the antichrist.* Christians love this two-fold theme because it makes for great storylines which are both entertaining and educational. Personally, I have serious reservations about the legitimacy of this narrative. Be that as it may, I can say with confidence that it is certainly not emphasized in Scripture.

When the Bible addresses the subject of the end of the age, its primary concern is the spiritual health of professing Christians.† The picture it presents is not very pretty. It describes a general climate of selfishness, worldliness, and apathy. The one thing that is stressed repeatedly is that there will be deception on a massive scale both outside and inside the Church "so as to mislead, if possible, even the elect."

---

* The "rapture" is an eschatological theory that was conceived in the early 1800s by a man named J.N. Darby. It quickly spread throughout the U.S. and has since become universally accepted as the de facto belief system of the end times.

† The primary passages of Scripture that discuss the spiritual condition of the Church can be found in Matthew 24-25; Luke 17 & 21; 2 Thessalonians 2; 2 Timothy 3-4; 2 Peter 2-3; Jude; and Revelation 17-18.

(Matthew 24:24) Why are Christians so unconcerned about something so strongly emphasized in Scripture?

One of those biblical passages that address this subject is 2 Thessalonians 2. In this portion of Scripture Paul mentions the antichrist in passing, but it is clear that his main concern is the spiritual peril of professing Christians alive during that time. It is a fascinating portion of Scripture because in it the apostle exposes what is occurring in the hearts of the multitudes of Christians who will fall away from God in the Last Days.

I should mention that there are four words that depict deception in this passage of seven verses.‡ That alone speaks loudly about the character of the Church of the great apostasy. In fact, these four terms for deception are used in end times' passages at least 42 times in the NT. Let's begin examining this portion of Scripture by looking at verse 3.

> Don't let anyone deceive [*expatao*] you in any way. For that day will not come unless the apostasy comes first and the man of lawlessness is revealed, the son of destruction.
> (2 Thessalonians 2:3 HSCB)

Paul opens this passage with the same warning Jesus used four times in the Olivet Discourse where He said, "See to it that no one misleads you." (Matthew 24:4; et al) Paul's very first concern is that his readers are not deceived about how the events of the Last Days will unfold. To curtail misunderstandings that were already beginning to emerge, Paul lays out a timeline of what will happen and lets his readers know that the "day of the Lord" (which he had just

‡ I will note these terms in the actual passages as we come to them. For a deeper explanation of them, please refer to Appendix #1.

mentioned in verse 2) would not occur until the apostasy had occurred. Then, sometime after this great falling away was well underway, the antichrist would appear.

It is easy when reading this passage to get the sense that everything described occurs all at once, but that is not the way it will be. As is so often the case, the prophet is only shown certain aspects of an event which would not occur until thousands of years later. He can only write down what he is shown. From his vantage point, it may even have seemed to him as though all of this would unfold quickly. But we know from other biblical passages that it will take a number of years for all of these events to develop.

> For the mystery of lawlessness is already at work; only he who now restrains will do so until he is taken out of the way. (2 Thessalonians 2:7)

It is widely accepted by scholars that this restraining force is the Holy Spirit. The mystery of lawlessness was at work in the first century but will become an ever-increasing force within the professing Church of the End Times. Jesus said that this increase of lawlessness will deaden the love of Christians. (Matthew 24:12) It will also correspond with the dramatic increase of self-love Paul warned about in 2 Timothy 3:1-7. The Holy Spirit will withdraw as lawlessness and self-centeredness increase within the professing Church.§ This, in turn, will make it possible for Satan to do his worst on earth as evil comes to a climax during the Tribulation Period.

> Then that lawless one will be revealed whom the Lord will slay with the breath of His mouth and bring to an end by the

---

§ A dramatic type of this withdrawal can be seen in Ezekiel chapters 9-11 when the glory of God withdrew from the Temple.

appearance of His coming; that is, the one whose coming is in accord with the activity of Satan, with all power and signs and false [*pseudos*] wonders. (2 Thessalonians 2:8-9)

Only those who are genuinely walking with the Lord will discern the true identity of the "lawless one." Those who are in the spirit of the world (aka *kosmos*) will not recognize him as being evil because he will be speaking their language. They will probably think of him as the most lovable and capable politician that they have ever seen. I spoke of this spiritual phenomenon in my book, *Intoxicated with Babylon*:

> A multitude of professing Christians in the U.S. are sound asleep, in a drug-induced stupor. They have been deceived by years of careful indoctrination via television and other media. Occasionally someone disturbs their slumber by ringing an alarm bell, but as a whole the Church has remained lethargic. It is all too easy to dismiss one's misgivings as unimportant. The sweet and soothing song of kosmos always allays their fears. "Now, now," he whispers, "there is nothing to be alarmed about. Go back to sleep. Everything is all right."
>
> Without realizing it, many who claim Christ as Lord and Savior are slowly being prepared to hear another voice, which will not sound much different than the one they have heard for years. It is not the Voice of the True Shepherd. One day a man will appear on television with a tone and message they recognize easily: the voice of kosmos.
>
> But this time he will speak with an unprecedented force of deception that will be irresistible to those who have been prepared for it. The intensity of his deceptive power is incomprehensible to our minds. The arrogant attitude of Christians will be their undoing. The hypnotic power

of the voice of *kosmos* PERSONIFIED will be more than they can resist. For many, it will be TOO LATE.[5]

When speaking of the deception of the Last Days, teachers and commentators focus on the "signs and false wonders" that the antichrist will perform. Of bigger concern is the "power" to deceive that the enemy will employ preceding this man's appearance. By the time he is revealed, Satan will have already led multitudes astray—including professing Christians. Deception is something that happens inwardly and the "signs and false wonders" will only serve as the final convincers of what people have already accepted as truth. Those who are living for the temporal pleasures of this world will be completely open to the message of the antichrist. Believers who love the truth will not be deceived by this man or the wicked spirit that possesses him.[C] These saints will see him for whom and what he is.

> And with all the deception [*apate*] of wickedness for those who perish, because they did not receive the love of the truth so as to be saved. (2 Thessalonians 2:10)

The wickedness Paul speaks of here is the fruit of a lawless nature. When people will not submit to the authority of God—whether they claim Christianity or not—their inward life will become a hothouse where sin can flourish. In the last chapter, we briefly looked at the spiritual condition of the Church in our day. Sin is running rampant and deception, which always goes hand-in-hand with sin, is increasing with it. The lack of submission to God and the love of the world have opened up the Christian Church to widespread deception.

This verse also provides further irrefutable evidence that this portion of Scripture is referring to professing Christians.

[C] See Daniel 12:10.

The people being spoken of here have been exposed to the truth. Nevertheless, they have not considered it important enough to earnestly seek it. It is not of great concern to them and therefore they do not value it.

One of the key words in this chapter that is typically overlooked is the word love—*agape*; a term that describes the ruling passion of a person's heart. They did not love [*agape*] the truth—it was not the ruling passion of their hearts. The truth being spoken of is not the superficial Bible knowledge which most Christians are satisfied to possess. It does not refer to traditional orthodoxy or one's favorite doctrinal opinions. It has much more to do with the reality of one's relationship with God. Truth is a deep and pure fountain that will take a seeking saint into the very depths of God. Jesus promised that the Holy Spirit would "guide" such believers "into all the truth." (John 16:13) Those who love God, love the truth, pursue the truth, and live by the truth.

> For this reason God will send upon them a deluding [*plane*] influence so that they will believe what is false [*pseudos*], in order that they all may be judged who did not believe the truth, but took pleasure in wickedness. (2 Thessalonians 2:11-12)

The actual Greek words in this phrase "deluding influence" are *plane energeia*. *Plane* is defined as being led astray or deceived. *Energeia* means activity and is the Greek term from which we get the word "energy." In other words, *the delusion these people have opened their hearts to will be activated and energized within them.* The day will come when the flood of lies they have taken in year after year will be galvanized into action within them, effectively sealing them off from the kingdom of Truth. It is a spiritual phenomenon similar to what is seen in Romans 1 where we are told that "God gave them over to degrading passions." (Romans 1:26) In both cases the Lord is simply giving people what they have shown they desire.

The overarching fact Paul is conveying in this chapter is that the majority of the professing Church of the Last Days will fall away from the Lord. This will happen to individuals in three primary ways.

MANY CHRISTIANS ARE NEGLECTING THE TRUTH

In God's economy, a person does not need to make an outright refusal to hear and act upon the truth in order to be sentenced to hell; he only needs to ignore it. As the farmer will lose his harvest through simple neglect, and in the same way that the businessman will go bankrupt through negligence, it takes little effort to lose the Lord's offer of salvation; it requires no more than simply ignoring it.

The prophet Amos lived in a time of great spiritual declension. He was actually from the tribe of Judah, but the Lord called him to go north and preach the truth to the wayward tribes of Israel. In one of those prophecies of "double reference," Amos warned of a time when a word from the Lord would be a rare occurrence:**

"Behold, days are coming," declares the LORD God, "When I will send a famine on the land, not a famine for bread or a thirst for water, but rather for hearing the words of the LORD." (Amos 8:11)

What the prophet was referring to was not a scarcity of Bibles; it was a famine of receiving a direct word from the Lord. This is certainly true in our day. It is becoming more and

---

** "Double reference" is a rule of exegesis. It means that the prophecy is meant for an upcoming period but is also pointing to events that will occur during the end of the age.

more rare to hear men with a fresh word from God. Sermons have become thirty minute sermonettes featuring biblical facts that do not touch the hearts of people, do not confront sin and worldliness, and do not call them into a life in God. We are already living in a famine of hearing from the Lord.

While it is true that starvation can come from a lack of available food, just as true is that it can happen because of a loss of appetite. For instance, you could put a plate of delicious food in front of someone with the flu and he would push it away in disgust. That is a picture of the day we live in. A disease of spiritual lethargy has been let loose upon the Church. There simply is very little hunger for the Word of God. Even sadder yet is that they don't even realize how badly they need it. They are turning to man's understanding for their direction in life, and they are filling up on the junk food of the world. It is no wonder then that their desire for true spiritual bread is minimal and that their spirit life is slowly waning away. Jesus spoke of this condition when he said to the Pharisees, "Hypocrites! You know how to discern the face of the sky, but you cannot discern the signs of the times." (Matthew 16:3 NKJV)

To discern the times means one must know how to hear the voice of the Lord. And to hear His voice a person must know how to listen. The Holy Spirit does not come shouting, like the spirit of the world does. He speaks in a still, small voice.

To hear the voice of the Lord one must know how to quiet oneself. A person must spend quality time soaking in the Word. And he must also limit the amount of time he subjects himself to the shouting voice of the world. Only those who are in the habit of sitting in God's presence have the love of the truth growing both in their outward lives and in the depths of their heart.

But the fact of the matter is that today's Christians are largely indifferent to truth. The biggest hindrance to receiving truth is that they are certain they have it. They have filled their minds with a myriad of meaningless minutiae of Bible facts and are missing what God really wants to say to them. It is very reminiscent of the Pharisees during Jesus' time. He told them, "You tithe mint and dill and cummin, and have neglected the weightier provisions of the law: justice and mercy and faithfulness." (Matthew 23:23) The particulars of the failure of the Jewish leaders were different than what besets the Church today. Christians don't "tithe mint and dill and cummin"; but, just like the Jews, they focus on unimportant information about religion rather than on what is valuable in God's sight. As Jesus put it, they "strain out a gnat and swallow a camel." (Matthew 23:24)

This bounty of head knowledge has only served to deceive people into thinking they have a walk with God that they simply do not possess. It has convinced them that they have the truth; therefore, they see no reason to seek it. Head knowledge has made people arrogant and indifferent to the reality of their spiritual condition. As I said elsewhere, "If you think you can't be deceived, you're already halfway there." We are living in the Last Days and the deception is deep, pervasive, and powerful; yet hardly anyone is concerned.

Another factor that contributes to so many neglecting the truth is the fact that the message of the world lines up perfectly with our natural thinking. The fallen human nature is wired to think selfishly and pridefully. A genuine believer is intentional about fighting against that natural tendency. This battle in the mind is not easily winnable, however.

Let me illustrate this truth from something I recently experienced in London. My morning devotions are a fixed habit in my life. I first spend at least an hour in the Word and then I go out for a prayer walk. I go through this routine every morning no matter where I might be.

While I was in London I would be walking along at 4:00 in the morning, trying to shut out distractions so I could focus on my conversation with the Lord. I would inevitably come up to a crosswalk and my natural tendency would be to look to the left to make sure no cars were coming. However, the British drive on the left side of the road, so I should have been looking to my right to avoid any danger. But this inclination to look left is so habitual that I would have to practically force my head to look to the right, instead of to the left. More than once I nearly stepped in front of an oncoming car! That really is a picture of how our natural thinking is so prone to go along with the lies of the world. We have to train ourselves to go against our natural thinking and the only way that is going to happen is by constantly subjecting ourselves to the influence of God's Word.

We cannot afford to neglect this gift. We must treat it with the love and respect it deserves. It is the one source of truth that we can depend upon.

It should be noted that the decision to neglect or even reject truth does not occur all at once. It is a pattern of life that comes about through millions of tiny decisions. A person who is in love with God is constantly concerned about walking in truth. A "Sunday Christian" is self-satisfied and feels no strong need to pursue truth any further. He is certain he has it.

MANY CHRISTIANS ARE TURNING AWAY FROM THE TRUTH

Earlier in the chapter, I quoted Paul as saying, "For this reason God will send upon them a deluding (*plane*) influence so that they will believe what is false (*pseudos*)." (2 Thessalonians 2:11) *Pseudos* is another one of those Greek terms that has been transliterated into the English language. The Greeks understood it to describe something fake or counterfeit just like we would.

The point the apostle was making was that people would not accept and embrace the love of the truth that God was offering because they preferred something counterfeit. This verse could easily be paraphrased, "God will send a powerful influence upon them to accept a pseudo-faith, a counterfeit version of Christianity."

Although we touched on this subject in Chapter Nine, I would like to return to it momentarily. In his second epistle to Timothy, Paul spent the better part of chapter 3 describing the self-centered culture within the apostate Church. He concluded that chapter and opened the next by earnestly sharing with his disciple how vital it is for believers to be immersed in Scripture. Then he gave the reason for his great concern:

> For the time will come when they will not endure sound doctrine; but wanting to have their ears tickled, they will accumulate for themselves teachers in accordance to their own desires, and will turn away their ears from the truth and will turn aside to myths. (2 Timothy 4:3-4)

The time *has* come and this is the reality of our situation right now. A huge portion of the professing Church is turning away from the truth in favor of a pseudo version of Christianity. In the next chapter I will be addressing the issue of false teachers, but I want to touch on it here in the context of why people will turn away from the truth.

The second epistle of Peter talks about *pseudoprophētēs* and *pseudodidaskalos*: fake preachers who will flood the Church with fake Christianity. He warned that "Many will follow their sensuality, and because of them the way of the truth will be maligned and in their greed they will exploit you with false words." (2 Peter 2:2-3) On this occasion, the word "false" is not *pseudos* but a different Greek term: *plastos*. It is the word from which our term "plastic" comes. So Peter is warning that the Last Days will be a time when plastic people will present a plastic rendition of Christianity. It has been molded into something carnal and worldly. This will lead to many people turning away from the truth.

I want to offer our passage in 2 Timothy again, but this time through a paraphrase that seems to reliably convey what Paul is saying:

> A time will come when some will no longer tolerate sound teaching. Instead, they will live by their own desires; they'll scratch their itching ears by surrounding themselves with teachers who approve of their lifestyles and tell them what they want to hear. They will turn away from the real truth because they prefer the sound of fables and myths. (2 Timothy 4:3-4 Voice)

I think the scholars who wrote this Bible translation really captured the situation with their rendition. Can you see what is happening here? The pseudo-prophets and pseudo-teachers that Peter and Jude warned would come are already at work in the Church today.

And why do people follow them? They listen to their message because it lines up with the lifestyle they want to lead. I can tell you from much painful experience that we live in an age when people demand this from their pastors. There is no question that the Church is glutted with self-serving, pseudo-teachers who are in the ministry for what they can get out of it for themselves. Just as true is the fact that there are also many sincere pastors who have been emotionally beaten into submission by carnal congregations who simply will not tolerate the preaching of the truth. The reality is that such people are, in essence, rejecting God, distorting God, and re-creating God into their own image and to their own liking.

What is God's response to this rejection? He gives them over to a deluding influence. I can see the Lord saying to people, "So, you don't want the truth? You prefer your own version of Christianity? You want pseudo-teachers and pseudo-prophets? Then I will let you have them until they are coming out of your nostrils." (Numbers 11:20) Not only will I allow them to swarm through the Church, but I will also send upon you a spirit of delusion." *The Pulpit Commentary* says this of the situation:

> The pleasures of sin cannot exist side by side with the love of the truth. Moral corruption has no sympathy for the lofty thirst for truth of a pure soul. Hence it may be concluded that indifference to truth is a sign of moral evil. The corrupt life is a false life, and its departure from truth reveals the baseness of the character beneath. They who do not love the truth shall not have it. Liars become incapable of knowing truth. The habit of indifference to truth so grows upon some people that the whole idea of truth becomes obscure and meaningless to them—the spiritual eye blinded and burnt out by the fires of falsehood and unrighteousness.[6]

MANY CHRISTIANS ARE SUPPRESSING THE TRUTH IN UNRIGHTEOUSNESS

When Paul wrote his treatise to the believers in Rome, one of the first things he wanted to address with them was the wickedness thriving in their own society. Sexual sin was rampant and he felt that it was important for them to see this culture from God's perspective.

This is not the time to look deeply into the first chapter of that great book, but I do want to examine one phrase he wrote regarding people in blatant sin. He said that they "suppress the truth in unrighteousness." (Romans 1:18) This might be a good opportunity to look at this phrase in other translations.

+ The Amplified Bible says that they
"repress and hinder the truth."
+ The Living Bible says that they "push away the truth."
+ The New English Bible says that they "stifle the Truth."
+ Wuest explains that they "hold down the truth."
+ The Voice says that they "keep God's truth in check."

These translations are all touching on different aspects of the same phenomenon of those who have sin in their lives. It is a further clarification of "the deceitfulness of sin" the book of Hebrews mentions. (Hebrews 3:13)

Suppressing the truth implies that these people have the truth, but whenever it begins to exert its influence upon them—starts to expose sin, idolatry, and lust—they "push it away." As someone said, "They strangle the disturbing voice of truth by argument and by denial."[7] Old time Baptist Bible scholar A.T. Robertson said that truth "is out in the open, but wicked men, so to speak, put it in a box and sit on the lid and 'hold it down in unrighteousness.' Their evil deeds conceal the open truth of God from men."[8]

After describing the horrible lifestyle of those given over to sexual sin, Paul returned once again to the subject of truth. In verse 25 he wrote that they exchange "the truth of God for a lie," a *pseudos*. They would prefer something fake so they can keep their beloved sin. This is the very lawlessness that Paul described in our passage in 2 Thessalonians 2. Do you know why many Christians will follow the antichrist one day? It is because they are in the same lawless spirit he is in—and they want nothing to do with submitting to God's authority.

These people exchange the truth of God for a lie and that lie—which is rampant now in the Church—is that people do not need to obey God, to submit to His authority, or to live out His will. In their minds, the only thing required is church attendance and belief in the traditional doctrines taught in the Church. If a person believes Jesus died for their sin, God's grace will cover anything and everything they might do—so they think.

Yet, Paul makes it abundantly clear that our only hope in this age of delusion is to love the truth with all our hearts. In such a climate of overwhelming deception, how will believers survive? God has thrown us a life preserver: it is the love of the truth. To love the truth means that I will be blameless before men and sincere towards God; I will love God in my heart and obey Him in my actions; I will embrace what He says about me—no matter how much it may hurt or demand change; I will serve Him with a good conscience and a sincere faith; and, I will immerse myself in the Eternal Word of Truth.

We live in a climate of unprecedented, pervasive deception. It is vital that we pursue the truth with all our hearts and that we stand on it no matter what. With eyes of faith, A.W. Tozer captured the great issues of our day:

> I see the time coming when all the holy men whose eyes have been opened by the Holy Spirit will desert worldly Evangelicalism, one by one. As the Church now stands, the man who sees this condition of worldliness in the church is written off as somewhat fanatical. But the day is coming when the house will be left desolate and there will not be a man of God left among them. I would like to live long enough to watch this develop and see how things turn out. I would like to live to see the time when the men and women of God—holy, separated and spiritually enlightened—walk out of the evangelical church and form a group of their own; when they get off the sinking ship and let her go down in her worldliness and form a new ark to ride out the storm.[9]

"The impenitent [see] those as their *friends* who speak smooth things to them and help them to deceive themselves."

-A.W. PINK[1]

"These [false prophets] were not necessarily predictors or soothsayers, but teachers having, as they said, a message from God.... Throughout the Christian ages heretics have always raised their evil voices, and the history of the Church is very much composed of accounts of such teachers, and of the efforts made to suppress them and to correct their pernicious doctrines."

-THE PULPIT COMMENTARY[2]

THREE:
SPURIOUS TEACHERS AND
FALSE PROPHETS

There is a reason Scripture calls people sheep: they are meant to be led; but just like sheep, people are easily led astray. To "be led" implies that there must be a leader, and it would be hard to underestimate the impact leaders have when it comes to shepherding the Lord's flock.

General Bernard Montgomery once asserted, "Leadership is the capacity and will to rally men and women to a common purpose, and the character which inspires confidence."[3] Most people want to be led, but they must also feel like they can trust the person who would lead them. Oswald Saunders wrote quite a lot on the subject of Christian leadership.

The overriding need of the church, if it is to discharge its obligation to the rising generation, is for a leadership that is authoritative, spiritual, and sacrificial. Authoritative, because people love to be led by one who knows where he is going and who inspires confidence... Spiritual because a leadership that is unspiritual, that can be fully explained in terms of the natural, although ever so attractive and competent, will result only in sterility and normal spiritual bankruptcy. Sacrificial because modeled on the life of the One who gave Himself a sacrifice for the whole world, who left us an example that we should follow His steps.[4]

The Apostle Paul delineated five different offices in the Church for the purpose of "equipping the saints" and "building up of the Body of Christ." (Ephesians 4:12) Those designated ministers are categorized as apostles, prophets, evangelists, pastors, and teachers. Any office of ministry is susceptible to deception; however, for the objectives of this chapter, we will limit our study to a brief look at prophets and teachers.

Although this may be a bit of an oversimplification, the basic difference between these two ministers has to do with the way each receives inspiration from the Lord and the way they communicate what they have received.

A Christian teacher (probably the equivalent of the OT priest and the NT scribe) is first and foremost a student of the written Word; i.e., the "*logos*." A good teacher spends a great deal of time researching subjects and poring over biblical texts. When he prepares a message, he will first accumulate an abundance of material which he then sifts through, discarding what is unnecessary, and finally organizing what he considers relevant to his audience. His main concern is what the *logos*, the written Word of God, has to say on a subject. Jesus said, "Therefore every scribe who has become a disciple of the kingdom of heaven is like a head of a household, who brings out of his treasure things new and old." (Matthew 13:52)

While humility is one of the great requirements of every minister, perhaps this can be an exceptional challenge to the teacher. Studying Scripture can easily become an academic exercise. In Paul's first epistle to the Corinthian church, he alluded to the fact that knowledge not lived out has a tendency to make a person prideful.* It is easy for teachers to fall into the trap of seeing the Bible as a resource of information rather than as a divine source to turn to for one's own spiritual growth.

---

* In 1 Corinthians 8:1, Paul said, "Knowledge makes arrogant, but love edifies."

Those who do so can easily fall into the trap of allowing truth into their minds but not into their hearts.

A New Testament prophet, like his OT brother, is typically a reformer. He is first and foremost a man of great consecration to the Lord, sometimes spending long periods of time seeking His face. The Bible sometimes refers to these brothers as "seers" because they have remarkable powers of perception into the spiritual realm. When the Lord speaks to such men it is usually about the spiritual condition of the Church. As Amos said, "Surely the LORD God does nothing unless He reveals His secret counsel to His servants the prophets." (Amos 3:7) As a reformer, God requires a prophet to confront His people when they are straying from the truth. A.W. Tozer spoke of such men:

> A thousand or ten thousand ordinary priests or pastors or teachers could labor quietly almost unnoticed while the spiritual life of Israel or the church was normal. But let the people of God go astray from the paths of truth, and immediately the specialist appeared almost out of nowhere. His instinct for trouble brought him to the help of the Lord and of Israel.
>
> Such a man was likely to be drastic, radical, possibly at times violent, and the curious crowd that gathered to watch him work soon branded him as extreme, fanatical, negative. And in a sense they were right. He was single-minded, severe, fearless, and these were the qualities the circumstances demanded. He shocked some, frightened others, and alienated not a few, but he knew who had called him and what he was sent to do. His ministry was geared to the emergency, and that fact marked him out as different, a man apart.[5]

Because of the level of intimacy such men have with the Lord, He is able to impress into their hearts what the Bible calls a *rhema* word. The challenge for these men is to make certain that anything they communicate to others lines up with Scripture (i.e., the *logos*).

A healthy church will have all five gifts (apostles, prophets, evangelists, pastors, and teachers) operating within it. The fact that such a church is rare in the U.S. is one more indicator of the serious trouble we are in.[†]

FALSE-HEARTED MINISTERS

The Church greatly needs godly teachers and prophets. Unfortunately, Church history has been replete with counterfeit versions of these offices. In his second epistle, the Apostle Peter indicates that these frauds have always plagued the people of God and will, by the end of the age, proliferate throughout the Church.[‡]

As one old-time preacher said, "wherever there is a Divine truth which saves, there will be a Satanic counterfeit which damns."[6] In other words, if there are godly teachers who are gifted at digging truth out of the Word, there will also be spurious teachers [Gk. *pseudodidaskalos*) who twist what Scripture says. And if there are true prophets who really walk with God, there will also be false prophets [Gk. *pseudoprophetes*) who "speak a vision of their own imagination, not from the mouth of the LORD." (Jeremiah 23:16)

A false teacher is someone who is quite possibly a gifted teacher but twists the meaning of Scripture to fit into his own preconceived notions. Jesus exposed the difference between the godly and the fake when He said, "The good man brings out of his good treasure what is good; and the evil man brings out of

---

† I believe at least three of these gifts are in operation on a regular basis at Pure Life Ministries.

‡ In 2 Peter 2:1, the Apostle says that "false prophets also arose among the people, just as there will also be false teachers among you..." As he wrote this, Peter moved from sharing past history to foretelling future events. It is clear by what he says throughout chapters 2 and 3 that he is referring to events occurring in the Last Days.

his evil treasure what is evil." (Matthew 12:35) And the Lord spoke of such men through Jeremiah when He said, "How can you say, 'We are wise, and the law of the LORD is with us'? But behold, the lying pen of the scribes has made it into a lie." (Jeremiah 8:8) These men had perverted Scripture to say something other than what was originally intended.

Not only are there pseudo-teachers, but there are also pseudo-prophets. A false prophet copies the authentic prophet in that he presents himself as having a fresh word from the Lord. He does have a "word," but it is a satanically inspired message that has the sole purpose of leading people away from God. The Lord spoke of these men through Jeremiah when He said, "I did not send these prophets, but they ran. I did not speak to them, but they prophesied. But if they had stood in My council, then they would have announced My words to My people, and would have turned them back from their evil way and from the evil of their deeds." (Jeremiah 23:21-22)

These men were present in biblical times and they continue to be involved in ministry today. They are not outside the Church but inside it, holding prominent positions in Christian media, seminaries, denominational headquarters, and large churches. Charles Spurgeon saw them at work during his time:

> They have risen in all ages; in these modern times they have risen in clouds, till the air is thick with them, as with an army of devouring locusts. These are the men who invent new doctrines, and who seem to think that the religion of Jesus Christ is something that a man may twist into any form and shape that he pleases. Alas, that such teachers should have any disciples! It is doubly sad that they should be able to lead astray "many." Yet, when it so happens, let us remember that the King said that it would be so.

Is it any wonder that, where such "iniquity abounds"

and such lawlessness is multiplied, "the love of many shall wax cold?" If the teachers deceive the people and give them "another gospel which is not another," it is no marvel that there is a lack of love and zeal. The wonder is that there is any love and zeal left after they have been subjected to such a chilling and killing process as that adopted by the advocates of the modern "destructive [higher] criticism." Verily, it is rightly named "destructive," for it destroys almost everything that is worth preserving.[7]

Biblical writers actually make quite a few statements about false teachers and false prophets. Many of these comments are mere passing references to them, but there are also entire sections of Scripture devoted to the subject (e.g., Jeremiah 23, 2 Peter 2, Jude, etc.). It is best to see these accumulated statements as a composite picture of a person, made up of bits and pieces mostly from various passages in the New Testament. Think of it as a puzzle that is incomplete until you see all the pieces in place. I have identified 45 characteristics of what these men are (i.e., character) and 63 different things that they do (i.e., activity).[§] For the sake of our chapter here, we will limit our study to nine tell-tale signs of a fraudulent minister.

1. THEY PRESENT A FALSE IMAGE

As mentioned, NT writers label these men *pseudodidaskalos* (spurious teachers) and *pseudoprophētēs* (false prophets), *pseudos* being the prefix common to both terms. In English, we understand that the word "pseudo" describes something that presents the appearance of being authentic but is actually bogus.[₵] Whatever their particular designation, they are all

---

§ To get the entire picture, please refer to Appendix # 3.

₵ For the most part, it is best to see these terms as used to describe any fake minister, regardless of his particular office.

counterfeits to what makes up a true man of God. As He wrapped up the fabulous Sermon on the Mount, Jesus warned:

> "Beware of the false prophets, who come to you in sheep's clothing, but inwardly are ravenous wolves. You will know them by their fruits. Grapes are not gathered from thorn bushes nor figs from thistles, are they? So every good tree bears good fruit, but the bad tree bears bad fruit. A good tree cannot produce bad fruit, nor can a bad tree produce good fruit. Every tree that does not bear good fruit is cut down and thrown into the fire. So then, you will know them by their fruits." (Matthew 7:15-20)

Our Lord was referring to ministers who appear one way to people, while being something altogether different inside. They present themselves as sheep: "an emblem of innocence, sincerity, and harmlessness,"[8] "with a bland, gentle, plausible exterior."[9] In other words, they have amiable personalities, have a thorough knowledge of orthodoxy, and instinctively know how to present themselves as spiritually-minded.

These false-hearted preachers are adept at seamlessly fitting into the flock. In front of others, they look the part, but they are driven by the kind of voracious appetite that compels a wolf to stalk its prey.**

** It is important to note the context of Jesus' warnings here. Just before He issued this alert, Jesus told His listeners that there are only two roads in the spiritual realm: the first is "narrow" and has "few" people on it; the second is "broad" which is preferred by many travelers. These false prophets are, in essence, standing at the "narrow gate" doing their utmost to direct traffic back onto the "broad way."

Just after the warning about false prophets is the vignette regarding professing Christians who are involved in many spiritual activities and yet do not live in "the will of God." Thus, the people Jesus called "false," are among those who are on the "broad way" and do not live in submission to the Lord.

Jesus was not alone in exposing these frauds. Paul said, they disguise "themselves as apostles of Christ," as "servants of righteousness," and, like Satan, "as an angel of light." (2 Corinthians 11:13-15) He told the Galatians that they "desire to make a good showing in the flesh." (Galatians 6:12) Referring to the inconsistency in how they present themselves to others as opposed to what they are truly like, he said they "take pride in appearance and not in heart." (2 Corinthians 5:12) They are, in short, "deceiving and being deceived." (2 Timothy 3:13)

Elsewhere I wrote the following:

> When most Christians think of false teachers, the descriptions that Jesus and Paul gave come to their minds. But instead of looking for sheep, they look for wolves. Instead of looking for angels of light, they look for servants of Satan, such as obvious cult leaders. What many fail to realize is that false teachers *appear* as sheep and angels. When Jesus warned of false prophets coming in the last days, He was not primarily referring to men like Jim Jones or David Koresh. He said, "*Many* false prophets will arise, and will mislead *many*." (Matthew 24:11, emphasis added) He was describing deception that would occur on a much grander scale than that of a few isolated cult leaders. The wolves in sheep clothing and the angels of light are not *outside* the Church but *inside* it! They are not recognized as deceivers because their behavior is not what the Church expects to see in a deceiver.[10]

2. ENEMIES OF THE CROSS

One of the Apostle Paul's greatest declarations is what he told the Corinthians: "For the word of the cross is foolishness to those who are perishing, but to us who are being saved it is the power of God." (1 Corinthians 1:18) It is a statement that divides the wheat from the tares, the sheep from the goats, and the true from the false.

To the sincere believer, the Cross means everything. It reflects God's hatred of sin and, at the same time, His love for mankind. The Cross characterizes the life of the follower of Christ who repents of his love of the world and sinful practices. It is in the repentance found at the foot of the Cross that believers find freedom from the hold of sin.

The Cross represents a mindset that is built upon the proper understanding of Self—the need for Self to be repented of, mortified, and denied. The Cross means that Jesus Christ is everything, receives all the glory, and directs all one's paths. It cuts against self-will, self-exaltation, and self-centeredness. Oswald Chambers grasped the significance of the Cross in the life of the believer. "If I do not put to death the things in me which are not of God," he insisted, "they will put to death the things that are of God."[11]

This is the spiritual reality that pseudo-Christians violently resist. "Those who are perishing" are willing to sing about the Cross or to wear one on their necks, but they want nothing to do with the lifestyle it represents.

Paul once said of the false teachers of his day: "For many walk, of whom I often told you, and now tell you even weeping, that they are enemies of the cross of Christ." (Philippians 3:18) He also spoke of those who are careful not to do anything that would cause them to "be persecuted for the cross of Christ." (Galatians 6:12) The Cross meant everything to him. He went on to tell the Galatians, "But may it never be that I would boast, except in the cross of our Lord Jesus Christ, through which the world has been crucified to me, and I to the world." (Galatians 6:14) Madame Guyon would later echo his sentiments: "If you will not savor the cross, you cannot savor the things of God. It is impossible to love God without loving the cross."[12]

3. EMPTY SUITS

In the first chapter, I mentioned the Hebrew word *shav*, which is defined as "emptiness, vanity, falsehood."[13] It is an important term because it furnishes us with one more prominent characteristic of false-hearted teachers: they are devoid of spiritual substance. The character of such men is empty and their message is vain.

This same thought is brought forth in the NT. Jude said of the false prophets of the Last Days that they will be "clouds without water, carried along by winds; autumn trees without fruit, doubly dead..." (Jude 12) Peter added that they are "springs without water and mists driven by a storm" who speak "out arrogant words of vanity." (2 Peter 2:17-18) All of these metaphors represent something that promises needed resources (e.g., rain, fruit, water), but actually provide nothing of value. "Empty suits" is a modern term which perfectly describes such people. Harry Ironside summed up such false ministers:

> There are many self-made ministers whose inner lives are in sad contrast to their ministry. Many, too, insist on taking the place belonging to a servant of God who have never spent any time in His school, learning His ways. Thus, their utterances are empty and disappointing in the extreme, as might be expected when coming from men who had not been sent by the Lord.[14]

4. SMOOTH TALKERS

Another distinctive of false preachers is that they have a natural ability to charm people. Part of this is their eloquent manner of speaking—whether it's in front of a congregation or simply conversing with another person.

Solomon once mused that "sweetness of speech increases persuasiveness." (Proverbs 16:26) Of course, he meant this proverb as a complimentary way of describing a diplomatic person. And it is true that pastors must be diplomatic in dealing with fussy parishioners. However, truth should trump diplomacy when preaching the Word of God.

Jesus alluded to this ability when He warned, "Woe to you when all men speak well of you, for their fathers used to treat the false prophets in the same way." (Luke 6:26) Those who are well spoken of in our day are too often the beloved ministers with ingratiating smiles and pleasant sermons. Upon hearing their man-pleasing messages, congregants walk away feeling good about themselves. But ministers who deliver such insincere commendations are guilty of flattering their flock. And this is exactly what Jude warned about when he said false teachers flatter "people for the sake of gaining an advantage." (Jude 16)

How different is the word from the Lord delivered by a true prophet! Such men are not afraid to confront sin, pride, selfishness, and worldliness. True believers love preaching that causes them to earnestly examine their hearts. In contrast, pseudo-Christians consider prophets to be legalistic, incorrigible cranks!

5. WORLDLY-MINDED

In John's day, there were members of his congregation who were "from the world" (1 John 4:5) system of the day. No wonder their message was received: they "speak as from the world, and the world listens to them." (1 John 4:5) Jude called such preachers "worldly minded." (Jude 19) The Apostle Paul warned the Philippians about those men whose "god is their appetite" as they "set their minds on earthly things." (Philippians 3:19)

Of course, John could never imagine American life, with all of the opportunities to indulge oneself in a plethora of worldly activities. One preacher, who later repented, confided to me that during his many years of pastoring he spent most of his time watching television. Since his carnal condition precluded him from receiving inspiration from the Lord, he went to the internet to find sermon material.

Christians who spend hours watching television, surfing the internet, and playing on social media have no discernment, which is why they can listen to such carnal messages without seeing the lack of substance they offer.

6. REBELLIOUS

Jude appealed to his readers to "contend earnestly for the faith… for certain persons have crept in unnoticed, those who were long beforehand marked out for this condemnation, ungodly persons who turn the grace of our God into licentiousness and deny our only Master and Lord, Jesus Christ." (Jude 3-4)

To "deny" the Lord is describing an unwillingness to submit to His authority over one's life. In essence, they say "no" to His commandments and to the lifestyle required of His followers. (Luke 9:23-25)

These are the lawless men (Matthew 7:21-23; 24:11-12) who help spread the false gospel of the great apostasy. These men have never submitted their lives, much less their ministries to the Lord. Peter said they "despise authority" and are "self-willed." (2 Peter 2:10) Paul called them "rebellious men" (Titus 1:10) and said that they are "impostors [who] will proceed from bad to worse, deceiving and being deceived." (2 Timothy 3:13) Their licentious, "grace covers everything" message serves to deepen people's bondage to sin, leading them right out of the house of God and into the domain of darkness.

7. SENSUOUS

Scripture presses the point over and over again that the lying preachers of the end times maintain a secret life of lust and sexual sin. These fakes have "eyes full of adultery that never cease from sin" (2 Peter 2:14) and "indulge the flesh in its corrupt desires." (2 Peter 2:10) Jude adds that they are "following after their own lusts" (Jude 16), "casting up their own shame like foam." (Jude 13)

Can there be any doubt that these men are addicted to pornography and are regularly involved in some form of sexual sin? These men have brought a vile atmosphere into the Church. In verse 19, Peter says they are "slaves of corruption [Gk. *phthora*]," a word that can also be defined as destruction. However, this term does not speak of sudden annihilation; it was used to describe rotting fruit or the decomposition of a dead person's body. When applied to a person's spiritual life, it refers to the putrefaction of one's character. In other words, they are being destroyed *from within*.

Not only do they corrupt the Christian communities they are a part of, but they also promote an antinomian lifestyle of living without godly restraint. Peter said that "many will follow their sensuality" and "because of them the way of the truth will be maligned." (2 Peter 2:2) How tragically this has come to pass in our day!

8. SELF-CONFIDENT

These charlatans also have an astounding amount of hutzpah. Paul said they are "conceited," that they "understand nothing," that they are "men of depraved mind and deprived of the truth." (1 Timothy 6:3-5) He told Timothy that they are prone to overreaching, "wanting to be teachers of the Law, even though they do not understand either what they are saying or the matters about which they make confident assertions." (1 Timothy 1:7)

Peter said they are "daring" and inferred that they are so cocky and brazen that they don't even "tremble when they revile angelic majesties"; "reviling where they have no knowledge." (2 Peter 2:10, 12) Jude said they "feast with you without fear, caring for themselves." (Jude 12) These are all characteristics of men who are full of pride and unwarranted self-confidence.

9. FULL OF COVETING LUST

Christian television is full of them: preachers who peddle "the word of God" (2 Corinthians 2:17) supposing "that godliness is a means of gain." (1 Timothy 6:5) Paul went on to tell Titus that they teach "things they should not teach for the sake of sordid gain." (Titus 1:11)

Peter would later describe them as "greedy" (2 Peter 2:3) and "having a heart trained in greed." (2 Peter 2:14) He said that they are possessed with the same "madness" that possessed Balaam, "who loved the wages of unrighteousness." (2 Peter 2:15)

The Greek term Peter used in these verses is *pleonexia*. Most Bibles translate this word as "greedy," which is certainly accurate. However, this is another case where the Greek and English languages do not perfectly correspond with each other. The New King James Version uses the word "covetous," which is slightly broader in its meaning than "greedy." Being money hungry is certainly a large part of being covetous, but I tend to think that the definition of the word offered by a modern dictionary is closer to the meaning of *pleonexia*: "eagerly desirous."[15] In other words, these people are driven by selfish motives and are in the ministry to get something for Self.

This underlying motivation is the compelling factor for many preachers. It could be the drive to be popular, an inordinate longing to be respected, or the eager desire to be seen and heard every Sunday. But it's hard not to think of prosperity preachers as those who are best described by the word *pleonexia*. One minister offered the following description of the "health and wealth" gospel:

In light of Scripture, the prosperity gospel is fundamentally flawed. At bottom, it is a false gospel because of its faulty view of the relationship between God and man. Simply put, if the prosperity gospel is true, grace is obsolete, God is irrelevant, and man is the measure of all things. Whether they're talking about the Abrahamic covenant, the atonement, giving, faith, or prayer, prosperity teachers turn the relationship between God and man into a *quid pro quo* transaction.[16]

CONCLUSION—JUDGMENT

These people are living their best life now, but unimaginable judgment is gathering like storm clouds, soon to break upon them. Paul simply said that their "end is destruction." (Philippians 3:19)

Peter used the same noun over and over again when he said they will bring "swift destruction upon themselves." (2 Peter 2:1) It seemed that he wanted to echo this sentiment in every way he could. He went on to say that "their judgment from long ago is not idle, and their destruction is not asleep." (2 Peter 2:3)

In spite of the fact that they tell themselves that God's grace covers them, Peter wanted to make it very clear that they would face retribution for the harm they have brought upon the Body of Christ. His argument was as follows: "For if God did not spare angels when they sinned, but cast them into hell..." and "did not spare the ancient world..." and "if He condemned the cities of Sodom and Gomorrah to destruction..." "then the Lord knows how... to keep the unrighteous under punishment for the day of judgment." (2 Peter 2:4-9) They will suffer "wrong as the wages of doing wrong." (2 Peter 2:13) They are those "for whom the black darkness has been reserved." (2 Peter 2:17) And finally, in words he once heard the Lord speak of the traitor, "For it would be better for them not to have known the way of righteousness, than having known it, to turn away from the holy commandment handed on to them." (2 Peter 2:21)

There simply is no getting around the fact that the Church is infested with rebels, false teachers, and heretics. Satan is using them very effectively, most especially in the propagation of three great lies.

SPURIOUS TEACHERS AND FALSE PROPHETS

"The greatest of God's demands on man is not for him to bear the cross, to serve, make offerings, or deny himself. The greatest demand is for him to obey."

-WATCHMAN NEE[1]

"The Christian life is narrow from the beginning to the end. There is no such thing as a holiday in the spiritual realm. We can take a holiday from our usual work; but there is no such holiday in the spiritual life. It is always narrow. As is starts, so it continues. It is a 'fight of faith' always, right to the end… It is narrow all the way; there will be foes and enemies attacking you right to the last minute… There will be subtle temptations on the road of life, and you will have to watch and be on guard, from the beginning to the end. You will never be able to relax!"

-D. MARTYN LLOYD-JONES[2]

FOUR:
SATAN'S FIRST GREAT LIE: OBEDIENCE IS OPTIONAL

A common metaphor used throughout Scripture is portraying a person's life as a journey. For instance, the terms "way" and "path" in the OT are used nearly 700 times, mostly in a figurative sense. There are another 100 usages of the term "way" in the NT.

We see the journey metaphor used in conveying one of the supreme truths the Lord wanted to impart to the Israelites when He brought them out of Egypt. It is found in the great address of Moses, just before he died and they crossed into the Promised Land: "Now, Israel, what does the LORD your God require from you, but to fear the LORD your God, to walk in all His ways and love Him, and to serve the LORD your God with all your heart and with all your soul." (Deuteronomy 10:12) He was describing a lifestyle that would be built around the fear of the Lord and a love for the Lord. This way of life must be embraced with all one's heart and soul.

Jesus carried this same concept into the NT as He wrapped up His own sermon: "Enter through the narrow gate; for the gate is wide and the way is broad that leads to destruction, and there are many who enter through it. For the gate is small and the way is narrow that leads to life, and there are few who find it." (Matthew 7:13-14)

In this illustration, Jesus explained that there are two roads, with two distinct groups of people marching along, heading toward destinations that are clearly opposite from each other. I have the sense that this was a sight into the unseen spiritual realm that was never far from His mind.

As obvious as it is, it should be noted that "narrow" does not mean "broad"; "few" is not a synonym of "many." John Bunyan, who languished in a damp, cold jail cell for years because of his refusal to stop preaching the Cross, painted a graphic picture of this spiritual reality in his classic book, *The Pilgrim's Progress*. His primary purpose was to represent the Narrow Way as a difficult path where an occasional lonely straggler is seen pushing on toward his heavenly calling against all obstacles.

As much as seeker sensitive pastors want to throw open the gates of heaven to anyone who ever showed the slightest inclination toward the things of God, it is clear that Jesus' parable precludes such a message. Adam Clarke said, "There are few who find the way to heaven; fewer yet who abide any time in it; fewer still who walk in it; and fewest of all who persevere unto the end."[3]

It is an interesting phenomenon that the very thing that Jesus used to illustrate the way to destruction is what false believers use to support the notion that they are saved. They convince themselves that because everyone else around them lives like they do, that means they must be in good standing with God. They are missing the point: the Broad Way is where the masses of religious people are found.*

A study of the context of this passage makes it abundantly clear that Jesus is talking about church people. The broad way

---

* Ray Comfort is convinced that even this first parable about the broad way is describing people who have had an experience with God—a false conversion. The point he makes is that these people also go through a gate—the wide gate—something that outright unbelievers would never do.

is not describing pagans who have no interest in the kingdom of God. No, it is referring to people who are attempting to enter the kingdom of God on their own terms. The narrow way is describing people who are entering the kingdom of God through repentance and saving faith and remain on the narrow path through obedience.

In spite of the fact that Jesus plainly tells us that it is a narrow path, there are many who are determined to create a road of their own making. Every day of their lives is spent furthering it in their own direction. But the "ancient path" is fixed precisely where God has ordained it to be. It will not be shifted around by the whims of man. If not one single human being ever traverses it again, it remains where God has established it.

Hanging a sign on the Broad Way which reads, "Narrow Path" does not make it so. It is sheer delusion and folly to think that just because everyone else is on the Broad Way that somehow it is acceptable to God. Its popularity should suggest the very opposite. As John Wesley said, "If many go with you, as sure as God is true, both they and you are going to hell!"[4]

The reason such people consider the true Christian life as being too restrictive is because their focus is entirely on what they may have to give up. They do not see the value of the "pearl of great price" (Matthew 13:45-46) and the ultimate emptiness of the things they are pursuing.

GOING ASTRAY

The upshot of all of this is that the Bible clearly delineates the Christian life as a path that is straight and is headed to heaven. It isn't that apostate Christians are never on the narrow path. I believe they do have times that they are there in some sense; they just do not want to be confined to it. The picture that presents itself to me about these people is that the narrow way is headed perfectly straight into the future, but their lives weave to and fro; yes, at times they are on the narrow way, but just as often they are wandering off track. They point to those times they are obedient to the Lord as proof that they are on the narrow way, but it is nothing more than self-flattery. The core issue is whether they are going God's appointed way, or whether they are going their own way.[†]

When Jesus spoke of the condition of the Church in the first section of His Olivet Discourse, His main concern was to warn end time Christians against going astray:

> Jesus answered, "At that time deception will run rampant. So beware that you are not fooled! For many will appear on the scene claiming my authority or saying about themselves, 'I am God's Anointed,' and they will lead many astray.
>
> "And many lying prophets will arise, deceiving multitudes and leading them away from the path of truth.
>
> "For there will be imposters falsely claiming to be God's 'Anointed One,' and false prophets will arise to perform miracle signs to lead astray, if possible, those God has chosen to be his." (Matthew 24:4-5, 11, 24 The Passion)

The key word used in all four verses is *planao*, which means to "roam (from safety, truth, or virtue): - go astray, deceive, err, seduce, wander, be out of the way."[5] The literal meaning is to go awry or be led off course (e.g., Matthew 18:12: "If any man has a hundred sheep, and one of them has gone astray..."). But its primary use in Scripture has to do with being led astray from

---

† Remember what Jesus said in Matthew 7:21-23. "Not everyone who says to Me, 'Lord, Lord,' will enter the kingdom of heaven, but he who does the will of My Father who is in heaven will enter. Many will say to Me on that day, 'Lord, Lord, did we not prophesy in Your name, and in Your name cast out demons, and in Your name perform many miracles?' And then I will declare to them, 'I never knew you; depart from Me, you who practice lawlessness.'"

Christ and His truth. About half its uses occur in passages regarding the Last Days.[†]

The writer of Hebrews also spoke of the danger of this tendency. He compared the Christian life to a sailor moored at a dock (which presumably would be the Truth). He said, "For this reason we must pay much closer attention to what we have heard, so that we do not drift away from it. For... how will we escape if we neglect so great a salvation?" (Hebrews 2:1-3a) The idea conveyed here is that it is a very subtle, gradual departure. The Pulpit Commentary paints the following picture of this declension:

At sunset the ship is close to shore and all is safe; without a warning it drops into the tide, and swings round, and with no sound but the ripple of the water is carried down the stream to the open sea, and the crew may sleep through it all. So, departure from Christ may be as involuntary and quiet as that; a silent, ceaseless, unconscious creeping back to old habits. There is its danger. Drifting away means leaving Christ without knowing it, till we find ourselves far out at sea, and a tide we cannot resist bearing us still further away. You have seen men who were once close to Christ, but whilst they slept they have unconsciously glided away, and by the current of worldliness been carried into the rapids and whirled along faster and faster, only waking to stare wildly at their helplessness, and close their eyes in despair for the final plunge into the eternal gulf.[6]

This commentator, who lived and ministered during the latter part of the 19th century warned about "the current of worldliness." His experience with the power of the spirit of the world would have been minimal compared to what you and

---

[†] Matthew 24:4-5, 11, 24; Mark 13:5-6; Luke 21:8; 2 Timothy 3:13; 2 Peter 2:15; Revelation 2:20; 12:9; 13:14; 18:23; 19:20; 20:3, 8, 10.

I face. Yet, even in those mild times there was that constant threat of drifting away. The danger is how imperceptible those currents are. It is a constant, quiet, subtle drawing away from Christ. You must not allow yourself to drift—you must stay firmly anchored into the Rock. Andrew Murray, discussing the overall message of the book of Hebrews, said the following:

> It was to meet the spirit of backsliding, to warn against the disease and its danger, and to make known the infallible cure, that our author takes up his pen. He saw that the one cause of all the feebleness and faithlessness was this: the want of the knowledge and the faith of what Christ and His salvation truly are.[7]

Adam Clarke, also commented on the concerns the author of the book of Hebrews shared about the tendency to fall away from the faith. He wrote:

> The writer's arguments against backsliding or apostasy are the most terrifying and powerful that can well be conceived, and are as applicable now to guard Christian believers against falling from grace as they were in the apostolic times.[8]

THE CALL TO PERSEVERANCE

False teachers are leading the way for the apostate Church and one of their primary strategies has been to remove the expectation of *faithfulness* out of the Christian faith. Nevertheless, in spite of man's determination to cheapen the faith, an honest student of the Bible must admit that Scripture is very clear that believers are expected to remain devoted to the Lord throughout the course of their lives. Only those who approach Scripture with the predetermined notion that they are "OK" will deny this. This inevitably leads to a doctrinal system that waters down the need for obedience and reinforces the delusion that the Narrow Way can also be broad.

One example is the parable of the Sower and the Seed, found in Matthew 13, Mark 4 and Luke 8. I won't take the time to write out and explain all that is involved with this well-known parable. I will just sum it up by pointing out that there are four soils mentioned, each of which is a metaphor for someone who has heard the Word of God. The first person is likened to seed that has fallen along the path but the devil steals the word right out of his heart and so he does not come into the faith. The second hearer is the one who "receives it with joy" but his faith is only temporary, "and when affliction or persecution arises because of the word, immediately he falls away." (Matthew 13:20-21) The third also receives the Word "but the worries of the world, and the deceitfulness of riches, and the desires for other things enter in and choke the word, and it becomes unfruitful." (Mark 4:19) Only the fourth type of hearers are approved. They are "the ones who have heard the word in an honest and good heart, and hold it fast, and bear fruit with perseverance." (Luke 8:15) The clear inference is that they alone will be saved.

Over and over again, using different terms, illustrations, and arguments, Scripture insists that people must remain obedient to God for the duration of their lives in order to be saved in the end.§

This was widely believed in OT times. There are many references to this, but what the Lord said to Ezekiel is an unescapable argument regarding this truth:

> But when a righteous man turns away from his righteousness, commits iniquity and does according to all the abominations

---

§ For a fuller study on this subject, please refer to Appendix #3.

that a wicked man does, will he live? All his righteous deeds which he has done will not be remembered for his treachery which he has committed and his sin which he has committed; for them he will die. (Ezekiel 18:24)

In the NT, it is expressed in various ways. Paul spoke of those who had "suffered shipwreck in regard to their faith" (1 Timothy 1:18b-19), "fall[en] away from the faith" (1 Timothy 4:1), "wandered away from the faith" (1 Timothy 6:10), and "gone astray from the faith" (1 Timothy 6:21)

This understanding of Scripture continued on into the Early Church. Consider what the following Church fathers thought about the need to persevere in the faith:

"Let us then practice righteousness so that we may be saved unto the end." Clement of Rome (c. first century)

"Even in the case of one who has done the greatest good deeds in his life, but at the end has run headlong into wickedness, all his former pains are profitless to him. For at the climax of the drama, he has given up his part." Clement of Alexandria (c. 150-215)

"Some think that God is under necessity of bestowing even on the unworthy what He has promised [to give]. So they turn His liberality into His slavery... For do not many afterwards fall out of [grace]? Is not this gift taken away from many?" Tertullian (c. 155-220)

"A man may possess an acquired righteousness, from which it is possible for him to fall away." Origen (c. 184-253)

"Those who do not obey Him, being disinherited by Him, have ceased to be His sons." Irenaeus (c. 130-202)[9]

The call to persevere in the faith has been a major part of God's dealings with His people from the earliest days right up to the present. However, nowhere is it stressed more emphatically than to believers who would be alive during the Last Days. In the Olivet Discourse Jesus said:

> "At that time many will fall away and will betray one another and hate one another. Many false prophets will arise and will mislead many. Because lawlessness is increased, most people's love will grow cold. But the one who endures to the end, he will be saved." (Matthew 24:10-13)

The context is clear: it is the final period before the return of Christ. Deception is rampant. People are falling away from the truth and forsaking the Lord. God's love inside professing Christians has grown icy—if it has even ever existed. In the midst of this apostasy, we are assured that those who persevere in the faith will be saved.

This call is also a major theme for believers referred to in the book of Revelation. Matthew Henry wrote:

> Perseverance in the faith of the gospel and true worship of God, in this great hour of trial and temptation, which would deceive all but the elect, is the character of those registered in the book of life. This powerful motive and encouragement to constancy, is the great design of the whole Revelation.[10]

THE LIE

One of the most predominate characteristics of the Apostate Church of the Last Days is that those professing Christians are "lovers of pleasure rather than lovers of God." (2 Timothy 3:4) Such people love the world and endure church services. The call found throughout Scripture to live a holy life falls on deaf ears when it comes to them. Once again I turn to words I wrote twenty years ago in my book, *Intoxicated with Babylon:*

> Tragically, there is another cry so deafening that hardly anyone can hear what God is saying to those "with ears to hear." That ungodly voice shouts out, "You don't have to be holy!" Entire denominations and church movements teach that a person does not really have to obey God. This false message is loudly proclaimed from pulpits, over Christian radio, and through a barrage of books aimed at giving churchgoers a false sense of security. Its vocal proponents shout down anyone who counters it. "You're teaching legalism! You're telling people they have to earn their way to heaven! There is nothing a person can do to save himself. It's all God's grace!"
>
> As with most deceptions there is usually enough truth embedded in the message to make it believable. And it should be acknowledged that a strongly legalistic presentation of Christianity lends itself to a "saved by works" understanding of the Gospel. But there isn't enough of that unbalanced teaching in church circles to warrant the overwhelming emphasis on grace that Christendom has heard in the last 20-30 years. One would think that legalism is the greatest threat the Church has ever faced, considering the inundation of teachings given on grace. The truth of the matter is that the real threat is from those teachings which have, in the name of Grace, encouraged believers to indulge themselves in a selfish and worldly lifestyle, far from the abundant life Jesus had in mind for His Bride.
>
> No doubt Satan in his subtlety has planned every aspect of this strategy for the last days. An outright statement that "sinning doesn't matter" would be too strong a poison

for believers to swallow. Satan instead concocted an entire doctrinal scheme that would allow for such worldly living. By leading Bible teachers to over-emphasize God's grace and de-emphasize the need for godliness and holiness, the devil has made compromised living acceptable in the eyes of the average churchgoer. Through the concerted efforts of many false teachers holiness is now politically incorrect and licentiousness the status quo.

There are those who will provide many plausible arguments for the unrighteousness at work in the Church right now. False teachers have always done their utmost to "strengthen the hands of evildoers, so that no one has turned back from his wickedness." (Jeremiah 23:14) I humbly and earnestly ask those who have been taken in by these liars to quiet themselves and meditate on the following verses, most of which come from the pen of the Apostle of Grace:

He who believes in the Son has eternal life; but he who does not obey the Son will not see life, but the wrath of God abides on him. (John 3:36)

But because of your stubbornness and unrepentant heart you are storing up wrath for yourself in the day of wrath and revelation of the righteous judgment of God, who will render to each person according to his deeds: to those who by perseverance in doing good seek for glory and honor and immortality, eternal life; but to those who are selfishly ambitious and do not obey the truth, but obey unrighteousness, wrath and indignation. (Romans 2:5-8)

Do you not know that when you present yourselves to someone as slaves for obedience, you are slaves of the one whom you obey, either of sin resulting in death, or of obedience resulting in righteousness? (Romans 6:16)

For this you know with certainty, that no immoral or impure person or covetous man, who is an idolater, has an inheritance in the kingdom of Christ and God. Let no one deceive you with empty words, for because of these things the wrath of God comes upon the sons of disobedience. (Ephesians 5:5-6)

...when the Lord Jesus will be revealed from heaven with His mighty angels in flaming fire, dealing out retribution to those who do not know God and to those who do not obey the gospel of our Lord Jesus. These will pay the penalty of eternal destruction, away from the presence of the Lord and from the glory of His power. (2 Thessalonians 1:7a-9)

And having been made perfect, He became to all those who obey Him the source of eternal salvation. (Hebrews 5:9)

For it is time for judgment to begin with the household of God; and if it begins with us first, what will be the outcome for those who do not obey the gospel of God? (1 Peter 4:17)

They profess to know God, but by their deeds they deny Him, being detestable and disobedient and worthless for any good deed. (Titus 1:16)

Satan's great purpose in life is to destroy people eternally. At the top of his target list are those who claim to follow Christ yet do not live in obedience to Him. "Do not be deceived, my beloved brethren." (James 1:16)

OBEDIENCE IS OPTIONAL

"O soul, He only who created thee can satisfy thee. If thou ask for anything else, it is thy misfortune, for He alone who made thee in His image can satisfy thee."

-AUGUSTINE[1]

"If [His presence] is all that God gives me, I am satisfied, but if all that He gave me was the [whole] world, I would not be satisfied."

-JEREMIAH BURROUGHS[2]

FIVE:
SATAN'S SECOND GREAT LIE: PERFECT FULFILLMENT IS FOUND IN PERFECT CIRCUMSTANCES

The satanic lie that "perfect fulfillment is found in perfect circumstances" represents a very powerful deception because it is built on a half-truth. In one sense, it shows how powerful truth is, in that even something that is only partially true can make a significant impact on a person's life. And there is truth to the statement that better circumstances tend to provide a more fulfilled life. The problem is that it is not the whole story.

For instance, let's say you have always had a dream of living in the wilds of Alaska. The remoteness of the wilderness, the abundance of big game, the thought of being out of the rat race of civilization are all part of the dream. This fantasy is so strong in you that, at great sacrifice, you save your money and make the move to Alaska. Upon arrival, you go house hunting and purchase the perfect place. The parcel is only fifty acres, but it is remote enough that you might as well be on a thousand acres. You find a job an hour away from the property that will pay you enough to keep up the monthly payments. And to your utter amazement, all your hopes have been accomplished!

When you first move into your dream house, everything is idyllic. You cannot believe that you actually live there! Every morning you go out and take in the view of the sun coming up over the mountains to the east. On the weekends you spend time exploring your property or the local area. You feel like you are in heaven.

Now fast forward six months. By now you have grown accustomed to life in Alaska. You still love your home, but not like when you first moved in. The sunrise no longer holds you in rapt attention. You have explored everything worth seeing in the vicinity. The excitement of living in the wilderness has waned. You are still happy to be there, but the thrill is gone.

Fast forward a few months later when winter sets in. Everything about life in this wilderness area is difficult. You are constantly fighting with freezing pipes. Your truck does not want to start. Blizzards come in on a fairly regular basis, blanketing your house and driveway with snow that is often measured in feet. The drive to work is difficult and treacherous. Now you are beginning to find out why so few people live there.

Chances are that you do not have this fantasy and really cannot even relate to someone being consumed with this idea. But it does not matter because the story I just painted is actually a spiritual formula that can be used for any earth-based aspiration: a perfect mate, a great career, a house full of kids, a beautiful car; in short, if it is a dream built on what the world offers, it can be plugged right into this formula.

Here's another way to look at it. Let's say science has invented a device that is able to measure the level of a person's sense of fulfillment in life. Generally speaking, if you rated a 57 on the happiness meter before you bought that dream house, it probably shot up into the 90s when you moved in. However, once the dust has settled a year later, you will most likely find yourself back down in the 60s on the meter. Yes, you do feel more fulfilled than before you got what you wanted; but it also is not the all-out game-changer you had fantasized it to be. The bottom line is that there are no perfect circumstances in life and even if there were, they would not bring lasting fulfillment. Everything in earth life loses its luster over time.*

The fact of the matter is that every human has been led through life by misleading promises. This is inevitable because we must deal with an ungodly triad that supports them. Our fallen nature believes there is something other than God that can satisfy its particular desires. The world provides a myriad of possibilities one might pursue. Demons offer perfectly timed suggestions, opportunities and temptations to encourage such idolatry.

The world tells us that we will be happy when we get the perfect career position; the Lord tells us that we will find fulfillment only in doing His will. The world tells us that we will be satisfied when we arrive at financial security; the Lord tells us that contentment will only be found in Him. The world tells us that we will be happy with the perfect mate—someone who will really love us and meet our needs; the Lord tells us that we will never have the capacity to receive love until we first learn to give it. The lie is that the things of this world can bring us fulfillment and happiness. The truth is that genuine fulfillment can only come from the Lord.

WARRING LIFESTYLES

It was God who instilled within the human heart the inherent drive to find fulfillment. His purpose for implanting this inside a person is to create a hunger to know Him. One hears this great heart-cry come forth through the psalm of David, "O God, You are my God; I shall seek You earnestly;

---

* Interestingly, this spiritual formula is very comparable to the second law of thermodynamics: everything within our universe is undergoing the process of decay. Anything alive is in the process of dying; anything with warmth is cooling; anything with energy is being drained of its vigor.

my soul thirsts for You, my flesh yearns for You, in a dry and weary land where there is no water." (Psalm 63:1) This deep love for the Lord and the fervent desire to have meaningful fellowship with Him which David expresses is arguably the Lord's greatest desire for His people. It is the indwelling Spirit of the true born-again believer that compels him to seek God in this way.

Satan will not allow this to happen unchallenged. He has masterfully used the world system to cater to the lusts of our lower nature. The flesh also has a deep yearning inherent within it that wishes to be satisfied. This lust is the motivating energy that drives a person to acquire, possess or experience some particular item or activity. The desire for sin always promises satisfaction and rarely delivers. Even when a person does find some level of enjoyment in experiences or acquired possessions, it rarely lasts. Lust for what the world offers does not produce satisfaction, but it does create a relentless state of agitation. The more a person indulges it, the more frustration he is sure to experience.

THE BATTLE

In his letter to the Galatian church, Paul shared the age-old fight that goes on within the soul of any person desiring to walk with God. I will offer his words in a paraphrased translation:

> Here's my instruction: walk in the Spirit, and let the Spirit bring order to your life. If you do, you will never give in to your selfish and sinful cravings. For everything the flesh desires goes against the Spirit, and everything the Spirit desires goes against the flesh. There is a constant battle raging between them that prevents you from doing the good you want to do. (Galatians 5:16-17 Voice)

As this passage indicates, a believer's soul becomes the theater of a daily battleground. It is an all-out fight for supremacy over a person's life. One can get the sense of the violence involved in this battle by the fact that later in the chapter the Apostle says: "Now those who belong to Christ Jesus have crucified the flesh with its passions and desires." (Galatians 5:24) It is clear that this is a winnable war, and, notwithstanding the battle involved in it, the true believer will prevail.

The present tense of the verb "walk" also infers that this is an ongoing lifestyle, a term that we inherently understand because walking is simply the habitual practice of taking steps over and over again. To "walk in the Spirit" implies that a believer's daily life is made up of spiritual activities, e.g., a solid devotional life that keeps one "in the Spirit." However, terminology can be misleading. Jessie Meldrum, a biblical counselor who has ministered to women for some forty years, shares from her experience:

> When praying with women in the church I often ask about their life in God. I no longer use the terms "devotional life" or "quiet time" because it does not mean the same thing to everyone, i.e., many do the "One-minute devotional" and have some sort of (distracted) prayer time on the way to work. I have learned to ask if they have a regular, consistent prayer life. When I suggest they commit to spending thirty minutes with the Lord in prayer and in the Word, the response is often anger. They think I just don't understand the real world and that devoting this kind of time for God is extreme. Personally, no matter how busy I might be, I cannot imagine making it through a day without that solid connection with God.

It is simply not possible to have any kind of meaningful relationship with the Lord without spending quality time with

Him, for it is in that quiet time that the Lord is able to speak and impart His energy and desire into a person's life.

The "flesh" is "the mind, the will, the emotions of man which act independent of God and against God, even in defiance of God.... In short, flesh as used in Galatians 5:16 is that ugly complex of human sinful desires with ungodly motives, affections, words, and actions that Sin generates in our bodies."[3] This is a good description, if not a little too confining because it is possible to be "in the flesh" even with activities that are not necessarily sinful in themselves: e.g., being overly focused on a favorite hobby, overindulging in junk food, making working out at the gym too high of a priority, and so on. In short, carnal living can describe any lifestyle that keeps God out of the central position.

Once Paul established the fact that a daily battle will take place within a believer's heart, he then described the two opposing lifestyles that are a result of which side is winning. The first is made up of the sort of attitudes and activities one would expect of carnal people:

> Now the deeds of the flesh are evident, which are: immorality, impurity, sensuality, idolatry, sorcery, enmities, strife, jealousy, outbursts of anger, disputes, dissensions, factions, envying, drunkenness, carousing, and things like these, of which I forewarn you, just as I have forewarned you, that those who practice such things will not inherit the kingdom of God. (Galatians 5:19-21)

Paul then quickly contrasts this horrid way of living with what the Spirit of God nurtures within the heart of a true believer:

> But the fruit of the Spirit is love, joy, peace, patience, kindness, goodness, faithfulness, gentleness, self-control; against such things there is no law. (Galatians 5:22-23)

It is obvious that the first list describes the moral atmosphere and mental state of people who walk "according to the course of this world" and are on the broad way "that leads to destruction." (Ephesians 2:2; Matthew 7:13)

By contrast, those who walk in the Spirit and are "led by the Spirit" (Romans 8:14), have lives that are consistent with the kingdom of God. This walk includes the guidance of the Spirit (Romans 8:14; Galatians 5:18), the strength of the Spirit (Ephesians 3:16), the help of the Spirit (John 14:16, 26; 16:7), and the truth that is taught by the Spirit. (John 15:26)

One of the great lies that Satan has so effectively propagated within the Christian community is that a believer can have a little of both worlds. This simply cannot be the case. Paul makes it clear that people who "practice" the deeds of the flesh will not inherit the kingdom of God—they are not part of the Body of Christ.

The reason this lie has been able to take such root within the evangelical realm is that, generally speaking, we have lost the sense of God's abhorrence of sin and have cheapened the fruit of the Spirit into little more than human emotions.

Another contrast between these conflicting lifestyles can be seen in the Beatitudes. Jesus pronounced heavenly blessings on eight different characteristics. For each of these statements, there is a contrasting thought that holds an equal amount of truth:

+ Jesus said, "Blessed are the poor in spirit," and equally true, "Miserable are those who are full of themselves."
+ Jesus said, "Blessed are those who mourn," and equally true, "Miserable are those who feel no remorse over their sinful nature."
+ Jesus said, "Blessed are the meek," and equally true, "Miserable are the self-willed, who always want their way."

- Jesus said, "Blessed are those who hunger and thirst for righteousness," and equally true, "Miserable are those who are indifferent and apathetic about the things of God."
- Jesus said, "Blessed are the merciful," and equally true, "Miserable are the self-centered who never leave their comfort zone."†
- Jesus said, "Blessed are the pure in heart," and equally true, "Miserable are those whose hearts are full of idols."
- Jesus said, "Blessed are the peacemakers," and equally true, "Miserable are the opinionated who regularly cause divisions."
- Jesus said, "Blessed are those who have been persecuted for the sake of righteousness," and equally true, "Miserable are those who protect their own rights, feelings, and lives no matter the cost." (Matthew 5:3-10)

With all of that in mind, let's take a look at the fruit of the Spirit. I will emphasize the first three because every human being is looking for these forms of fulfillment: love, happiness and security.

THE PURSUIT OF LOVE

I have spent the past thirty-four years of my life ministering to those whose passions for sex had controlled and dominated their lives. Nowhere is the contrast clearer between the life God offers and what the world proposes than in the realm of love. Men tend to look for it in pornography and cheap sex; women are more prone to seek it in shallow relationships fueled by needy emotions. The world's idea of love is all built around the Self-life and driven by selfish lust. This is clearly demonstrated in a worldly marriage when a husband (or a wife) comes to his

---

† To live out the love of God to others implies the willingness to put their needs before one's own desires.

mate and announces that he is filing for divorce. Why? "I can't help it; I've fallen in love with someone else."

What a contrast God's idea of love presents! "God is love," John tells us. (1 John 4:8, 16) So when the Bible speaks of believers being filled with the Holy Spirit, it is saying that they will likewise be full of His love.

As I said earlier, the secret to receiving love is to give it out. My wife Kathy once counseled a young lady who would have been best described with the word "needy." Any discerning person who spent time with this girl would sense this fairly quickly.

The redeeming attribute of this young woman was a sincere and earnest desire to become more Christ-like. As Kathy worked with her, a real transformation began to take place. She was one of those people who, once shown what she needed to do, would gladly follow instructions. Over the course of a couple of years, she simply became a different person. And I can tell you that now she spends her life sacrificially ministering to younger women. The neediness that once characterized her was replaced with the deep sense of fulfillment that comes from giving one's life away. The infilling of God's love that she experienced is fairly typical of any true believer who will give of themselves for the sake of others.

I am sure you have heard of the term "clean energy." In a secular sense, it is used to describe energy that is produced in such a way that it does not cause pollution to the atmosphere. But in the spiritual realm, it is a good metaphor for God's love. Yes, there is a passion involved, but it is not soul-polluting lust; it is the clean, soul-cleansing love produced by the Spirit of God.

THE PURSUIT OF HAPPINESS

According to the National Institute of Mental Health, 16.2 million American adults deal with depression.[4] In 2017, there were 47,173 suicides[5] and 70,237 accidental overdoses[6] in the

U.S. These statistics tell me that—with all of our prosperity—the United States is not the land of happiness Third World people might imagine it to be.

It is not hard to see that something is missing in our nation. The mad pursuit of pleasure, entertainment, and merriment that characterizes so much of American life is not delivering what it promises. Lust will not be denied, however. It is a mania that constantly and relentlessly drives people to seek more pleasure, more entertainment, and more possessions. It is an itch that cannot be satisfied, no matter how much it is scratched.

Jesus once admonished: "Woe unto you that laugh now, for you shall mourn and weep." (Luke 6:25) The laughter He is referring to is a representation of an overall frivolous and superficial mindset. He is describing people who are always on the hunt for the next opportunity to laugh and live it up, whether it comes from watching entertaining television or carousing with other shallow-minded people.

Let's face it: the best the world can offer are short stints of temporary happiness or satisfaction. It knows nothing of the deep sense of joy that comes from a genuine walk with God. So the first aspect of this lie is that worldly happiness will fulfill.

There is another wrong perception I should touch on as well. We all know people who are positive and buoyant by nature. They tend to see the bright side of everything. They are quick to smile, easy to get along with and enjoy being with other people. Such individuals would be what the world considers happy. I do not mean to infer there is anything wrong with having this natural disposition, but it is important for believers to understand that this is not the joy which Paul was referring to. The "joy of the Lord" is not something a person is born with; it only comes as a direct result of the work of the Holy Spirit in a person's life.

Here again a comparison is helpful. Natural happiness can be empty, while the joy of the Lord is fulfilling. Natural happiness is typically focused on receiving something for Self, while the joy of the Lord is built around the principle that it is more blessed to give than to receive. Natural happiness tends to be shallow, while the joy of the Lord is deep and rewarding. Natural happiness is temporal, while the joy of the Lord is eternal.

Another mistaken notion is to think a person is experiencing this joy because things are going his way. Perhaps he just received a promotion at work, or delivered a healthy baby, or was just engaged to someone he loves. There is nothing wrong with being happy about positive circumstances, but that also is not equivalent to the joy of the Lord.

God's joy is not an emotional response to positive experience. It comes from the Holy Spirit and produces a deep sense of contentment, fulfillment and delight that is not dependent upon favorable circumstances. It is a deep fountain within that abides with a person through the good times and the bad times; through times of peace and times of war; through times of happiness and times of sorrow.

The one thing that should not be missed is that it is the joy of the Lord: i.e., His joy! *The Pulpit Commentary* says this about God:

The brightness and beauty of the world are reflections from the blessedness of God. Because he is glad, nature is glad, flowers bloom, birds sing, puppies and kittens frolic. Look at the beauty of nature that hasn't been marred by the curse: rich green forest cities of busy insect life, flashing ocean waves, and the pure blue sky above, and all that is sweet and lovely in creation swells into a grand symphony of gladness, because the mighty Spirit that haunts it is himself overflowing with joy.[7]

God is joyful and His people are invited to enter into His joy. In fact, when Jesus was painting the picture of the faithful servant being rewarded with eternal life, He used these very words: "Enter into the joy of your Lord." (Matthew 25:21, 23 NKJV) One can only imagine what the home of God will be like! David said to the Lord, "In Your presence is fullness of joy." (Psalm 16:11) In Luke 15, Jesus spoke of heaven being a place full of God's joy when a sinner repents. (Luke 15:7, 10) Paul said "for the kingdom of God is not eating and drinking, but righteousness and peace and joy in the Holy Spirit." (Romans 14:17) And in the book of Revelation one sees the angels and saints continually rejoicing around the throne of God. The truth is that anywhere the Lord manifests Himself is going to be a place of fulfilling joy for those who love Him.

THE PURSUIT OF SECURITY

The third element of life that one looks to for fulfillment is peace. Feeling loved and happy in life is wonderful, but how much does it mean if a person is regularly succumbing to fear or anxiety?

Let's face it: earth can be a frightening place. How could we expect it to be otherwise? It's mostly controlled by the Prince of Darkness. Even in America there is plenty to be concerned about. For instance, in 2018, there were 1.2 million violent crimes and 7.1 million property crimes.[8] Millions have experienced the fear of assault against their person or their property. And this is just one small example.

The fear of physical suffering and death is very real for many Americans. But that is not all people worry about. According to the National Institute of Mental Health, some 40 million American adults are affected by various "anxiety disorders."[9] In 2017, the American Psychiatric Association conducted a poll of U.S. adults regarding stress. Here is what they discovered:

Sixty-eight percent of respondents were worried about safety, 67% about paying their bills, 56% about the American political landscape, and 48% about interpersonal relationships. Other sources of stress were health care (43%), the economy (35%), trust in government (32%), hate crimes (31%), wars (30%), terrorist attacks (30%), high taxes (28%), Social Security (26%), government scandals (25%), and low wages (22%).[10]

I should mention that all of this anxiety is helping fuel what some consider to be an epidemic in the long-term use of prescription drugs. In 2013, the Medical Expenditure Panel Survey discovered that some 40 million Americans were regularly taking some form of psychiatric drugs.[11] That is a number that has undoubtedly risen significantly since. Anti-anxiety pills such as Valium, Xanax, Zoloft, and Prozac make up the majority of those numbers. And, of course, these numbers do not even touch the multitudes of people addicted to illicit drugs and alcohol.

Medication is the best solution the world can offer to people who are dominated by fear and worry. The world's answer to that desire for inward peace is to numb the mind through drugs and drinking. But of course when the person comes down off their high, he still must face himself, he still must deal with his inner turmoil, and he still must come to grips with the fact that his life is not right with God.

Jesus tells His followers not to worry (Matthew 6:25) and not even to fear "those who kill the body." (Matthew 10:28) The only fear that should have any real control over the believer's life is the fear of God. Christians often allow fear to debilitate them simply by allowing the media to dominate their thinking. Secular news does its utmost to perpetuate people's fear and sensationalize its stories to keep them coming back for the latest information. I am writing this as the coronavirus panic has ground our nation to a halt. It is to be expected that unredeemed souls would give in to such hysteria but believers have access to the peace "which surpasses all comprehension." (Philippians 4:7)

True peace with God only comes about when a person lives in submission to the Lord's will and has a vibrant life in God. "In Me you may have peace," Jesus said. (John 16:33) In other words, if you look for it elsewhere, you will not find it. It is only by abiding in Christ and living in the will of God that one enjoys a life of spiritual tranquility. Paul expressed it in different terms, but he was making the same point: "For the mind set on the flesh is death, but the mind set on the Spirit is life and peace." (Romans 8:6) Isaiah conveyed the same message: "You will keep him in perfect peace, whose mind is stayed on You, because he trusts in You." (Isaiah 26:3 NKJV) The Psalmist brought out yet one more important aspect of this lifestyle when he wrote, "Those who love Your law have great peace, and nothing causes them to stumble." (Psalm 119:165) All of these inspired writers were looking at the same object from different angles: true, fulfilling peace can only come from the Lord.

In a thousand ways, Satan wishes to assure us that the world which he controls can offer love, happiness and peace. No, it is a lie. True fulfillment only comes about through walking with the Lord and allowing Him to meet all of our needs.

PERFECT FULFILLMENT IS FOUND IN PERFECT CIRCUMSTANCES

"Truth is indeed more than what we say; it ought to be what we are.... We know what it means to have truth but stagger at the idea of being true. We are far more at home with the religion that is occupied with having and doing. We know how to go about acquiring more and more truths. But the religion of God is animated foremost by a desire to be, not merely to do or acquire."
-PAUL VOLK[1]

"Truth is not only something that we believe; it is also something that we are called upon to speak and to practice. This connection between truth and action is found throughout the NT.... Christians are expected to be truthful in this way, being honest and having actions that reflect the commitment to truth."
-WILLIAM D. MOUNCE[2]

SIX:
SATAN'S THIRD GREAT LIE: THE KNOWLEDGE OF TRUTH COMES THROUGH OSMOSIS

I n 2003, an assistant and I spent nearly a month traveling throughout South America, doing whatever we could to provide biblical solutions to the problem of sexual sin in the Latin Church. Having grown up in California, I understood a smattering of Spanish, but my ability to speak it was very limited. However, by the end of our trip, I had unwittingly absorbed the language into my being. In fact, I was beginning to *think* in Spanish.

Language experts say that "immersion learning" is the best way to grasp a new language. It is also a valuable way of becoming acquainted with a new culture. In other words, the best way to understand the Chinese people would be to live in China for an extended period of time. A person would learn far more about the country that way than simply by reading books about it.

This principle also holds true when entering the Christian community. There is a way of thinking and a value system in the Church that, for the most part, holds true in the Christian community of any nation in the world. A newcomer to Christianity quickly learns the "ins-and-outs" of acceptable and unacceptable behavior. This comes about by being immersed in the Christian culture.

A word that describes this phenomenon is "osmosis," defined as "a usually effortless often unconscious assimilation."[3] Another dictionary says it is "a subtle or gradual absorption."[4]

While there are some definite benefits to this natural learning process, there are also inherent dangers when it comes to the things of God. I fear that multitudes have joined the American Church, have become thoroughly acquainted with her ways, but have never really been converted to Christ. This is especially true of children raised in Christian homes.

GENERATIONAL CHRISTIANITY

It goes without saying that Christian parents want what is best for their kids. So they familiarize them with the Bible and raise them to believe in the Lord. They also do their utmost to protect them from harmful influences. They can and should try to influence them in the right way, but ultimately, following Christ is a personal decision a young person must make for himself.

One need only look at the wicked sons of Aaron, Eli, Samuel, David, Hezekiah and Josiah—all of them godly men—to know that leading a devout life is no guarantee that a child will follow in one's footsteps.

What happened in the Ephesian church during the first century is a fascinating illustration of this truth. The apostle Paul visited Ephesus in about 54 A.D. What he found was a wicked city given over to all sorts of idolatry and witchcraft. In fact, many of these people were demon possessed. However, when he began preaching in the marketplace, people started getting saved—radically saved! They were so impacted by the power of God through the apostle's preaching that they immediately began burning their books on witchcraft and sorcery. It was a mighty revival that swept through Ephesus. Those new believers were so on fire for the Lord that they took the gospel out all over the region of Asia Minor.

Now fast-forward 40 years later when Jesus addressed the church of Ephesus in Revelation 2. Listen to what He said to these people:

"I know your deeds and your toil and perseverance, and that you cannot tolerate evil men, and you put to the test those who call themselves apostles, and they are not, and you found them to be false; and you have perseverance and have endured for My name's sake, and have not grown weary. But I have this against you, that you have left your first love." (Revelation 2:2-4)

All those years later the believers at Ephesus were still solid doctrinally. They continued to believe in the Lord and hold fast to the teachings of Scripture. They even recognized and rejected the gnostic teachers so prevalent at the time. But there was one vital element they were now missing: a genuine and vibrant love for God. Apparently, those early believers—who were clearly on fire for the Lord—either died off or simply lost their passion for God over time.

The amazing thing is that while the love for God was dissipating in the Ephesian church, the form of Christianity remained intact. A good illustration of this would be a bucket of water with a pinhole in the bottom. Over time the water drains out, but the bucket remains. That's a picture of people who have maintained the form of Christianity but whose hearts have drifted away from the Lord.

Now take this a step further. By 95 A.D., when John received the Revelation, most of the congregation of Ephesus was undoubtedly made up of the children and grandchildren of those early believers. Just like most American Christians today, those first believers raised their kids to believe in God. They took them to church and taught them biblical truth. But somewhere along the way the fire had died off. Either those original parents lost their enthusiasm, or their children never really came to love God for themselves.

Apparently, the children of those early believers came to see Christianity as a good belief system but not really worth getting excited about. The passion for God diminished even further with the third generation of professing Christians. They continued the orthodoxy of the church and identified themselves as believers but lacked a true love for God. They basically learned to do church without passion and without love. They came to adopt the attitude that, as long as they avoided obvious sin, they could give their hearts to the things of the world without concern.

Actually, the Christians of all seven of the churches Jesus addressed in Revelation faced this same challenge. Only the believers of Smyrna and Philadelphia maintained their love for the Lord throughout those 40 years. Somehow they managed to pass along their fervency to their children and grandchildren.

In Ephesus, however, a cold, religious mindset had set into the church. For all their religious law-keeping, they had forsaken the most important law of all: "You shall love the Lord your God with all your heart and with all your soul and with all your might." (Deuteronomy 6:5) According to Jesus, this was more important than anything else Scripture commanded. (Matthew 22:38)

Lost love leads to the dead formalism of organized religion. And it should be noted that it was organized religion that put Jesus on the Cross. It was organized religion that threatened to rip the early Church apart. It was organized religion that persecuted Wycliffe, Luther, Tyndale, the Moravians and many other God-loving saints. And it was organized religion that opposed every revival the Church has ever experienced.

I believe that what happened to the church of Ephesus has happened in America as well. In the early Seventies, a revival called the Jesus Movement swept across the nation. Thousands of young people—disillusioned by drugs, promiscuity and materialism—began turning to the Lord. My wife and I both came to the Lord during this time.

That revival eventually faded and the church transitioned into a period dominated by Christian media and megachurches. The evangelical movement was going corporate, and those early Jesus freaks were now becoming respectable church members. Even though the fire died out for most of them, they still maintained the form of godliness, just like the Ephesian Christians. However, what they were lacking was the power of the Holy Spirit working in their lives. (2 Timothy 3:5)

This form of Christianity—with all its correct doctrine and outward spirituality—became the new norm in the American Church. And this is what was passed along to their children and grandchildren—a form without love; a form without fire; a form without the power of a godly life.

FULL KNOWLEDGE OF THE TRUTH

The great need of our day is for a fresh fire from God to sweep through the Church. We need to come into a deeper comprehension of God's truth. Being affected by truth requires more than intellectually absorbing what it is communicating—no matter how accurate our assessment of it might be. Yes, we must comprehend what the Bible teaches, but many, if not most, professing Christians never go beyond this shallow level. They are content to be doctrinally correct and knowledgeable about general facts regarding the Christian faith. Stopping at this point in the trek is fatal because the truth still has not reached the heart where it can actually transform a person's life.

In one brief passage, the Apostle Paul laid out the essence of the issue which people face today. He said that God "desires all men to be saved and to come to the knowledge of the truth." (1Timothy 2:4) That expresses the heart of God as well as any statement ever spoken.*

It is an important passage because it presents the truth as God sees it and implies why it is that people do not come to the truth. When Paul speaks of "the knowledge of the truth," he is not referring to interesting tidbits about the spiritual realm or head knowledge about the Lord. He is talking about the kind of knowledge that gets into a person, overthrows long-held falsehoods, and brings about an internal revolution.

Elsewhere he instructed Timothy that he should gently correct "those who are in opposition, if perhaps God may grant them repentance leading to the knowledge of the truth, and they may come to their senses and escape from the snare of the devil, having been held captive by him to do his will." (2 Timothy 2:25-26) Whatever this truth is he is speaking of, it is clear that people cannot be saved until they come into it. They are held captive by the devil and they will only find freedom from his icy grip as their minds and hearts are expanded with a true understanding of the ways of God.

To really grasp what the apostle was saying to his readers, we must acquire a better understanding of the word "knowledge." The Greek term generally used by NT writers to describe knowledge is *gnosis*, which they used to describe knowledge in the same way the English languages uses it.

However, that is not the word Paul used when he referred to the "knowledge of the truth." The word used in those passages is *epignosis*, which is a strengthened form of *gnosis*. In this conjunction, the prefix "epi" means "fully." Let me offer an

---

* There are only a small handful of instances where Scripture explicitly expresses something that God desires. Two of them have to do with truth. We have already examined the first: "Behold, You desire truth in the innermost being..." (Psalm 51:6)

example of the difference in the verb tense of these two words. In the famous "Love Chapter," Paul told the Corinthians, "For now we see in a mirror dimly, but then face to face; now I *know* [*ginosko*] in part, but then I will *know fully* [*epiginosko*] just as I also have been *fully known*. [*epiginosko*]" (1 Corinthians 13:12)

So when Paul was talking about coming into a "knowledge of the truth," he was describing a deep and profound comprehension of truth—something at the extreme other end from the head knowledge so prevalent in the American Church.

Regarding *epignosis*, Marvin Vincent says, "Always of a knowledge which powerfully influences the form of the religious life and hence containing more of the element of personal sympathy than the simple gnósis knowledge, which may be concerned with the intellect alone without affecting the character."[5] Kenneth Wuest adds the following:

> *Epignosis* is full, perfect, precise knowledge as opposed to *gnósis*, imperfect, partial knowledge... [*Epignosis*] is not a mere intellectual knowledge of the facts concerning Him acquired by a study of the Gospels, for instance, but a heart experience of what and who He is gained by such a study plus a personal association with Him by means of the Word and the ministry of the Holy Spirit.[6]

THE ENTRANCE

I fear that the American Church has largely become apostate. I would characterize the two predominant groups of pseudo-Christians within it as "insiders" and "outsiders." The "insiders" are the multitudes of young people who have been raised in church. The "outsiders" are the masses of unbelievers who have come into the evangelical community and learned to adopt its language and lifestyle. These groups are similar in that both are comprised of people who have become assimilated into the Church without ever truly being converted to Christ.

As these people intermingle with each other, they strengthen their conviction that they all share a saving faith. As nominal Christians continue to populate our churches, this false belief system will become progressively stronger. Little do they realize that they are the very ones Paul warned about in the apostate church as "always learning and never able to come to the knowledge [*epignosis*] of the truth." (2 Timothy 3:7)

One of the fatal mistakes many people make is the notion that possessing a great deal of Christian information means that they really know the Lord. Such people have heard sermons by the thousands and read spiritual books by the hundreds, but something vital is missing: they have not yet crossed the line into true Christianity evidenced by a transformed heart and life. James was very concerned about this in his day. He wrote:

> Therefore, ridding yourselves of all moral filth and the evil that is so prevalent, humbly receive the implanted word, which is able to save your souls. But be doers of the word and not hearers only, deceiving yourselves. (James 1:21-22 CSB)

The test of true Christianity is not found in the realm of head knowledge but in the reality of Christ dwelling within and His life being reflected and lived out in every aspect of one's daily life.

From our vantage point, it is difficult to discern genuine believers from pseudo-Christians. Since we have all absorbed the evangelical culture, we look and sound alike. As I discussed in the fifth chapter of Book Two, some people have the natural ability to seamlessly melt into this culture with little effort. This makes discerning the difference between wheat and tares all the more challenging.

My wife, Kathy, has faced this dilemma many times over the years while counseling the wives of men in sexual sin. She eventually learned that the best way to find out the reality of a person's Christian experience is to ask them to share with her their testimony about how they came to the Lord. Many of these women have been raised in Christian homes and cannot remember a specific time when they really repented of their sins and came into the faith.[†] Others can recall what transpired that brought them to the point of habitual church attendance, but their memory of actually being born again is vague and full of Christian platitudes. Still other women can precisely articulate a time when they came to an end of themselves, saw their sinful condition, repented of self-will, and put their faith in Christ. Kathy knows she is dealing with an authentic believer when she hears a testimony like that.[‡]

Whether or not we can discern the difference between wheat and tares, in the spiritual realm which our Lord inhabits, there is an enormous gulf lying between the two. At the end of the day, every person who belongs to Christ has, in one form or another, experienced true repentance of their former life. This is the only path into "the knowledge of the truth."

True repentance means that something dramatic has occurred in the person's Self-life. In order for Jesus Christ to reign in a person's heart, his ego must first be crushed.

Jesus exposed the insincerity of many of His listeners one day

† One friend of ours told us that she had been involved with the planning for a ladies group luncheon in her church. She suggested that one of the longtime members should share her testimony. When she asked for volunteers, not one of them could recall actually being born again!

‡ This technique is good at substantiating a true believer but is not necessarily a foolproof method of discerning a false Christian (c.f. Matthew 13:27-29). Presumably, a person who can articulate her salvation experience is the real deal. Nevertheless, there are true believers who cannot remember a particular experience of crossing into the Kingdom of Light. The evidence that authenticates their Christian life is seen in the way they live.

by telling them a parable about the wicked tenants of a vineyard who murdered the owner's son. (Luke 20:9-16) He followed this up by asking them, "What then is this that is written: 'The stone which the builders rejected, this became the chief corner stone'? Everyone who falls on that stone will be broken to pieces; but on whomever it falls, it will scatter him like dust." (Luke 20:17-18)

The clear message is that people who were faced with the reality of who Jesus was had two options opened to them: they would either be "broken to pieces" by falling on Him or they would reject Him and eventually face utter destruction. This spiritual truth is just as relevant in our current evangelical culture as it was in Israel of the first century.

The radical transformation that occurs when a person has been broken over his sin is the Narrow Gate entrance into true Christianity. The humbled mindset that occurs in such an encounter with Christ is then lived out on the Narrow Way. That kind of life in God is a far different thing than the carnal, world-loving attitude of a churchgoer who is full of head knowledge but utterly lacking in the kind of heart knowledge that comes through the process of repentance.

This third great fraud Satan has perpetuated on the American Church is that just because a person has renounced certain sins, has embraced the basic belief system of the Christian religion, and has adopted the lifestyle of typical evangelicals, he is a bona fide, born again believer. It is a lie of enormous and devastating proportions.

There are many church going people of our time who have learned the Christian language and lifestyle but never truly became a part of the Body of Christ. Such people have indeed entered a gate and perhaps developed a new lifestyle, but, in the end, it will prove to be "the gate [that] is wide and the way [that] is broad that leads to destruction, and there are many who enter through it." (Matthew 7:13)

EPILOGUE

My constant prayer through the writing of this book has been that the Lord would help me to present the many ways that Satan, the Master Deceiver, has successfully attacked not only the culture, but the Church and the people of God. His subtle lies and deceptive schemes have already stolen, hollowed or demolished the faith of multitudes.

We should all pause before the throne of God and let Him show us our responsibility in these things: How have I allowed his lies to gain entrance in my heart? How have these lies affected me in my relationship with the Lord and others? Are there ways I have even intentionally or unwittingly participated in the enemy's success?

We tend to want to believe that it is only secular and pagan persons who are in trouble. But most of Scripture's numerous warnings against being deceived in the Last Days are aimed squarely at the people of God. And the way out of such deception is to pursue the Truth, to immerse ourselves in the Truth, to constantly cultivate a love of the Truth.

When Jesus ascended to the Father, He said it was better for us that He leave so that the Holy Spirit could be sent. Then, on three occasions during His last 24 hours on earth, Jesus explicitly referred to the Holy Spirit as the "Spirit of Truth":

+ I will ask the Father, and He will give you another Helper, that He may be with you forever; that is *the Spirit of truth*, whom the world cannot receive, because it does not see Him or know Him, but you know Him because He abides with you and will be in you. (John 14:16-17)
+ When the Helper comes, whom I will send to you from the Father, that is *the Spirit of truth* who proceeds from the Father, He will testify about Me... (John 15:26)
+ But when He, *the Spirit of truth*, comes, He will guide you into all the truth; for He will not speak on His own initiative, but whatever He hears, He will speak; and He will disclose to you what is to come. (John 16:13)

The Holy Spirit is our essential guide for *Walking in Truth in a World of Lies*. I believe that our convictions about the truth will be tested in the months and years ahead. The floodwaters of deception are rising. We are coming into a time when our only hope of enduring to the end is to sandbag ourselves against the lies that permeate our world and to embrace the truth as if our very eternal lives depend upon it—because they do! As you walk in the truth, you will discover, as I have, that only the truth can set you free and keep you free.

A PRAYER

Lord, as You well know we live in a world that is laden with falsehood; and we are constantly being fed fabrications of the truth; half-truths; lies; twisted and altered perceptions of reality—with just enough truth in them to make them plausible.

Many of us have believed falsehoods about You; falsehoods about ourselves, falsehoods about our relationship with You; false concepts about Scripture; false concepts about life.

I pray that spiritual reality would be impressed into the hearts and minds of every person who has read this book. Help these dear brothers and sisters absorb truth in such a way that they will be able to discern falsehood when it is presented to them—whether it comes from our culture or from someone in the church.

Lord, as You know, we love many things in this world that we shouldn't love. Help us to love the truth. Let that love become greater than the love we have for the things of this world. Please remove anything in us the enemy can use as a hook to draw us away from the truth.

I pray that Your Spirit of Truth would rest upon every reader. Lead them into Your truth. Put Your Truth into their innermost being. Help them to accept Your gift of the love of the truth. In Jesus' mighty name, Amen.

APPENDICES

APPENDIX ONE:
TRUTH IN THE BIBLE

Truth and falsity are subjects of enormous importance to the Lord. He is Truth, He perfectly represents truth, and He demands it of His people. Therefore, the Lord spared no expense in furnishing interested readers a fairly exhaustive supply of terms in both Hebrew and Greek to effectively communicate the facts about truth and falsehood. If we are to understand what He has to say to us regarding these subjects, it is important that we not gloss over the terms.

TRUTH IN HEBREW

The primary word depicting truth in the OT is *emeth*. But before we look at this important term, we must first consider its etymology.

Emeth is actually a derivative of the word *aman*. This is a fascinating word in the Hebrew language. As I mentioned in the first chapter of Book One, the technical meaning of *aman* is "firmness, certainty, and solidness." It is used 117 times and translated in the NASB with various words, the most prominent being "believe." For instance, speaking of Abraham we are told "Then he believed [Heb. *aman*] in the LORD; and He reckoned it to him as righteousness." (Genesis 15:6) And later, the biblical account says: "When Israel saw the great power which the LORD had used against the Egyptians, the people feared the LORD, and they believed [Heb. *aman*] in the LORD and in His servant Moses." (Exodus 14:31) But this was a wavering people. "The LORD said to Moses, 'How long will this people spurn Me? And how long will they not believe [Heb. *aman*] in Me, despite all the signs which I have performed in their midst?'" (Numbers 14:11)

Aman is also often translated as "faithful." The Lord told Aaron and Miriam, "Not so, with My servant Moses, he is faithful [Heb. *aman*] in all My household." (Numbers 12:7) Moses later returned the compliment: "Know therefore that the LORD your God, He is God, the faithful [Heb. *aman*] God, who keeps His covenant and His lovingkindness to a thousandth generation with those who love Him and keep His commandments." (Deuteronomy 7:9)

This foundational term is also translated into other English words. Moses remonstrated with the people of Israel as they prepared to enter the Promised Land: "But for all this, you did not trust [Heb. *aman*] the LORD your God." (Deuteronomy 1:32) And David later exclaimed, "The law of the LORD is perfect, restoring the soul; the testimony of the LORD is sure [Heb. *aman*], making wise the simple." (Psalm 19:7)

As I said, *aman* is an important root word in the Hebrew language. But *emeth* isn't its only derivative; there are a couple of others worth mentioning.

Emun is used 5 times and translated in the NASB as "faithful" (2), "trustworthy" (2), and "faithfulness" (1). We find the Lord employing it in Deuteronomy: "Then He said, 'I will hide My face from them, I will see what their end shall be; for they are a perverse generation, sons in whom is no faithfulness [Heb. *emun*].'" (Deuteronomy 32:20) Solomon said, "A trustworthy [Heb. *emun*] witness will not lie, but a false witness utters lies." (Proverbs 14:5) He also noticed, "Many a man proclaims his own loyalty, but who can find a trustworthy [Heb. *emun*] man?" (Proverbs 20:6)

Emunah is used 48 times and is nearly always translated in the NASB with the word "faithful" or a derivative. It is often used to describe the Lord: "The Rock! His work is perfect, for all His ways are just; a God of faithfulness [Heb. *emunah*] and without injustice, righteous and upright is He." (Deuteronomy 32:4) "For the word of the LORD is upright, and all His work is done in faithfulness [Heb. *emunah*]." (Psalm 33:4)

His people are also expected to prove faithful. David told Saul: "The LORD will repay each man for his righteousness and his faithfulness [Heb. *emunah*]..." (1 Samuel 26:23) He later admonished his people, "Trust in the LORD and do good; dwell in the land and cultivate faithfulness [Heb. *emunah*]." (Psalm 37:3) The psalmist wrote, "I have chosen the faithful [Heb. *emunah*] way; I have placed Your ordinances before me." (Psalm 119:30) He also acknowledged the inscrutable ways of the Lord: "I know, O LORD, that Your judgments are righteous, and that in faithfulness [Heb. *emunah*] You have afflicted me." (Psalm 119:75)

And how could we leave out the famous words of Habakkuk? "Behold, as for the proud one, his soul is not right within him; but the righteous will live by his faith [Heb. *emunah*]." (Habakkuk 2:4)

So we can see that the various derivatives of the Hebraic term *aman* are similar and yet each retains its distinct characteristics. It might be helpful to think of it as a family where a man has sired four children. This man, Aman, received his name because he was seen to be solid in his convictions, not deviating from reality. Although his sons each have their own personalities, they also have taken on his characteristics as well. His first son, Emeth, is unshakeable like his father as far as seeing the state of things. Emun and Emunah are non-identical twins who are solid in their faithfulness. Amen is known for always affirming that which is real to the facts. Each brother retains his own individual character traits while, at the same time, sharing a deep resemblance to each other. On the whole, this family is known for being committed to reality and unshakeable in their convictions.

With all of that in mind, let's get back to *emeth*. As a refresher, let's revisit what the *Theological Wordbook of the Old Testament* (TWOT) says about this Hebraic term *emeth*:

> This very important concept in biblical doctrine gives clear evidence of the biblical meaning of "faith" in contradistinction to the many popular concepts of the term. At the heart of the meaning of the root is the idea of certainty. And this is borne out by the NT definition of faith found in Heb 11:1 ['Now faith is the assurance of things hoped for, the conviction of things not seen.'].[1]

The *Theological Dictionary of the New Testament* (TDNT) says this about *emeth*: "The common OT word for truth appears some 126 times. It denotes a reality that is firm, solid, binding, and hence true. With reference to persons it characterizes their action, speech or thought, and suggests integrity."[2]

Emeth is used 127 times. The NASB uses various words, the most prominent being "truth" and its derivatives, 104 times and "faithful" with its derivatives 19 times. In one of the most profound moments of Moses' life, he was allowed to see God: "Then the LORD passed by in front of him and proclaimed, 'The LORD, the LORD God, compassionate and gracious, slow to anger, and abounding in lovingkindness and truth [Heb. *emeth*].'" (Exodus 34:6) Joshua admonished Israel, "Now, therefore, fear the LORD and serve Him in sincerity and truth [Heb. *emeth*]; and put away the gods which your fathers served beyond the River and in Egypt, and serve the LORD." (Joshua 24:14) Later, Samuel would tell them, "Only fear the LORD

TRUTH IN THE BIBLE

and serve Him in truth [Heb. *emeth*] with all your heart; for consider what great things He has done for you." (1 Samuel 12:24)

David would later cry out, "O LORD, who may abide in Your tent? Who may dwell on Your holy hill? He who walks with integrity, and works righteousness, and speaks truth [Heb. *emeth*] in his heart." (Psalm 15:1-2) The Truth of God was very real to David. He would later implore the Lord, "Lead me in Your truth [Heb. *emeth*] and teach me, for You are the God of my salvation; for You I wait all the day." (Psalm 25:5) And then exclaimed: "All the paths of the LORD are lovingkindness and truth [Heb. *emeth*] to those who keep His covenant and His testimonies." (Psalm 25:10) Prophetically, he would speak the very words His Lord would later utter on the cross: "Into Your hand I commit my spirit; You have ransomed me, O LORD, God of truth [Heb. *emeth*]." (Psalm 31:5) Finally, David would affirm: "The LORD is near to all who call upon Him, to all who call upon Him in truth [Heb. *emeth*]." (Psalm 145:18)

There is one more Hebraic term used to define truth which is also part of the *aman* family. It is a word we're all very familiar with because it was transliterated into Greek and later into the English language. It is the word *amen*, which is used 30 times, nearly always retaining its Hebrew form "amen" in the NASB.

Isaiah called the Lord "the God of *Amen*" (Isaiah 65:16), but more typically the word was used in the same manner that we use it. For instance, when David had the ark returned to Jerusalem, he concluded his tremendous prayer with these words: "'Blessed be the LORD, the God of Israel, from everlasting even to everlasting.' Then all the people said, 'Amen,' and praised the LORD." (1 Chronicles 16:36) Hundreds of years later, Ezra opened the Word of God in front of the people: "Then Ezra blessed the LORD the great God. And all the people answered, 'Amen, Amen!' while lifting up their hands; then they bowed low and worshiped the LORD with their faces to the ground." (Nehemiah 8:6)

Four different psalmists employed the term, each using it as an exclamation point to his praise to the God of Israel. David exclaimed, "Blessed be the Lord, the God of Israel, from everlasting to everlasting. Amen and Amen." (Psalm 41:13) An unnamed psalmist added: "And blessed be His glorious name forever; and may the whole earth be filled with His glory. Amen, and Amen." (Psalm 72:19) Ethan cried out, "Blessed be the Lord forever! Amen and Amen." (Psalm 89:52) And finally, another unnamed psalmist poured out his heart: "Blessed be the Lord, the God of Israel, from everlasting even to everlasting. And let all the people say, 'Amen.' Praise the Lord!" (Psalm 106:48)

As I previously mentioned, this practice of emphasizing some truthful statement with the word "amen" was carried forth into the NT. It is actually used some 150 times in the NT, 31 of which retain its Hebrew word ("amen"). Jesus was never recorded using the term to emphasize a statement.* However, He did use the word "amen" frequently, usually as an affirmation in the midst of a statement, rather than as a concluding emphatic. For instance, in the Sermon on the Mount He said, "For truly [Heb. *amen*] I say to you, until heaven and earth pass away, not the smallest letter or stroke shall pass from the Law until all is accomplished." (Matthew 5:18) He also told His listeners, "When you pray, you are not to be like the hypocrites; for they love to stand and pray in the synagogues and on the street corners so that they may be seen by men. Truly [Heb. *amen*] I say to you, they have their reward in full." (Matthew 6:5)

It seems that each time Jesus employed the word "amen," it was in conjunction with an important truth. When speaking of the lack of responsiveness to the preaching of His disciples, He remarked, "Truly [Heb. *amen*] I say to you, it will be more

---

* It is used to conclude the Lord's Prayer in Matthew 6:13, but this verse was almost certainly a later addition.

tolerable for the land of Sodom and Gomorrah in the day of judgment than for that city." (Matthew 10:15) And when sharing the parables with His disciples He affirmed to them, "For truly [Heb. *amen*] I say to you that many prophets and righteous men desired to see what you see, and did not see it, and to hear what you hear, and did not hear it." (Matthew 13:17)

Salvation was a subject of tremendous importance that Jesus wanted to emphasize. He doubled its usage when He told Nicodemus, "Truly [Heb. *amen*], truly [Heb. *amen*], I say to you, unless one is born again he cannot see the kingdom of God." (John 3:3) He repeated this method when He spoke of Judgment Day: "Truly [Heb. *amen*], truly [Heb. *amen*], I say to you, he who hears My word, and believes Him who sent Me, has eternal life, and does not come into judgment, but has passed out of death into life." (John 5:24) He later shared with His disciples a kingdom truth when He insisted, "Truly [Heb. *amen*] I say to you, unless you are converted and become like children, you will not enter the kingdom of heaven." (Matthew 18:3)

Other NT writers also used the term, but it was usually in the traditional manner of affirming the truth of a statement regarding the Lord. For instance, the Apostle Paul told the Romans, "For from Him and through Him and to Him are all things. To Him be the glory forever. Amen." (Romans 11:36) And to Timothy he wrote, "Now to the King eternal, immortal, invisible, the only God, be honor and glory forever and ever. Amen." (1 Timothy 1:17) He also used the term in his final written words: "The Lord will rescue me from every evil deed, and will bring me safely to His heavenly kingdom; to Him be the glory forever and ever. Amen." (2 Timothy 4:18)

In the Revelation, Jesus called Himself, "The Amen, the faithful and true Witness, the Beginning of the creation of God." (Revelation 3:14) He concluded the great Revelation with the words, "He who testifies to these things says, 'Yes, I am coming quickly.'" John quickly responded, "Amen. Come, Lord Jesus." (Revelation 22:20)

TRUTH IN GREEK

As I mentioned in the first chapter of Book One, the primary Greek word for truth is *aletheia* which is derived from *alethes*. And again, it is a compound of the Greek prefix "a," (corresponding to the English prefix "un") and the word *lanthano*, meaning concealed or hidden. So *alethes* literally means unconcealed.

The TDNT says, "Etymologically *aletheia* has the meaning of non-concealment. It thus indicates a matter or state to the extent that it is seen, indicated or expressed, and that in such seeing, indication or expression it is disclosed, or discloses itself, as it really is, with the implication, of course, that it might be concealed, falsified, truncated, or suppressed. *Aletheia*, therefore, denotes the 'full or real state of affairs.'"[3]

The *Complete Biblical Library Greek-English Dictionary* offers a slightly different view of it: "*Alētheia* not only stands for irrefutable facts, but it also expresses the truth itself, that which is unattainable to the human mind and which can only be perceived in ecstasy or through divine revelation."[4]

In his study on the Septuagint (Greek) version of the OT, Everett Harrison offers the following fascinating explanation about how *emeth* and *alētheia* work together:

> That which is *true* corresponds with the nature of things. In this sense the *truth* is eternal and divine, for the Greek recognized no distinction between the natural and the supernatural. These values are continued in the Septuagint use of aletheia but because of the circumstance that it was often used to translate 'emeth, a Hebrew word for truth which stresses the elements of reliability and

trustworthiness, a new content becomes added... whereas the classical aletheia largely serves as an intellectual term, the same word in its Septuagint setting has often a decidedly moral connotation, especially when used with reference to the divine. New Testament writers draw from both streams of meaning, so that the exegete must be constantly on the alert to detect, if he can, whether aletheia means reality or trustworthiness. John and Paul make largest use of the term. The Greek sense seems clearly present in passages like Romans 1:25, whereas a comparison of Romans 3:3 and 3:4 shows with equal clearness that here the Hebraic background is powerfully operative. Paul is especially fond of linking the word truth with the gospel. Here the two strains may be said to unite, for the gospel message corresponds to reality that is, it is ultimate truth... but even more so because the gospel originates with God and possesses His own guarantee.[5]

Aletheia is used 98 times in the NT, nearly always translated as "truth." Jesus utilized the term 23 times. He told Nicodemus, "But he who practices the truth [Gk. *aletheia*] comes to the Light, so that his deeds may be manifested as having been wrought in God." (John 3:21) Not long after this, He shared with the Samaritan woman a great insight into God's Kingdom: "But an hour is coming, and now is, when the true [Gk. *alethinos*] worshipers will worship the Father in spirit and truth [Gk. *aletheia*]; for such people the Father seeks to be His worshipers. God is spirit, and those who worship Him must worship in spirit and truth [Gk. *aletheia*]." (John 4:23-24)[†] To a skeptical Jewish crowd He asserted, "If you continue in My word, then you are truly [Gk. *alethos*] disciples of Mine;

† Alethinos is another important term which is utilized to express the validity of a person; but we must leave it to the reader to do his own study of this word.

and you will know the truth [Gk. *aletheia*], and the truth [Gk. *aletheia*] will make you free." (John 8:31b-32) And then shared with them a profound truth about Satan: "...the devil... does not stand in the truth [Gk. *aletheia*] because there is no truth [Gk. *aletheia*] in him..." (John 8:44) He later promised His disciples that they would not be left alone upon His death: "But when He, the Spirit of truth [Gk. *aletheia*], comes, He will guide you into all the truth [Gk. *aletheia*]..." (John 16:13)

The Apostle Paul included *aletheia* in the Love Chapter: "[Love] does not rejoice in unrighteousness, but rejoices with the truth [Gk. *aletheia*]." (1 Corinthians 13:6) He assured Timothy that "[God] desires all men to be saved and to come to the knowledge of the truth [Gk. *aletheia*]." (1 Timothy 2:4) He also gave insight into one of the great purposes of the Body of Christ: "... the household of God, which is the church of the living God, the pillar and support of the truth [Gk. *aletheia*]." (1 Timothy 3:15)

James spoke of the tremendous victory of winning a backslider back to the Lord: "My brethren, if any among you strays from the truth [Gk. *aletheia*] and one turns him back, let him know that he who turns a sinner from the error of his way will save his soul from death and will cover a multitude of sins." (James 5:19-20) While John shared that love must be expressed sincerely: "Little children, let us not love with word or with tongue, but in deed and truth [Gk. *aletheia*]. We will know by this that we are of the truth [Gk. *aletheia*], and will assure our heart before Him." (1 John 3:18-19)

COMMENTS REGARDING TRUTH

Oswald Chambers wanted everyone to understand that truth was a Person: "*The* Truth is our Lord Himself, consequently any part of the truth may be a lie unless it leads to a relation to *the* Truth. Salvation, sanctification, the Second Coming are all parts of the Truth, but none is the Truth; and they are only parts of the Truth as they are absorbed by the Truth, our Lord Himself."[6]

Lewis Sperry Chafer posited, "Apart from the element of truth in God there would be no certainty whatsoever in this life, and men would wander on in comfortless perplexity not knowing whence they came or whither they are going."[7]

Wayne Detzler asserts, "No Christian can either know or practice truth, apart from constant reliance on the One who is Truth. He is Truth, because He conforms to and indeed creates ultimate reality."[8]

In speaking of *aletheia*, Ralph Martin writes,

> Whereas truth in Western cultures often concerns facts that can be proven logically or scientifically, truth in the NT may deal with genuine, dependable, faithful behavior or 'things as they really are' in contrast to something that has been hidden or concealed... A matter of truth is rarely defended with logical arguments, but instead the author often appeals to the source of revealed truth or assumes the veracity of the claims. Furthermore, whereas today it is commonplace to question the truth of God's existence, this existence was typically assumed in NT contexts.[9]

A.W. Tozer shared the following important thoughts about the Word of God and its relationship to truth:

> The Bible is, among other things, a book of revealed truth. That is, certain facts are revealed that could not be discovered by the most brilliant mind. These facts are of such a nature as to be past finding out. These are facts that were hidden behind a veil, and until certain men who spoke as they were moved by the Holy Ghost took away that veil no mortal man could know them. The lifting of

the veil of unknowing from undiscoverable things we call divine revelation.

What is generally overlooked among humankind is that truth as set forth in the Christian Scriptures is a moral thing; it is not addressed to the intellect only, but to the will also. It addresses itself to the total man, and its obligations cannot be discharged by grasping it mentally.

Truth engages the citadel of the human heart and is not satisfied until it has conquered everything there. The will must come forth and surrender its sword. It must stand at attention to receive orders, and those orders it must joyfully obey. Short of this, any knowledge of Christian truth is inadequate and unavailing.

Bible exposition without moral application raises no opposition. It is only when the hearer is made to understand that truth is in conflict with his heart that resistance sets in. As long as people can hear orthodox truth divorced from life they will attend and support churches and institutions without objection![10]

Dr. Bruce Hurt talks of the truthfulness, reliability, and trustworthiness of the Lord:

He is absolutely dependable, without falseness of any kind. God's plan, principles, and promises are completely reliable, accurate, real, and factual. God is real, not imaginary, vain and empty like the idols of the pagans, who represent a so-called god of their own vain imagination... The practical aspect of God's unchanging truthfulness is that we can stand on His promises with full assurance of faith no matter how we feel, no matter how dire our circumstances... God deals in truth, but Satan traffics in lies.[11]

APPENDIX TWO:
DECEPTION IN THE BIBLE

A scan of stories through the narrative sections of Scripture indicates roughly a hundred stories of various biblical characters telling falsehoods. Most of these incidents were people who used deception to further their own selfish or even evil purposes. There were a handful of others who lied out of fear. These lies began during the advent of man in the Garden of Eden and are discussed right up to the final chapter of the Bible.

When looking at biblical terms, one must keep in mind that the Hebrew tongue is more elaborate than the Greek or English languages.* So it should come as no surprise that there are twenty distinct word groups in the OT (amounting to nearly 400 verses) representing different aspects of deception. As we work our way through these various terms, notice the different nuances of the words that represent deception.

DECEPTION IN THE OLD TESTAMENT

Unquestionably, the first word to consider is *sheqer*. Out of the 115 times this word is used in the OT, 37 of those occurrences are found in the book of Jeremiah. As we saw in Book Three, chapter one, deception had become entrenched

---

* For example, according to the Strong's Concordance, there are 5,624 different Greek words in the New Testament while there are 8,674 Hebraic words in the Old Testament.

in the nation by this time. Political leaders, religious leaders, and the population had all given over to deception. "…from the prophet even to the priest," Jeremiah exclaims, "everyone deals falsely [*sheqer*]." (Jeremiah 6:13) "How can you say, 'We are wise, and the law of the LORD is with us'? But behold, the lying [*sheqer*] pen of the scribes has made it into a lie [*sheqer*]." (Jeremiah 8:8) The Lord lamented, "The prophets are prophesying falsehood [*sheqer*] in My name. I have neither sent them nor commanded them nor spoken to them; they are prophesying to you a false [sheqer] vision, divination, futility and the deception of their own minds." (Jeremiah 14:14)

The TWOT says the following of *sheqer*: "Used of words or activities which are false in the sense that they are groundless, without basis in fact or reality."[1] A very insightful word study is to look up every verse using *sheqer* and replace the English word with this phrase ("groundless, without basis in fact or reality") as I have included below. In many occasions I think you will find this exercise breathing new life into the verses. Here are a number of examples:[†]

> The LORD said to him, "How?" And he said, "I will go out and be a <u>deceiving</u> spirit in the mouth of all his prophets."… ["…a spirit that speaks what is groundless, without basis in fact or reality" in the mouth…] (1 Kings 22:22)

> Behold, he travails with wickedness, and he conceives mischief and brings forth <u>falsehood</u>. […brings forth what is groundless, without basis in fact or reality.] (Psalm 7:14)

> You love evil more than good, <u>falsehood</u> more than speaking what is right. Selah. [You love… that which is groundless, without basis in fact or reality…] (Psalm 52:3)

---

† *Sheqer* is underlined in each verse.

Remove the <u>false</u> way from me, and graciously grant me
Your law. [Remove the way which is groundless, without
basis in fact or reality" from me...] (Psalm 119:29)

Therefore I esteem right all Your precepts concerning
everything, I hate every <u>false</u> way. [...I hate every way
which is groundless, without basis in fact or reality.] (Psalm
119:128)

I hate and despise <u>falsehood</u>, but I love Your law. [I hate
and despise that which is groundless, without basis in fact
or reality...] (Psalm 119:163)

Truthful lips will be established forever, but a <u>lying</u>
tongue is only for a moment. [...a tongue that speaks that
which is groundless, without basis in fact or reality...]
(Proverbs 12:19)

<u>Lying</u> lips are an abomination to the LORD, but those
who deal faithfully are His delight. [Lips that speak that
which is groundless, without basis in fact or reality are an
abomination...] (Proverbs 12:22)

A righteous man hates <u>falsehood</u>, but a wicked man acts
disgustingly and shamefully. [A righteous man hates that
which is groundless, without basis in fact or reality...]
(Proverbs 13:5)

Yet in spite of all this her treacherous sister Judah did not
return to Me with all her heart, but rather in <u>deception</u>,"
declares the LORD. [Judah returned to Me... in that
which is groundless, without basis in fact or reality...]
(Jeremiah 3:10)

The prophets prophesy <u>falsely</u>, and the priests rule on their *own* authority; and My people love it so! But what will you do at the end of it? [The prophets prophesy that which is groundless, without basis in fact or reality...] (Jeremiah 5:31)

Behold, you are trusting in <u>deceptive</u> words to no avail. [...you are trusting in words that are groundless, without basis in fact or reality...] (Jeremiah 7:8)

...from the least even to the greatest everyone is greedy for gain; from the prophet even to the priest everyone practices <u>deceit</u>. [...everyone practices that which is groundless, without basis in fact or reality.] (Jeremiah 8:10)

I have heard what the prophets have said who prophesy <u>falsely</u> in My name, saying, "I had a dream, I had a dream!" [...who prophesy in My name that which is groundless, without basis in fact or reality...] (Jeremiah 23:25-26)

Because you disheartened the righteous with <u>falsehood</u> when I did not cause him grief, but have encouraged the wicked not to turn from his wicked way and preserve his life, [...disheartened the righteous with that which is groundless, without basis in fact or reality...] (Ezekiel 13:22)

The meaning of the next term, *râmâh*, takes a slightly different turn. Literally, *râmâh* means to throw or shoot, but from there it is figuratively used to depict a deceiver causing someone to fall from truth by beguiling or deceiving them. However, it is its derivatives that are used more often.

One of them is *mirmâh*, which can describe activity that is either deceitful or treacherous. So Isaac explains to Esau, "Your brother came deceitfully [Heb. *mirmâh*] and has taken away your blessing." (Genesis 27:35) David says to the Lord, "You destroy those who speak falsehood; the LORD abhors the man of bloodshed and deceit [Heb. *mirmâh*]." (Psalm 5:6) Solomon claims, "The thoughts of the righteous are just, but the counsels of the wicked are deceitful [Heb. *mirmâh*]." (Proverbs 12:5) And in Jeremiah, the Lord says, "Your dwelling is in the midst of deceit [Heb. *mirmâh*]; through deceit [Heb. *mirmâh*] they refuse to know Me," declares the LORD." (Jeremiah 9:6) But it is Daniel who surprises with this term, using it to describe the schemes of the antichrist: "And through his shrewdness he will cause deceit [Heb. *mirmâh*] to succeed by his influence; and he will magnify himself in his heart, and he will destroy many while they are at ease. He will even oppose the Prince of princes, but he will be broken without human agency." (Daniel 8:25)

The sense of deceitful treachery is carried on with *remîyâh*, another derivative of râmâh. David exclaims, "How blessed is the man to whom the LORD does not impute iniquity, and in whose spirit there is no deceit [Heb. *remîyâh*]!" (Psalm 32:2) He later resolves, "He who practices deceit [Heb. *remîyâh*] shall not dwell within my house; he who speaks falsehood shall not maintain his position before me."

The final term found in this word group is *tarmûth*. It refers to the kind of deception that is used in fraudulent words and practice. As we saw above, the Psalmist cries out, "You have rejected all those who wander from Your statutes, for their deceitfulness [Heb. *tarmûth*] is useless (*sheqer*)." (Psalm 119:118) Jeremiah laments, "Why then has this people, Jerusalem, turned away in continual apostasy? They hold fast to deceit [Heb. *tarmûth*], they refuse to return." (Jeremiah 8:5)

The *kâzab* word group is also important. The TWOT says, "The basic meaning is to speak that which is untrue and therefore false to reality."[2] Moses reveals the enormous gap between God and mankind when he said, "God is not a man, that He should lie [Heb. *kâzab*]..." (Numbers 23:19)[‡] The Psalmist continued this same thought when he exclaimed, "I said in my alarm, 'All men are liars [Heb. *kâzab*].'" (Psalm 116:11) David wanted to make sure everyone knew that this included everyone—from the least to the greatest—when he wrote, "Men of low degree are only vanity and men of rank are a lie [Heb. *kâzab*]; in the balances they go up; they are together lighter than breath." (Psalm 62:9)

Another fascinating Hebraic term is *pâthâh*. Of this word, the TWOT says, "The basic verb idea is 'be open, spacious, wide,' and might relate to the immature or simple one who is open to all kinds of enticement, not having developed a discriminating judgment as to what is right or wrong."[3] Moses warns the children of Israel, "Beware that your hearts are not deceived [Heb. *pâthâh*], and that you do not turn away and serve other gods and worship them." (Deuteronomy 11:16) But it can also carry the sense of attempting to cause someone's heart to be open to deception. For instance, Solomon told his son, "My son, if sinners entice [Heb. *pâthâh*] you, do not consent." (Proverbs 1:10) In other words, "My son, if sinners [attempt to open your heart to deception,] do not consent."

One of the most perplexing stories of the Bible uses this term:

The LORD said, "Who will entice [Heb. *pâthâh*] Ahab to go up and fall at Ramoth-gilead?" And one said this while

---

‡ This is another word that can be replaced with its definition: "God is not a man, that He should speak [that which is untrue and therefore false to reality.]" Or, Ezekiel 13:9a, "So My hand will be against the prophets who see false visions and utter *kâzab* ("lying") divinations..." could be changed to read: "So My hand will be against the prophets who see false visions and utter divinations [that are untrue and therefore false to reality....]"

another said that. Then a spirit came forward and stood before the LORD and said, "I will entice [Heb. *pâthâh*] him." The LORD said to him, 'How?' And he said, "I will go out and be a deceiving [*sheqer*] spirit in the mouth of all his prophets." Then He said, "You are to entice [Heb. *pâthâh*] him and also prevail. Go and do so." (1 Kings 22:20-22)

A similar term is *nâshâ*, which carries the sense of being deceived through seduction. In the Garden, Eve attempted to blame-shift when she said, "The serpent deceived [Heb. *nâshâ'*] me, and I ate." (Genesis 3:13) Jeremiah told the Jewish people, "'For thus says the LORD of hosts, the God of Israel, 'Do not let your prophets who are in your midst and your diviners deceive [Heb. *nâshâ'*] you, and do not listen to the dreams which they dream." (Jeremiah 29:8) Obadiah warned the Edomites, "The arrogance of your heart has deceived [Heb. *nâshâ'*] you..." (Obadiah 1:3)

The *shô'âh* word group introduces another facet of deception: its vanity. One of the most famous statements in the Bible is found in the Ten Commandments: "You shall not take the name of the LORD your God in vain [Heb. shav], for the LORD will not leave him unpunished who takes His name in vain [Heb. *shav*]." (Deuteronomy 5:11) Job uses it in a slightly different sense: "Surely God will not listen to an empty [Heb. *shav*] cry, nor will the Almighty regard it." (Job 35:13) The Psalmist pleads, "Turn away my eyes from looking at vanity [Heb. *shav*], and revive me in Your ways." (Psalm 119:37) Solomon shares a powerful spiritual truth when he says, "Unless the LORD builds the house, they labor in vain [Heb. *shav*] who build it; unless the LORD guards the city, the watchman keeps awake in vain [Heb. *shav*]." (Psalm 127:1) The Lord exclaims, "Bring your worthless [Heb. *shav*] offerings no longer, incense is an abomination to Me. New moon and sabbath, the calling of assemblies—I cannot endure iniquity and the solemn assembly." (Isaiah 1:13) Later, Isaiah says, "Woe to those who drag iniquity with the cords of falsehood [Heb. *shav*], and sin as if with cart ropes." (Isaiah 5:18)

Other terms and word groups are used as well, but I will only mention one. Jeremiah, overwhelmed with the level of deception in his people, indicted all of mankind when he said, "The heart is more deceitful [Heb. *'âqôb*] than all else and is desperately sick; who can understand it?" (Jeremiah 17:9)

DECEPTION IN THE NEW TESTAMENT

As I said before, the Greek language is simpler and only two primary word groups describing deception are used in the NT.§

The first word family we should be familiar with begins with the term *apatao*. The basic sense these terms represent is that of deception. In the Septuagint version of the OT, the Philistine leaders offered Delilah eleven hundred pieces of silver if she would deceive Samson into telling her the secret of his power: "Entice [Gk. *apate*] him, and see where his great strength lies..." (Judges 16:5)

In the New Testament, Jesus warned of the deceitfulness [Gk. *apate*] of riches" (Mark 4:19), while Paul told the Colossians, "See to it that no one takes you captive through philosophy and empty deception [Gk. *apate*]..." (Colossians 2:8)

The Greek term *exapatao* is a strengthened form of *apate*. The apostle Paul really brings this out when he told Timothy, "And it was not Adam *who* was deceived [Gk. *apate*], but the woman being deceived [Gk. *exapatao*], fell into transgression." (1Timothy 2:14) What's the difference between what Adam (*apate*) and Eve (*exapatao*) experienced? Adam was led to

§ A third word, *planao*, will be covered in Appendix #4.

believe something false through what his wife told him, but Eve was "thoroughly seduced" (the idea behind *exapatao*) by the serpent. Paul used the same term when warning the Corinthian Christians: "But I am afraid that, as the serpent deceived [Gk. *exapatao*] Eve by his craftiness, your minds will be led astray from the simplicity and purity of devotion to Christ." (2 Corinthians 11:3)

The second term we'll take a brief look at is *pseudos*, which carries roughly the same meaning as we are accustomed to in the English language. In our language, it is often used in the formation of compound words defining something as false. For instance, when an author wishes to remain anonymous, he uses a pseudonym—a false name. Or a wannabe philosopher might be called a pseudointellectual. This same usage is also in play in Greek New Testament, always used in a negative sense, we are warned about *pseudoprophētēs* (spurious prophets), *pseudodidaskalos* (teachers delivering a false message), *pseudapostolos* (fake apostles), *pseudologos* (propagating an errant teaching), or even *pseudochristos* (false Christs).

In the English language, pseudo is usually used to create compound terms. However, in the Greek, *pseudos* is mostly employed as a standalone word, primarily referring to something false. The following are some examples:

+ "...Whenever [the devil] speaks a lie [Gk. *pseudos*], he speaks from his own nature, for he is a liar [Gk. *pseustes*] and the father of lies." (John 8:44)
+ "For they exchanged the truth of God for a lie [Gk. *pseudos*]..." (Romans 1:25)
+ "...the one whose coming is in accord with the activity of Satan, with all power and signs and false [Gk. *pseudos*] wonders." (2 Thessalonians 2:9)

English Bibles often use the word "lie" when translating *pseudos*, but, personally, I feel terms such as "false" or "falsehood" more accurately express what the writer meant.

There are a number of other terms in the NT. One fascinating word is *plastos*, which means what you would expect it to mean: artificial, something "plastic" as opposed to real.

APPENDIX THREE:
FALSE PROPHETS, TEACHERS, AND APOSTLES

C ertainly, no study of the condition of the Apostate Church would be complete without acquiring at least a basic understanding of what the Bible says about its leaders.

The Old Testament certainly offers stories—mostly found during the final days of the nation of Judah—about the activities of false prophets, but it is the New Testament that presents a plethora of vital information about them.

The Lord really only said one thing about these imposters, and it is revealing that His main focus was on what they are like in the secret realm of their "inside world": "inwardly" He said, they "are ravenous wolves." (Matthew 7:15)

The apostle Paul warned the Ephesian leaders that "savage wolves will come in among you..." (Acts 20:29) To the Corinthians, he offered four different characterizations of them: "false apostles, deceitful workers, disguising themselves as apostles of Christ," going on to refer to them as servants of Satan. (2 Corinthians 11:13-15) He told the Philippians that these men were "enemies of the cross of Christ." (Philippians 3:18) In his letter to Timothy, he said they were "conceited," that they "understand nothing," that they are "men of depraved mind and deprived of the truth." (1 Timothy 6:3-5) He followed this up with Titus by saying they were "...rebellious men, empty talkers and deceivers..." (Titus 1:10)

Towards the end of his life, Peter was swept up into a Holy Spirit inspired vision of *pseudoprophētēs* (fake prophets) and *pseudodidaskalos* (spurious teachers). He called them false (2 Peter 2:1), greedy (2 Peter 2:3) and "daring and self-willed" (2 Peter 2:10). He said they are "like unreasoning animals, born as creatures of instinct..." (2 Peter 2:12). He went on to call them "stains and blemishes," (2 Peter 2:13), "having eyes full of adultery that never cease from sin,"... "having a heart trained in greed, accursed children (2 Peter 2:14)." They are possessed with the same "madness" that possessed Balaam. (2 Peter 2:16) He labeled them "springs without water and mists driven by a storm." (2 Peter 2:17) They are sensuous, "slaves of corruption." (2 Peter 2:18-19) Furthermore, they are just like "a dog [that] returns to its own vomit" and "a sow [that] returns to wallowing in the mire." (2 Peter 2:22)

The apostle John spoke of "false prophets," who are "from the world," (1 John 4:1, 5) and "deceivers" who share the characteristics of "the antichrist." (2 John 1:7)

Jude, the brother of our Lord, shared Peter's sentiments of these pseudo-ministers.* Jude accused them of being "ungodly." (Jude 1:4) He said they will be "hidden reefs in your love feasts" and "clouds without water, carried along by winds; autumn trees without fruit, doubly dead, uprooted; wild waves of the sea, casting up their own shame like foam; wandering stars..." (Jude 1:12-13) He also claimed they are "worldly minded, devoid of the Spirit." (Jude 1:19)

That is what they are, but just as important is what they do. Jesus said that they "come to you in sheep's clothing." (Matthew 7:15) "You will know them by their fruits," He said, going on to say that they bear "bad fruit," and cannot "produce good fruit." (Matthew 7:16-18)

---

* It seems that Jude wrote his epistle and Peter followed along his basic ideas.

Paul told the Ephesians that they would not spare the flock. (Acts 20:29) They would speak "perverse things, to draw away the disciples after them." (Acts 20:30) He warned the Roman believers that these deceivers would "cause dissensions and hindrances contrary to the teaching which you learned." (Romans 16:17) He told the Corinthians that they peddle "the word of God" (2 Corinthians 2:17), later claiming that they "take pride in appearance and not in heart."(2 Corinthians 5:12) He said that they will lead "your minds astray from the simplicity and purity of devotion to Christ," and will "preach another Jesus whom we have not preached" (2 Corinthians 11:3-4), and said they disguise "themselves as apostles of Christ," as "servants of righteousness," and, like Satan, "as an angel of light." (2 Corinthians 11:13-15)

Speaking of Judaisers, the Apostle to the Gentiles told the Galatians that these pseudo-preachers "wish to shut you out so that you will seek them." (Galatians 4:17) They "desire to make a good showing in the flesh," but are careful not to do anything that would cause them to "be persecuted for the cross of Christ." (Galatians 6:12)

He told the Ephesians that false teachers use "trickery," "craftiness," and "deceitful scheming." (Ephesians 4:14)

They "proclaim Christ out of selfish ambition," (Philippians 1:17) Paul told the Philippians. Their "god is their appetite," as they "set their minds on earthly things." (Philippians 3:19)

He warned the Colossians that they were adept at taking people "captive through philosophy and empty deception, according to the tradition of men, according to the elementary principles of the world, rather than according to Christ." (Colossians 2:8)

He told Timothy that they are prone to overreaching, "wanting to be teachers of the Law, even though they do not understand either what they are saying or the matters about which they make confident assertions." (1 Timothy 1:7) He also told him that they "advocate a different doctrine [that] does not agree with sound words, those of our Lord Jesus Christ, and with the doctrine conforming to godliness." (1Timothy 6:3) They "suppose that godliness is a means of gain." (1Timothy 6:5) Referring to false teachers of our day, he said they "will proceed from bad to worse deceiving and being deceived." (2Timothy 3:13) He reiterated their selfish motives to Titus when he said that they teach "things they should not teach for the sake of sordid gain." (Titus 1:11)

Peter's heart was full of concern for believers living during the end of the age. It was probably with tear-filled eyes that he said they would "secretly introduce destructive heresies, even denying the Master who bought them," (2 Peter 2:1) warning that they will "exploit you with false words." (2 Peter 2:3)

These *pseudoprophētes* "indulge the flesh in its corrupt desires and despise authority." In fact, he said, they are so brazen, that they don't even "tremble when they revile angelic majesties... reviling where they have no knowledge." (2 Peter 2:10, 12) These are people who live for the good times, counting "it a pleasure to revel in the daytime... in their deceptions, as they carouse with you... enticing unstable souls." (2 Peter 2:13-14) "Forsaking the right way," Peter continued, "they have gone astray, having followed the way of Balaam, the son of Beor, who loved the wages of unrighteousness." (2 Peter 2:15) "For speaking out arrogant words of vanity they entice by fleshly desires, by sensuality, those who barely escape from the ones who live in error, promising them freedom while they themselves are slaves of corruption; for by what a man is overcome, by this he is enslaved." (2 Peter 2:18-19)

It really is a sad story because there was a time that they had "escaped the defilements of the world by the knowledge of the Lord and Savior Jesus Christ," but they couldn't tolerate the thought of living without their sin, so they will once again become "entangled in them and... overcome." (2 Peter 2:20)

In John's day, there were members of his congregation who had gone back "out into the world" system that they loved. (1 John 4:1) No wonder their message is received, because they "speak as from the world, and the world listens to them." (1 John 4:5)

Jude said that "certain persons have crept in unnoticed... ungodly persons who turn the grace of our God into licentiousness and deny our only Master and Lord, Jesus Christ." (Jude 1:4) They "revile the things which they do not understand." (Jude 1:10) "Woe to them! For they have gone the way of Cain, and for pay they have rushed headlong into the error of Balaam." (Jude 1:11)

Watch out for them, says Jude, because they will "feast with you without fear, caring [only] for themselves." (Jude 1:12) Because they are full of themselves, they are always "finding fault" with others. (Jude 1:16) Life to them is all about "following after their own lusts." (Jude 1:16) Depending on the circumstances, sometimes these men "speak arrogantly," while at other times they flatter "people for the sake of gaining an advantage." (Jude 1:16) Jude says that the divisions in the Church are because of these men. (Jude 1:19)

Peter tells us that the outcome of their efforts will be that "many [Gk. *polus*] will follow their sensuality" and "because of them the way of the truth will be maligned." (2 Peter 2:2) He basically reiterated what Jesus foretold of the last days when He said that "Many [Gk. *polus*] false prophets will arise and will mislead many [Gk. *polus*]." (Matthew 24:11)

These people are living their best life now, but unimaginable judgment is gathering like storm clouds, soon to break out upon them. Paul simply said that their "end is destruction." (Philippians 3:19)

APPENDIX FOUR:
PERSEVERING IN THE TRUTH

One of the great subjects of Scripture is the need to persevere in one's commitment to the truth and to the Lord. The truth about God and His Kingdom must be accepted by faith and one must maintain that belief throughout life. The person who has accepted what the Bible claims about God will show forth that conviction by the way he lives his life. As Andrew Murray said, "We must live and experience truth in order to know it."[1] Charles Finney offers the same sentiments conversely: "Anyone who does not practice what he admits to be true is self-deceived."[2]

The concept of perseverance is addressed in Scripture from both a positive and negative perspective. We will look at the positive first.

PERSEVERANCE IN THE BIBLE

The words "perseverance" and "endurance" are not used as such in the OT. While perseverance in the NT carries with it the sense of staying faithful in the midst of adversity or even pressure to renounce one's faith, OT writers approached the subject with the idea of patiently waiting on the Lord. The Hebraic term used to express this subject is *qâvâh*.

David certainly understood what it meant to patiently endure hardship as he escaped from Saul's demonic rage and ran for his life. For thirteen years he remained faithful to the Lord in spite of having to live in hiding. He testified, "Indeed, none of those who wait [Heb. *qâvâh*] for You will be ashamed..." (Psalm 25:3) He then prayed, "Lead me in Your truth and teach me, for You are the God of my salvation; for You I wait [Heb. *qâvâh*] all the day." (Psalm 25:5) He later admonished: "Wait [Heb. *qâvâh*] for the LORD; be strong and let your heart take courage; yes, wait [Heb. *qâvâh*] for the LORD." (Psalm 27:14) He brought forth a more eschatological sense when he said, "Wait [Heb. *qâvâh*] for the LORD and keep His way, and He will exalt you to inherit the land; when the wicked are cut off, you will see it." (Psalm 37:34) And finally, he testified, "I waited [Heb. *qâvâh*] patiently for the LORD; and He inclined to me and heard my cry." (Psalm 40:1)

Isaiah exclaimed, "Indeed, while following the way of Your judgments, O LORD, we have waited [Heb. *qâvâh*] for You eagerly; Your name, even Your memory, is the desire of our souls." (Isaiah 26:8) And what an encouraging word he brought when he promised, "Yet those who wait [Heb. *qâvâh*] for the LORD will gain new strength; they will mount up with wings like eagles, they will run and not get tired, they will walk and not become weary." (Isaiah 40:31) Jeremiah expressed the same thought a little differently: "The LORD is good to those who wait [Heb. *qâvâh*] for Him, to the person who seeks Him." (Lamentations 3:25) Finally, Hosea cried out to backslidden Israel, "Therefore, return to your God, observe kindness and justice, and wait [Heb. *qâvâh*] for your God continually." (Hosea 12:6)

In the NT, the concept is more directed to those who must be encouraged to remain faithful to the Lord—even in the face of severe adversity or persecution. The primary term utilized by first century writers is *hupomone*. The TDNT says the following about this word:

Hupomone is naturally a basic attitude of NT believers in view of the eschatological orientation of their faith. Over against a hostile world, they wait confidently for the fulfillment of the kingdom and their own salvation.... Unlike Greek ethics, which regards the passive suffering of evil as shameful, Christians know that they are called to suffer (Acts 14:22), and they show their faith by persevering all the same.... If hope focuses on the future, the steadfastness of hope is its expression in the present time of affliction.... In Mk. 13:13 endurance will be needed in the trials of the last period if one is to be saved.... Revelation, the book of the martyr church, extols hupomone as right and necessary for believers. On the one side, it is waiting for Jesus (1:9; 3:10). On the other, it is the enduring of suffering and persecution (2:2-3, 19). The final clash is the supreme test and demands supreme steadfastness if all is not to be for nothing (13:10; 14:12).[3]

Paul tied *hupomone* to one's salvation when he spoke of "the day of wrath and revelation of the righteous judgment of God, who will render to each person according to his deeds: to those who by perseverance [Gk. *hupomone*] in doing good seek for glory and honor and immortality, eternal life; but to those who are selfishly ambitious and do not obey the truth, but obey unrighteousness, wrath and indignation." (Romans 2:5b-8)

The writer of Hebrews exhorted, "For you have need of endurance [Gk. *hupomone*], so that when you have done the will of God, you may receive what was promised." (Hebrews 10:36)

As the TDNT mentioned, perseverance is a major theme in the book of Revelation. In the chapter describing the terrible time that will soon be upon us, we are told, "If anyone is to be taken captive, to captivity he goes; if anyone is to be slain with the sword, with the sword must he be slain. Here is a call for the endurance and faith of the saints." (Revelation 13:10 ESV) The same thought is repeated in the following chapter, where the tribulation period is shown—not from the devil's perspective, but from God's: "Here is the perseverance [Gk. *hupomone*] of the saints who keep the commandments of God and their faith in Jesus." (Revelation 14:12)

Of this subject Matthew Henry writes,

> Perseverance in the faith of the gospel and true worship of God, in this great hour of trial and temptation, which would deceive all but the elect, is the character of those registered in the book of life. This powerful motive and encouragement to constancy, is the great design of the whole Revelation.[4]

A close cousin of *hupomone* is *hupomeno*, which carries the same basic idea. In Matthew, Jesus twice called on His people to persevere in their faith during the Last Days: "And you will be hated by all on account of My name, but it is the one who has endured [Gk. *hupomeno*] to the end who will be saved." (Matthew 10:22) James exclaims, "Blessed is a man who perseveres under trial; for once he has been approved, he will receive the crown of life, which the Lord has promised to those who love Him." (James 1:12)

FORSAKING THE TRUTH IN THE OLD TESTAMENT

As mentioned previously, the Bible deals with the subject of perseverance both positively and negatively. In the OT, the subject is dealt with extensively. In typical Hebraic fashion, there are a number of different terms to reflect various nuances of the concept of departing from the truth: *'azab* [forsaking], *tâ'âh* [straying], *shâgâh* [wandering], *meshubah* [backsliding], *sug* [going back] are the primary verbs we will look at regarding this subject. To forsake the Lord one must first abandon Truth. Let's take a brief look at these verbs.

The literal sense of 'azab means "to loosen." It is used over 200 times, and depending on the setting it is used in different ways. When regarding the subject of perseverance, it always has the sense of abandoning one's commitment to the Lord. When Moses threatened the children of Israel with the curses that would fall on them if they returned to idolatry, he said, "The Lord will send upon you curses, confusion, and rebuke, in all you undertake to do, until you are destroyed and until you perish quickly, on account of the evil of your deeds, because you have forsaken [Heb. 'azab] Me." (Deuteronomy 28:20) This did indeed happen many times in subsequent years. No sooner had Joshua died than the people returned to idolatry.

> Then the sons of Israel did evil in the sight of the Lord and served the Baals, and they forsook [Heb. 'azab] the Lord, the God of their fathers, who had brought them out of the land of Egypt, and followed other gods from among the gods of the peoples who were around them, and bowed themselves down to them; thus they provoked the Lord to anger. So they forsook [Heb. 'azab] the Lord and served Baal and the Ashtaroth. (Judges 2:11-13)

The prophet Samuel led the Jewish people for many years, but, wanting to be like the pagan nations surrounding them, they demanded to be ruled by a king. This hurt and offended the man of God, but the Lord immediately comforted Samuel.

> Listen to the voice of the people in regard to all that they say to you, for they have not rejected you, but they have rejected Me from being king over them. Like all the deeds which they have done since the day that I brought them up

from Egypt even to this day—in that they have forsaken [Heb. *azab*] Me and served other gods—so they are doing to you also. (1 Samuel 8:7-8)

The psalmist proclaimed, "Burning indignation has seized me because of the wicked, who forsake [Heb. *azab*] Your law." But he soon added, "They almost destroyed me on earth, but as for me, I did not forsake [Heb. *azab*] Your precepts." (Psalm 119:53, 87)

Solomon warned the young men of his day about abandoning "the paths of uprightness" (Proverbs 2:13), "reproof" (Proverbs 10:17), "the way" (Proverbs 15:10), and "the law" (Proverbs 28:4).

Who could forget the sad pronouncement Yahweh made about His people during the final years of Judah? "For My people have committed two evils: They have forsaken [Heb. *azab*] Me, the fountain of living waters, to hew for themselves cisterns, broken cisterns that can hold no water." (Jeremiah 2:13) Then followed an ominous warning: "'Your own wickedness will correct you, and your apostasies will reprove you; know therefore and see that it is evil and bitter for you to forsake [Heb. *azab*] the LORD your God, and the dread of Me is not in you,' declares the LORD God of hosts." (Jeremiah 2:19)

The next word, *tâ'âh*, carries the sense of wandering or straying. It is used literally to describe when Hagar wandered [Heb. *tâ'âh*] about in the wilderness of Beersheba. (Genesis 21:14) But, for our purposes, we are more concerned with its figurative sense of straying away from or being led away from truth. One of the worst periods of Jewish history was when "Manasseh seduced [Heb. *tâ'âh*] [the Jewish people] to do evil more than the nations whom the LORD destroyed before the sons of Israel." (2 Kings 21:9) David claimed, "The wicked are estranged from the womb; these who speak lies go astray [Heb. *tâ'âh*] from birth." (Psalm 58:3) The earnest Psalmist acknowledged, "I have gone astray [Heb. *tâ'âh*] like a lost sheep; seek Your servant, for I do not forget Your commandments." (Psalm 119:176) Solomon warned young men to stay far from the prostitute: "Do not let your heart turn aside to her ways, do not stray [Heb. *tâ'âh*] into her paths." (Proverbs 7:25) He also had much to say regarding the wicked: "…he who ignores reproof goes astray [*tâ'âh*]." (Proverbs 10:17) "…the way of the wicked leads them astray [Heb. *tâ'âh*]." (Proverbs 12:26) "Will they not go astray [Heb. *tâ'âh*] who devise evil?" (Proverbs 14:22) And who could ever forget the tremendous statement Isaiah made under inspiration? "All of us like sheep have gone astray [Heb. *tâ'âh*], each of us has turned to his own way; but the LORD has caused the iniquity of us all to fall on Him." (Isaiah 53:6)

A completely different Hebraic term, *shâgâh*, carries the same basic meaning. The Psalmist declared, "With all my heart I have sought You; do not let me wander [Heb. *shâgâh*] from Your commandments." (Psalm 119:10) He later asserted, "You rebuke the arrogant, the cursed, who wander [Heb. *shâgâh*] from Your commandments." (Psalm 119:21) Solomon said, "His own iniquities will capture the wicked, and he will be held with the cords of his sin. He will die for lack of instruction, and in the greatness of his folly he will go astray [Heb. *shâgâh*]." (Proverbs 5:22-23) He warned, "Cease listening, my son, to discipline, and you will stray [Heb. *shâgâh*] from the words of knowledge." (Proverbs 19:27) This was followed with another warning, "He who leads the upright astray [Heb. *shâgâh*] in an evil way will himself fall into his own pit, but the blameless will inherit good." (Proverbs 28:10)

The next verb to look at is *meshubah*, which simply means "apostasy." Solomon did warn the young men of his day: "For the apostasy [Heb. *meshubah*] of the inexperienced will kill them, and the complacency of fools will destroy them." (Proverbs 1:32 CSB) But this term is used almost entirely in the prophets.

As we saw above, Jeremiah warned the people of his day, "Your own wickedness will correct you, and your apostasies [Heb. *meshubah*] will reprove you..." (Jeremiah 2:19) In the following chapter, the Lord spoke to Jeremiah about the spiritual condition of Judah: "The Lord said also to me in the days of Josiah the king: 'Have you seen what backsliding [Heb. *meshubah*] Israel has done? She has gone up on every high mountain and under every green tree, and there played the harlot.... Then I saw that for all the causes for which backsliding [Heb. *meshubah*] Israel had committed adultery, I had put her away and given her a certificate of divorce; yet her treacherous sister Judah did not fear, but went and played the harlot also.'" (Jeremiah 3:6, 8 NKJV) The dialog continued: "Then the Lord said to me, 'Backsliding [Heb. *meshubah*] Israel has shown herself more righteous than treacherous Judah. Go and proclaim these words toward the north, and say: 'Return, backsliding [Heb. *meshubah*] Israel,' says the Lord; 'I will not cause My anger to fall on you. For I am merciful,' says the Lord; 'I will not remain angry forever.'" (Jeremiah 3:11-12 NKJV)

In the final days of the northern tribes of Israel, the Lord lamented, "So My people are bent on turning from [Heb. *meshubah*] Me..." (Hosea 11:7) And yet He still offered hope if they would repent: "I will heal their apostasy [Heb. *meshubah*], I will love them freely, for My anger has turned away from them." (Hosea 14:4)

Sug is a primary root word which literally means "to flinch"; from there it has the sense of "going back" or figuratively, "to backslide." It is used 24 times in the OT.

The psalmist was keen to assure the Lord, "Our heart has not turned back [Heb. *sug*], and our steps have not deviated from Your way." (Psalm 44:18) David spoke of fallen mankind: "Every one of them has turned aside [Heb. *sug*]; together they have become corrupt; there is no one who does good, not even one." (Psalm 53:3) Asaph spoke of the treachery of the Israelites in the wilderness when he said that they "...turned back [Heb. *sug*] and acted treacherously like their fathers; they turned aside like a treacherous bow." (Psalm 78:57) Solomon offered important insight into the consequences people will face when they turn away from the Lord: "The backslider [Heb. *sug*] in heart will have his fill of his own ways, but a good man will be satisfied with his." (Proverbs 14:14)

Isaiah shared a powerful indictment on the faithless Israelites of his day:

> "Behold, the LORD's hand is not so short that it cannot save; nor is His ear so dull that it cannot hear. But your iniquities have made a separation between you and your God, and your sins have hidden His face from you so that He does not hear.... Transgressing and denying the LORD, and turning away from [Heb. *sug*] our God..." (Isaiah 59:1-2, 13)

Another word used to describe those who fall away is *set*, which means "a departure." David affirmed to the Lord, "I will set no worthless thing before my eyes; I hate the work of those who fall away [Heb. *set*]; it shall not fasten its grip on me." (Psalm 101:3) Later, the Lord said, "The revolters [Heb. *set*] have gone deep in depravity, but I will chastise all of them." (Hosea 5:2) The word *set* is actually a derivative of *sut*, which is only used once, where David affirms, "How blessed is the man who has made the LORD his trust, and has not turned to the proud, nor to those who lapse [Heb. *sut*] into falsehood." (Psalm 40:4)

The word *zur* is typically used as "adultery," but in Isaiah the Lord used it figuratively in His opening address to Judah: "Alas, sinful nation, people weighed down with iniquity, offspring of evildoers, sons who act corruptly! They have abandoned [Heb. *'azab*] the LORD, they have despised the Holy One of Israel, they have turned away [Heb. *zur*] from Him." (Isaiah 1:4)

Ironically, the verb *shub*, used 1299 times in the OT—often in the sense of calling the wayward Jews to return to the Lord—is also used negatively.

But when a righteous man turns away [Heb. *shub*] from his righteousness, commits iniquity and does according to all the abominations that a wicked man does, will he live? All his righteous deeds which he has done will not be remembered for his treachery which he has committed and his sin which he has committed; for them he will die." (Ezekiel 18:24)

FORSAKING THE TRUTH IN THE NEW TESTAMENT

The first word to consider is *planos*, which contains the idea of roaming or going astray from the path of Truth. Paul told Timothy, "But the Spirit explicitly says that in later times some will fall away from the faith, paying attention to deceitful [Gk. *planos*] spirits and doctrines of demons." (1 Timothy 4:1) The Apostle John added, "For many deceivers [Gk. *planos*] have gone out into the world, those who do not acknowledge Jesus Christ as coming in the flesh. This is the deceiver [Gk. *planos*] and the antichrist." (2 John 1:7)

The primary derivative of *planos* is *planeo*, which is used 37 times in the NT. The secular idea behind this word is simply straying, drifting or wandering off. This can be seen in Hebrews 11 where men of God are said to have been "wandering in deserts and mountains and caves and holes in the ground."

(Hebrews 11:38) But, of course, Scripture uses it nearly entirely to speak of spiritual wandering. For instance, Jesus said, "What do you think? If any man has a hundred sheep, and one of them has gone astray [Gk. *planao*], does he not leave the ninety-nine on the mountains and go and search for the one that is straying [Gk. *planao*]?" (Matthew 18:12)

Jesus used this verb four times in the Olivet Discourse as warnings to not be misled. (Matthew 24:4, 5, 11, 24) Paul was very concerned that some Christians were using his teachings about grace to deceive themselves into thinking they could indulge in ongoing sin without consequence. He told the Corinthian church, "Or do you not know that the unrighteous will not inherit the kingdom of God? Do not be deceived [Gk. *planao*]; neither fornicators, nor idolaters, nor adulterers, nor effeminate, nor homosexuals, nor thieves, nor the covetous, nor drunkards, nor revilers, nor swindlers, will inherit the kingdom of God." (1 Corinthians 6:9-10) He made the same point to the Galatians from a slightly different perspective: "Do not be deceived [Gk. *planao*], God is not mocked; for whatever a man sows, this he will also reap. For the one who sows to his own flesh will from the flesh reap corruption, but the one who sows to the Spirit will from the Spirit reap eternal life." (Galatians 6:7-8)

James really captured the meaning of *planao* when he wrote, "My brethren, if any among you strays [Gk. *planao*] from the truth and one turns him back, let him know that he who turns a sinner from the error [Gk. *plane*] of his way will save his soul from death and will cover a multitude of sins." (5:19-20) These verses really bring out the proper biblical sense of the term because they show what the person has strayed from: namely, "the truth."

In the Revelation, *planao* is usually used with the idea of being deceived or misled. Only once does the New American

Standard Bible use the more literal sense of being led astray (Revelation 2:20). The English word preferred by the NASB translators in the other seven usages is "deceive." But these usages—used to describe the actions of "Babylon the great," the "beast," and the devil—take on an interesting change in meaning if you insert the idea of being led astray:

+ "...Satan, who [leads] the whole world [astray]..." (12:9)
+ The antichrist "[leads] those who dwell
  on the earth [astray]..." (13:14)
+ And Babylon was told that, "all the nations
  were [led astray] by your sorcery." (18:23)

What does this triumvirate of evil lead people away from? They are led away from the truth established by Jesus Christ.

Plane has a slightly different form than that of *planao*. In the first chapter of Romans, Paul told of those who were given over to a wanton lifestyle of sexual sin. He said, "And in the same way also the men abandoned the natural function of the woman and burned in their desire toward one another, men with men committing indecent acts and receiving in their own persons the due penalty of their error [Gk. *plane*]." (Romans 1:27) Peter spoke of false teachers: "For speaking out arrogant words of vanity they entice by fleshly desires, by sensuality, those who barely escape from the ones who live in error [Gk. *plane*]." (2 Peter 2:18)

A word study for *planao* (similar to the one I suggested in Appendix #4 with the Hebrew word *sheqer*) would be to replace the English word with the appropriate rendering of the phrase "going astray from the truth" as I have included below. For grammar's sake, there will be times you will need to alter the wording. For instance, Ephesians 4:14 reads: "As a result, we are no longer to be children, tossed here and there by waves and carried about by every wind of doctrine, by the trickery of men, by craftiness in deceitful [Gk. *plane*] scheming." It could be made more clear by inserting our defining phrase thus: As a result, we are no longer to be children, tossed here and there by waves and carried about by every wind of doctrine, by the trickery of men, by craftiness [...using devious scheming, leading others away from the truth of God.] I'll offer one more example. The Apostle John wrote, "We are from God; he who knows God listens to us; he who is not from God does not listen to us. By this we know the spirit of truth and the spirit of error [Gk. *plane*]. (1 John 4:6) What John was saying could be more expressive this way: "We are from God; he who knows God listens to us; he who is not from God does not listen to us. By this we know the spirit of truth and [the spirit which leads away from the truth of God.]"

The next Greek term carries with it a wide latitude of application, depending on the situation. *Skandalizo* can mean "stumble," "cause to sin," or, even more seriously, "fall away." I have discussed this term at length in my book, *At the Altar of Sexual Idolatry*, so I will confine my comments here to a couple of instances where it is regarding falling away. In the parable of the Sower and the Seed, Jesus spoke of the person who receives the word on "rocky" ground: "The one on whom seed was sown on the rocky places, this is the man who hears the word and immediately receives it with joy; yet he has no firm root in himself, but is only temporary, and when affliction or persecution arises because of the word, immediately he falls away [Gk. *skandalizo*]. (Matthew 13:20-21) And in the Olivet Discourse, Jesus foretold, "At that time many will fall away [Gk. *skandalizo*] and will betray one another and hate one another." (Matthew 24:10)

The literal meaning of *aphistemi* is simply to "remove"; figuratively, it means to "depart" or "withdraw." In Luke's rendition of the rocky soil hearer in the Sower and the Seed parable, he chose to use this term rather than *skandalizo*. "Those on the rocky soil are those who, when they hear, receive the word with joy; and these have no firm root," Jesus said; "they believe for a while, and in time of temptation fall away [Gk. *aphistemi*]." (Luke 8:13) The Apostle Paul told Timothy, "But the Spirit explicitly says that in later times some will fall away [Gk. *aphistemi*] from the faith, paying attention to deceitful spirits and doctrines of demons." (1 Timothy 4:1) Finally, the writer of Hebrews warned his readers: "Take care, brethren, lest there should be in any one of you an evil, unbelieving heart, in falling away [Gk. *aphistemi*] from the living God.... For we have become partakers of Christ, if we hold fast the beginning of our assurance firm until the end." (Hebrews 3:12, 14)

The next word we should briefly look at is *apostrepho*, which usually has the sense of "turning away" or "turning back." This is the term Paul used when he spoke of the Church of the Last Days: "For the time will come when they will not endure sound doctrine; but wanting to have their ears tickled, they will accumulate for themselves teachers in accordance to their own desires; and will turn away their ears from the truth, and will turn aside [Gk. *apostrepho*] to myths." (2 Timothy 4:3-4) He also employed this term writing to Titus while speaking of Cretan Christians. Take note of what he is concerned about them turning away from: "For this reason reprove them severely so that they may be sound in the faith, not paying attention to Jewish myths and commandments of men who turn away [Gk. *apostrepho*] from the truth." (Titus 1:13b-14) And, once again, we find the author of Hebrews addressing the subject of falling away: "See to it that you do not refuse Him who is speaking. For if those did not escape when they refused him who warned them on earth, much less shall we escape who turn away [Gk. *apostrepho*] from Him who warns from heaven." (Hebrews 12:25)

The next three terms are only used once regarding our subject matter. The first one is the apostasy we discussed in the second chapter of Book Three. The word *apostasia* is a derivative of *apostasion*, which means "divorce." That is clearly in Paul's mind when he wrote: "Let no one in any way deceive you, for it will not come unless the apostasy [Gk. *apostasia*] comes first, and the man of lawlessness is revealed, the son of destruction." (2 Thessalonians 2:3) The second word is only used once in the NT. *Hupostole* literally means "shrinkage," but in biblical terms it carries the idea of shrinking away from one's commitment to the truth: "But we are not of those who shrink back [Gk. *hupostole*] to destruction, but of those who have faith to the preserving of the soul." (Hebrews 10:39) The last word is also only used once in the NT, and it is used in a perplexing passage of Scripture that has caused alarm in the hearts of many people: "For in the case of those who have once been enlightened and have tasted of the heavenly gift and have been made partakers of the Holy Spirit, and have tasted the good word of God and the powers of the age to come, and then have fallen away [Gk. *parapipto*], it is impossible to renew them again to repentance, since they again crucify to themselves the Son of God and put Him to open shame." (Hebrews 6:4-6)

VARIOUS RELATED PASSAGES

"So Jesus was saying to those Jews who had believed Him, 'If you continue in My word, then you are truly disciples of Mine.'" (John 8:31)

"Behold then the kindness and severity of God; to those who fell, severity, but to you, God's kindness, if you continue in His kindness; otherwise you also will be cut off." (Romans 11:22)

"But I discipline my body and make it my slave, so that, after I have preached to others, I myself will not be disqualified." (1 Corinthians 9:27)

"Now I make known to you, brethren, the gospel which I preached to you, which also you received, in which also you stand, by which also you are saved, if you hold fast the word which I preached to you, unless you believed in vain." (1 Corinthians 15:1-2)

"And although you were formerly alienated and hostile in mind, engaged in evil deeds, yet He has now reconciled you in His fleshly body through death, in order to present you before Him holy and blameless and beyond reproach—if indeed you continue in the faith firmly established and steadfast, and not moved away from the hope of the gospel..." (Colossians 1:21-23)

"...keeping faith and a good conscience, which some have rejected and suffered shipwreck in regard to their faith." (1 Timothy 1:19)

"For the love of money is a root of all sorts of evil, and some by longing for it have wandered away from the faith and pierced themselves with many griefs." (1 Timothy 6:10)

"O Timothy, guard what has been entrusted to you, avoiding worldly and empty chatter and the opposing arguments of what is falsely called 'knowledge'—which some have professed and thus gone astray from the faith..." (1 Timothy 6:20-21)

"For if we go on sinning willfully after receiving the knowledge of the truth, there no longer remains a sacrifice for sins, but a terrifying expectation of judgment and the fury of a fire which will consume the adversaries. Anyone who has set aside the Law of Moses dies without mercy on the testimony of two or three witnesses. How much severer punishment do you think he will deserve who has trampled under foot the Son of God, and has regarded as unclean the blood of the covenant by which he was sanctified, and has insulted the Spirit of grace? For we know Him who said, 'vengeance is Mine, I will repay.' And again, 'The LORD will judge His people.' It is a terrifying thing to fall into the hands of the living God." (Hebrews 10:26-31)

"For if, after they have escaped the defilements of the world by the knowledge of the Lord and Savior Jesus Christ, they are again entangled in them and are overcome, the last state has become worse for them than the first. For it would be better for them not to have known the way of righteousness, than having known it, to turn away from the holy commandment handed on to them. It has happened to them according to the true proverb, 'a dog returns to its own vomit,' and, 'A sow, after washing, returns to wallowing in the mire.'" (2 Peter 2:20-22)

"By this we know that we have come to know Him, if we keep His commandments. The one who says, 'I have come to know Him,' and does not keep His commandments, is a liar, and the truth is not in him." (1 John 2:3-4)

"No one who abides in him keeps on sinning; no one who keeps on sinning has either seen him or known him. Little children, let no one deceive you. Whoever practices righteousness is righteous, as he is righteous. Whoever makes a practice of sinning is of the devil, for the devil has been sinning from the beginning. The reason the Son of God appeared was to destroy the works of the devil. No one born of God makes a practice of sinning, for God's seed abides in him, and he cannot keep on sinning because he has been born of God." (1 John 3:6-9 ESV)

"But I have this against you, that you have left your first love. Therefore remember from where you have fallen, and repent and do the deeds you did at first; or else I am coming to you and will remove your lampstand out of its place—unless you repent." (Revelation 2:4-5)

"He who overcomes will thus be clothed in white garments; and I will not erase his name from the book of life, and I will confess his name before My Father and before His angels." (Revelation 3:5)

"I am coming quickly; hold fast what you have, so that no one will take your crown. He who overcomes, I will make him a pillar in the temple of My God, and he will not go out from it anymore; and I will write on him the name of My God, and the name of the city of My God, the new Jerusalem, which comes down out of heaven from My God, and My new name." (Revelation 3:11-12)

I realize there are godly ministers who believe it is not possible to forfeit one's salvation, but in light of all of the preceding passages, I would only say that we would all be wise to remain as far from the cliff of apostasy as possible. As Jesus said in regards to End Time believers like you and I: "The one who endures to the end, he will be saved." (Matthew 24:13)

NOTES
BOOK ONE

INTRODUCTION

1. Jeremiah 9:6 (CSB).
2. Dictionary.com. (n.d.) Disinformation. In *Dictionary.com dictionary*. Retrieved November 28, 2019, from www.Dictionary.com/browse/disinformationDictionary.com. (n.d.) Doublespeak. In *Dictionary.com*. Retrieved December 27, 2019, from https://www.dictionary.com/browse/doublespeak
3. Dictionary.com. (n.d.) Duplicity. In *Dictionary.com dictionary*. Retrieved November 28, 2019, from www.Dictionary.com/browse/duplicity
4. Merriam-Webster. (n.d.). Fabricate. In *Merriam-Webster.com dictionary*. Retrieved November 28, 2019, from www.Merriam-Webster.com/dictionary/fabricate
5. Webster's Dictionary 1828. (n.d.). Falsehood. In *Webstersdictionary1828.com dictionary*. Retrieved January 19, 2020, from http://webstersdictionary1828.com/Dictionary/Falsehood
6. Dictionary.com. (n.d.) Fraud. In *Dictionary.com dictionary*. Retrieved November 28, 2019, from www.Dictionary.com/browse/fraud
7. Dictionary.com. (n.d.) Half-Truth. In *Dictionary.com dictionary*. Retrieved January 11, 2020, from https://www.dictionary.com/browse/half-truth
8. Webster's Dictionary 1828. (n.d.). Hypocrisy. In *Webstersdictionary1828.com dictionary*. Retrieved January 19, 2020, from http://webstersdictionary1828.com/Dictionary/hypocrisy
9. Webster's Dictionary 1828. (n.d.). Lie. In *Webstersdictionary1828.com dictionary*. Retrieved January 19, 2020, from . http://webstersdictionary1828.com/Dictionary/Lie
10. Dictionary.com. (n.d.) Scam. In *Dictionary.com dictionary*. Retrieved November 28, 2019, from www.Dictionary.com/browse/scam
11. Dictionary.com. (n.d.) Subterfuge. In *Dictionary.com dictionary*. Retrieved November 28, 2019, from www.Dictionary.com/browse/subterfuge
12. University of Massachusetts Amherst. (2002, June 10). *UMass Amherst Researcher Finds Most People Lie in Everyday Conversation*. https://www.umass.edu/newsoffice/article/umass-amherst-researcher-finds-most-people-lie-everyday-conversation
13. University of Massachusetts Amherst. (2002, June 10). *UMass Amherst Researcher Finds Most People Lie in Everyday Conversation*. https://www.umass.edu/newsoffice/article/umass-amherst-researcher-finds-most-people-lie-everyday-conversation
14. Douglas, J., & Olshaker, M. (2016). *The Cases That Haunt Us: From Jack the Ripper to JonBenet Ramsey, the FBI's Legendary Mindhunter Sheds Light on the Mysteries That Won't Go Away* (M. Hillgartner, Narrator) [Audiobook]. Blackstone Audio, Inc.

BOOK THREE: APPENDICES

CHAPTER ONE

1. Idleman, S. (2012). *Answers for a Confused Church*. El Paseo Publications. Page 22.
2. Guiness, O. Cited in MacArthur, J. (2003). *Truth: The Sphere of Existence* [Sermon]. Gracetoyou.org. https://www.gty.org/library/sermons-library/63-2/truth-the-sphere-of-existence%20on%204/12/20
3. Oxford University Press. (2016) *Word of the Year*. https://languages.oup.com/word-of-the-year/
4. Viner, K. (2016, July 12). *How technology disrupted the truth*. The Guardian. https://www.theguardian.com/media/2016/jul/12/how-technology-disrupted-the-truth Retrieved 2/14/2020.
5. Relativism. (2019, December 7). In *Wikipedia*. https://en.wikipedia.org/wiki/Relativism
6. Pew Research Center. (2019, October 17). *In U.S., Decline of Christianity Continues at Rapid Pace*. https://www.pewforum.org/2019/10/17/in-u-s-decline-of-christianity-continues-at-rapid-pace/
7. Harris, R. L., Harris, R. L., Archer, G. L., & Waltke, B. K. (1980). *Theological Wordbook of the Old Testament* [eBook edition]. Moody Press. Page 51.
8. Harris, R. L., Archer, G. L., & Waltke, B. K. (1980). *Theological Wordbook of the Old Testament* (Vol. #2). Moody Press. Page 2462.
9. Dictionary.com. (n.d.) Truth. In *Dictionary.com dictionary*. Retrieved May 9, 2020, from https://www.dictionary.com/browse/truth
10. MacArthur, J. (2007). *The Truth War*. Thomas Nelson. Pages 10-11.
11. Tozer, A.W. (1960) *The Best of A.W. Tozer* (Vol. #2). Christian Publications, Inc. Page 21.
12. Henry, M. *Matthew Henry's Commentary on the Whole Bible*. 3 John 3. e-Sword.

CHAPTER TWO

1. *Propaganda, Lies, Deceit and Half Truths*. (n.d.). Tentmaker.org. Retrieved December 11, 2019, from https://tentmaker.org/Quotes/propaganda_lies_deceit_halftruths_quotes.htm
2. Ryle, J. C. Cited in *2 Timothy 2:15 Commentary* (2019, November 8). Preceptaustin.org. Retrieved May 14, 2020, from https://www.preceptaustin.org/2_timothy_215-19#t
3. Kober, M. (2018, February 2). *Letter: The Bible was America's first textbook*. Des Moines Register. https://www.desmoinesregister.com/story/opinion/readers/2018/02/02/letter-bible-americas-first-textbook/301765002/
4. Marquand, R. (1985, September 5). *The rise and fall of the Bible in US classrooms....* The Christian Science Monitor. https://www.csmonitor.com/1985/0905/dback3-f.html
5. Age of Enlightenment. (2020, May 8). In *Wikipedia*. https://en.wikipedia.org/wiki/Age_of_Enlightenment
6. Age of Enlightenment. (2020, May 8). In *Wikipedia*. https://en.wikipedia.org/wiki/Age_of_Enlightenment
7. Marquand, R. (1985, September 5). *The rise and fall of the Bible in US classrooms....*

NOTES

The Christian Science Monitor. https://www.csmonitor.com/1985/0905/dback3-f.html

8. Merriam-Webster. (n.d.). Socialism. In *Merriam-Webster.com dictionary*. Retrieved January 20, 2020, from https://www.merriam-webster.com/dictionary/socialism

9. Bowers, C. (Director). (2016). *Agenda 2, Masters of Deceit* [Film]. Black Hat Films.

10. Bowers, C. (Director). (2016). *Agenda 2, Masters of Deceit* [Film]. Black Hat Films.

11. Merriam-Webster. (n.d.). Diversity. In *Merriam-Webster.com dictionary*. Retrieved December 11, 2019, from https://www.merriam-webster.com/dictionary/diversity

12. Queensborough Community College. (2020). *Definition for Diversity*. The City University of New York. https://www.qcc.cuny.edu/diversity/definition.html

13. Hardiman, K. (2017 April, 14). *Universities require scholars pledge commitment to diversity*. The College Fix. https://www.thecollegefix.com/universities-require-scholars-pledge-commitment-diversity/

14. Sneed, D. (2019, January 1). *The Case for Creation*. Answersingenesis.org. https://answersingenesis.org/creation-vs-evolution/case-creation/

15. MacArthur, J. (1999, March 28). *Creation: Believe It or Not, Part 2*. Gracetoyou.org. https://www.gty.org/library/sermons-library/90-209/creation-believe-it-or-not-part-2

16. MacArthur, J. (1999, March 28). *Creation: Believe It or Not, Part 2*. Gracetoyou.org. https://www.gty.org/library/sermons-library/90-209/creation-believe-it-or-not-part-2

17. Meyrat, A. (2019, October 26). *How Public Schools Indoctrinate Kids Without Almost Anyone Noticing*. The Federalist. https://thefederalist.com/2018/10/26/public-schools-indoctrinate-kids-without-almost-anyone-noticing/

18. Meyrat, A. (2019, October 26). *How Public Schools Indoctrinate Kids Without Almost Anyone Noticing*. The Federalist. https://thefederalist.com/2018/10/26/public-schools-indoctrinate-kids-without-almost-anyone-noticing/

19. Riley, A. (2019, December 5). *OPINION: Shoutdown culture shuts down traditional academic virtues*. Campus reform. https://www.campusreform.org/?ID=14064

20. Riley, A. (2019, December 5). *OPINION: Shoutdown culture shuts down traditional academic virtues*. Campus reform. https://www.campusreform.org/?ID=14064

21. Anti-Defamation League. (2020). *Who are Antifa?* Anti-Defamation League. https://www.adl.org/resources/backgrounders/who-are-antifa

CHAPTER THREE

1. Martindale, W., & Root, J. (Eds). (1990) *The Quotable Lewis*. Tyndale House Publisher, Inc. Page 151.

2. Courtemanche, G. Cited in *Quote by Gil Courtemanche: "Propaganda is as powerful as heroin; it surrept..."*. (n.d.). Goodreads.com. Retrieved May 15, 2020, from https://www.goodreads.com/quotes/545633-propaganda-is-as-powerful-as-heroin-it-surreptitiously-dissolves-all

3. Leach, W. (1993). *Land of Desire: Merchants, Power, and the Rise of a New American Culture*. Vintage Books.

4. Bernays, E. (2005). *Propaganda*. Liveright Publishing Company.

5. Edward Bernays. (2019, December 14). In *Wikipedia*. https://en.wikipedia.org/wiki/Edward_Bernays.

6. Edward Bernays. (2019, December 14). In *Wikipedia*. https://en.wikipedia.org/wiki/Edward_Bernays.

7. Bernays, E. (2005). *Propaganda*. Liveright Publishing Company.

8. Lanham Act, 15 USC § 1125 (1946).

9. *False Advertising Examples*. (2020). Yourdictionary.com. Retrieved December 14, 2019, from https://examples.yourdictionary.com/false-advertising-examples.html

CHAPTER FOUR

1. Kierkegaard, S. Cited in Wells, A.M. (Ed.). (1988). *Inspiring Quotations Contemporary and Classical*. Thomas Nelson Publishers. Page 197.

2. Adenay, W. F. *The Pulpit Commentary*. Jeremiah 1:1. e-Sword.

3. Postman, N. (1985). *Amusing Ourselves to Death: Public Discourse in the Age of Show Business*. Penguin Group. Page xix.

4. Riley, L. (n.d.). *History of Radio Advertising*. Study.com. Retrieved December 14, 2019, from https://study.com/academy/lesson/history-of-radio-advertising.html

5. Radio Advertisement. (December 14, 2019). In *Wikipedia*. https://en.wikipedia.org/wiki/Radio_advertisement

6. Radio Advertisement. (December 14, 2019). In *Wikipedia*. https://en.wikipedia.org/wiki/Radio_advertisement

7. Radio Advertisement. (December 14, 2019). In *Wikipedia*. https://en.wikipedia.org/wiki/Radio_advertisement

8. Stephens, M. (2020). *History of Television*. Nyu.edu. https://www.nyu.edu/classes/stephens/History%20of%20Television%20page.htm

9. The White House. (2020, March 14). *Proclamation on the National Day of Prayer for all Americans Affected by the Coronavirus Pandemic and for our National Response Efforts*. The White House. https://www.whitehouse.gov/presidential-actions/proclamation-national-day-prayer-americans-affected-coronavirus-pandemic-national-response-efforts/

10. Denison, J. (2020, April 21). *Gov. Cuomo explains declining COVID-19 cases in New York: 'God did not do that'*. Denison Forum. https://www.denisonforum.org/columns/daily-article/gov-cuomo-explains-declining-covid-19-cases-in-new-york-god-did-not-do-that

11. Decision Magazine. (2020, April 17). *Cuomo: 'God Did Not Stop the Spread of the Virus'*. Decision Magazine. https://decisionmagazine.com/cuomo-god-did-not-stop-the-spread-of-the-virus/

12. Fake news. (2019, December 16). In *Wikipedia*. https://en.wikipedia.org/wiki/Fake_news

13. Postman, N. (1985). *Amusing Ourselves to Death: Public Discourse in the Age of Show Business*. Penguin Group.

NOTES

14. Taibbi, M. (2019, July 7). *The Media's 10 Rules of Hate*. The Washington Spectator. https://washingtonspectator.org/taibbi-10rulesofhate/?gclid=EAI aIQobChMItobMxoW45gIVRNbACh3sGw9REAAYASAAEgJBivD_BwE.
15. Taibbi, M. (2019, July 7). *The Media's 10 Rules of Hate*. The Washington Spectator. https://washingtonspectator.org/taibbi-10rulesofhate/?gclid=EAI aIQobChMItobMxoW45gIVRNbACh3sGw9REAAYASAAEgJBivD_BwE.
16. Tremblay, J. (Director). (2012) *Shadows of Liberty* [Film]. Docfactory.
17. Tremblay, J. (Director). (2012) *Shadows of Liberty* [Film]. Docfactory.
18. Stephens, M. (2020). *History of Television*. Nyu.edu. https://www.nyu.edu/ classes/stephens/History%20of%20Television%20page.htm
19. Graham, B. Cited in Wells, A.M. (Ed.). (1988). *Inspiring Quotations Contemporary and Classical*. Thomas Nelson Publishers. Page 197.

CHAPTER FIVE

1. *Lies Politics Quotes*. (n.d.). Goodreads.com. Retrieved May 15, 2020, from https://www.goodreads.com/quotes/tag/lies-politics
2. Weishaupt, A. (2016) *Contra Mundum*. Hyperreality Books
3. Ellis, E.G. (2019, September 10). *Fighting Instagram's $1.3 Billion Problem—Fake Followers*. Wired. https://www.wired.com/story/instagram-fake-followers/
4. Wells, H.G. (n.d.). *World Brain: The Idea of a Permanent World Encyclopedia*. Berkley.edu. Retrieved December 15, 2019, from https://sherlock.ischool. berkeley.edu/wells/world_brain.html
5. Taylor, M.A. (Director). (2018) *The Creepy Line* [Film]. Wandering Foot Productions.
6. Curran, D. (2019, March 28). *Are you ready? Here is all the data Facebook and Google have on you*. The Guardian. https://www.theguardian.com/ commentisfree/2018/mar/28/all-the-data-facebook-google-has-on-you-privacy.
7. Curran, D. (2019, March 28). *Are you ready? Here is all the data Facebook and Google have on you*. The Guardian. https://www.theguardian.com/ commentisfree/2018/mar/28/all-the-data-facebook-google-has-on-you-privacy.
8. Taylor, M.A. (Director). (2018) *The Creepy Line* [Film]. Wandering Foot Productions.

CHAPTER SIX

1. Hitler, A. Cited in *Adolf Hitler Quotes*. (n.d.). Quotes.net. Retrieved March 3, 2020, from https://www.quotes.net/quote/7430.
2. Wise, D. (1973) *The Politics of Lying: Government Deception, Secrecy, and Power*. Random House. Page 18.
3. Ellsberg, D. Cited in *Government Lies Quotes*. (n.d.) Azquotes.com. Retrieved November 28, 2019, from https://www.azquotes.com/quotes/topics/ government-lies.html
4. Poynter Institute. (n.d.). *truth-o-meter*. PolitiFact. Retrieved November 28, 2019, from https://www.politifact.com/truth-o-meter/
5. Poynter Institute. (n.d.). *truth-o-meter*. PolitiFact. Retrieved November 28, 2019, from https://www.politifact.com/truth-o-meter/

6. Poynter Institute. (n.d.). *truth-o-meter.* PolitiFact. Retrieved November 28, 2019, from https://www.politifact.com/truth-o-meter/
7. Poynter Institute. (n.d.). *truth-o-meter.* PolitiFact. Retrieved November 28, 2019, from https://www.politifact.com/truth-o-meter/
8. Poynter Institute. (n.d.). *truth-o-meter.* PolitiFact. Retrieved November 28, 2019, from https://www.politifact.com/truth-o-meter/
9. Poynter Institute. (n.d.). *truth-o-meter.* PolitiFact. Retrieved November 28, 2019, from https://www.politifact.com/truth-o-meter/
10. Poynter Institute. (n.d.). *truth-o-meter.* PolitiFact. Retrieved November 28, 2019, from https://www.politifact.com/truth-o-meter/
11. Poynter Institute. (n.d.). *truth-o-meter.* PolitiFact. Retrieved November 28, 2019, from https://www.politifact.com/truth-o-meter/
12. Poynter Institute. (n.d.). *truth-o-meter.* PolitiFact. Retrieved November 28, 2019, from https://www.politifact.com/truth-o-meter/
13. Poynter Institute. (n.d.). *truth-o-meter.* PolitiFact. Retrieved November 28, 2019, from https://www.politifact.com/truth-o-meter/
14. Poynter Institute. (n.d.). *truth-o-meter.* PolitiFact. Retrieved November 28, 2019, from https://www.politifact.com/truth-o-meter/
15. Stafford, S. Cited in *Fooling Public Quotes.* (n.d.). Goodreads.com. Retrieved March 3, 2020, from https://www.goodreads.com/quotes/tag/fooling-public
16. Holan, A.D., & Qiu, L. (2015, December 21). 2015 *Lie of the Year: the campaign misstatements of Donald Trump.* PolitiFact. https://www.politifact.com/article/2015/dec/21/2015-lie-year-donald-trump-campaign-misstatements/
17. H.J. Resolution 1145, 88th Cong. (1964)
18. Vietnam War. (March 4, 2020). In *Wikipedia.* https://en.wikipedia.org/wiki/Vietnam_War
19. American Foreign Relations. (n.d.). *Presidential Power - Presidential war in Vietnam.* Retrieved March 4, 2020, from https://www.americanforeignrelations.com/O-W/Presidential-Power-Presidential-war-in-vietnam.html
20. Guardian News & Media Limited. (2002, August 27). *Full text of Dick Cheney's speech.* The Guardian.
21. Schwartz, Jon. (2016, February 18). *Trump is Right, Bush Lied: A Little-Known Part of the Bogus Case for War.* The Intercept. https://theintercept.com/2016/02/18/trump-is-right-bush-lied-a-little-known-part-of-the-bogus-case-for-war/
22. Schwartz, Jon. (2016, February 18). *Trump is Right, Bush Lied: A Little-Known Part of the Bogus Case for War.* The Intercept. https://theintercept.com/2016/02/18/trump-is-right-bush-lied-a-little-known-part-of-the-bogus-case-for-war/
23. Drogin, B., & Goetz, J. (2005, November 20). How U.S. Fell Under the Spell of 'Curveball.' *Los Angeles Times.* https://www.latimes.com/world/middleeast/la-na-curveball20nov20-story.html
24. Post-truth politics. (2020, January 18). In *Wikipedia.* https://en.wikipedia.org/wiki/Post-truth_politics
25. American-Israeli Cooperative Enterprise. (n.d.) *Joseph Goebbels: On the "Big Lie."* Jewish Virtual Library. Retrieved January 18, 2020, from https://www.

jewishvirtuallibrary.org/joseph-goebbels-on-the-quot-big-lie-quot.
26. Reilly, M. (2013, June 11). *James Clapper: I Gave 'Least Untruthful' Answer Possible On NSA Surveillance* (VIDEO). Huffpost. https://www.huffpost.com/entry/james-clapper-nsa-surveillance_n_3424620
27. Graham, B. (2016, April 20). *How our government has used deceit to withhold truth.* USA Today. https://www.usatoday.com/story/opinion/nation-now/2016/04/20/government-deceit-withhold-truth/83307394/

CHAPTER SEVEN

1. Lubben, S. (n.d.). *The Truth Behind the Fantasy.* Blazinggrace.org. Retrieved March 4, 2020, from https://www.blazinggrace.org/the-truth-behind-the-fantasy/
2. Jenkins, J. P. (n.d.). Encyclopedia Britannica. In *Encyclopedia Britannica.* Retrieved June 12, 2020, from https://www.britannica.com/topic/pornography
3. Gallagher, K. (2018) *When His Secret Sin Breaks Your Heart.* Pure Life Ministries.

BOOK TWO

INTRODUCTION

1. Wells, A.M. (Ed.). (1988). *Inspiring Quotations Contemporary and Classical.* Thomas Nelson Publishers.
2. Fenelon, F. *The Royal Way of the Cross.* Page 55.

CHAPTER ONE

1. Moody, J.C. Cited in Beckstrom, K., & Wirt, E. W. (Eds.). (1982). *Topical Encyclopedia of Living Quotations.* Bethany House Publishers. Page 215.
2. Wells, A.M. (Ed.). (1988). *Inspiring Quotations Contemporary and Classical.* Thomas Nelson Publishers. Page 57.
3. Matlock, P. Cited in Beckstrom, K., & Wirt, E. W. (Eds.). (1982). *Topical Encyclopedia of Living Quotations.* Bethany House Publishers. Page 215.
4. Henry, M. *Matthew Henry's Commentary on the Whole Bible.* Genesis 3. e-Sword.
5. Barnes, A. John 8:44. e-Sword.

CHAPTER TWO

1. Wesley, S. Cited in Beckstrom, K., & Wirt, E. W. (Eds.). (1982). *Topical Encyclopedia of Living Quotations.* Bethany House Publishers. Page 54.
2. *91 Quotes About Temptation.* (n.d.) ChristianQuotes.com. Retrieved February 5, 2020, from https://www.christianquotes.info/quotes-by-topic/quotes-about-temptation
3. Knutson, M. (n.d.) *The Remarkable Criminal Financial Career of Charles Ponzi.* Retrieved June 12, 2020, from https://www.mark-knutson.com/blog/wp-content/uploads/2014/06/ponzi.pdf
4. Gallagher, S. (2006) *Intoxicated with Babylon.* Pure Life Ministries.

BOOK THREE: APPENDICES

5. Hall, T. Cited in *The Biblical Illustrator*. 2 Timothy 4:3. e-Sword.

CHAPTER THREE

1. *91 Quotes About Temptation*. (n.d.). Christianquotes.com. Retrieved February 5, 2020, from https://www.christianquotes.info/quotes-by-topic/quotes-about-temptation
2. *91 Quotes About Temptation*. (n.d.). Christianquotes.com. Retrieved February 5, 2020, from https://www.christianquotes.info/quotes-by-topic/quotes-about-temptation
3. Ligonier Ministries. (n.d.). *Confronting Satan's Deception*. Ligonier.org. Retrieved January 22, 2020, from https://www.ligonier.org/learn/devotionals/confronting-satans-deception/
4. MacArthur, J. (2000). *The Fall of Man, Part 1* [Sermon]. Gracetoyou.org. The Fall of Man: https://www.gty.org/library/sermons-library/90-238/the-fall-of-man-part-1. Retrieved 11/1/18.
5. Poonen, Z. (n.d.). *How to Escape Deception* [Sermon]. Retrieved May 9, 2020, from http://ia800504.us.archive.org/20/items/SERMONINDEX_SID7764/SID7764.mp3

CHAPTER FOUR

1. Holmes, O. W. Cited in *Oliver Wendell Holmes, Sr. Quotes*. (n.d.). Brainyquote.com. Retrieved January 26, 2020, from http//www.brainyquote.com/quotes
2. *91 Quotes About Temptation*. (n.d.). Christianquotes.com. Retrieved February 5, 2020, from https://www.christianquotes.info/quotes-by-topic/quotes-about-temptation
3. Brown, D., Fausset, R., & Jamieson R. *Jamieson, Fausett and Brown Commentary*. Hebrews 3:13. e-Sword.
4. Copeland, R. Cited in Wells, A.M. (Ed.). (1988). *Inspiring Quotations Contemporary and Classical*. Thomas Nelson Publishers.
5. Shaw, S. Cited in Wells, A.M. (Ed.). (1988). *Inspiring Quotations Contemporary and Classical*. Thomas Nelson Publishers.
6. Barnes, A. Romans 2:4. e-sword.

CHAPTER FIVE

1. Simpson, A.B. Cited in *A.B. Simpson on The Heart*. (n.d.). oChristian.com. Retrieved May 17, 2020, from http://christian-quotes.ochristian.com/christian-quotes_ochristian.cgi?find=Christian-quotes-by-A.B.+Simpson-on-The+Heart
2. Poonen, Z. (n.d.). *How to Escape Deception* [Sermon]. Retrieved May 9, 2020, from http://ia800504.us.archive.org/20/items/SERMONINDEX_SID7764/SID7764.mp3
3. Strong, J. *Strong's Exhaustive Concordance of the Bible*. Hupokrisis. e-sword.
4. Renz, Dustin. (2016). *Pile of Masks: Exposing Christian Hypocrisy*. Make Way Ministries. Pages 39-40.

NOTES

5. Renz, Dustin. (2016). *Pile of Masks: Exposing Christian Hypocrisy*. Make Way Ministries. Page 40.
6. Renz, Dustin. (2016). *Pile of Masks: Exposing Christian Hypocrisy*. Make Way Ministries. Page 63.
7. Spurgeon, C. (1859) *Hypocrisy*. [Sermon]. Retrieved January 8, 2020, from https://www.spurgeon.org/resource-library/sermons/hypocrisy#flipbook/

CHAPTER SIX

1. Ryle, J.C. Cited in (2016, June 29). *Ignorance of the Bible Leads to Error*. Jcryle. info. http://www.jcryle.info/2016/06/ignorance-of-bible-leads-to-error.html
2. Murray, A. (1984). *The Inner Life*. Whitaker House. Page 39.
3. *John Wesley on the Bible, "O give me that book!"* (n.d.) Exiledpreacher.blogspot. com. Retrieved January 13, 2020, from http://exiledpreacher.blogspot. com/2006/03/john-wesley-on-bible-o-give-me-that.html
4. Havner, V. *The Best of Vance Havner*. Page 16.
5. Robertson, A. T. *Word Pictures in the New Testament*. e-sword.
6. Gill, J. *John Gill's Exposition of the Entire Bible*. e-sword
7. Clarke, A. *Adam Clarke's Commentary on the Bible*. e-sword.
8. Barnes, A. *Albert Barnes' Notes on the Bible*. e-sword.
9. Findlay, G. G. (1891). *The Epistle to the Galatians*. Hodder and Stoughton. Cited in *The Expositor's Bible*. AGES Software.
10. Torrey, R. A. (1982). *How to Obtain Fullness of Power*. Whitaker House. Page 55.
11. Tozer, A. W. (1978). *The Best of A.W. Tozer*. W. W. Wiesrbe (Comp.). Baker Book House, Grand Rapids. Page 61.

CHAPTER SEVEN

1. Galatians 4:16.
2. McVey, J. Cited in *Truth Hurts Quotes* (n.d.). Goodreads.com. Retrieved January 31, 2020, from https://www.goodreads.com/quotes/tag/truth-hurts
3. *The Pulpit Commentary*. 2 Samuel 11:1. e-Sword.
4. *The Pulpit Commentary*. 2 Samuel 11:18, e-Sword Bible program.
5. *The Pulpit Commentary*. 2 Samuel 12:1. e-Sword.

CHAPTER EIGHT

1. Havner, V. Cited in 20 *Quotes About Brokenness*. (n.d.). Christianquotes.com. Retrieved February 7, 2020, from https://www.christianquotes.info/quotes-by-topic/quotes-about-brokenness
2. MacArthur, J. (2007). *The Truth War*. Thomas Nelson. Page 2.
3. Gallagher, S. (2008) *Standing Firm through the Great Apostasy*. Pure Life Ministries.
4. Harris, R. L., Harris, R. L., Archer, G. L., & Waltke, B. K. (1980). *Theological Wordbook of the Old Testament* [eBook edition]. Moody Press.
5. MacLaren, A. *Expositions of Holy Scripture*. Psalm 51. e-Sword

BOOK THREE

INTRODUCTION

1. Hosea 4:1 NKJV.
2. Isaiah 59:14-16a CSB.
3. Michael, C. Cited in *Justice System Quotes*. (n.d.). Goodreads.com. Retrieved March 1, 2020, from https://www.goodreads.com/quotes/tag/justice-system
4. Murphy, P. *Practical Guide to Evidence*. Cited in Adversarial System. (2020, April 28). In Wikipedia. https://en.wikipedia.org/w/index.php?title=Adversarial_system&oldid=953680907

CHAPTER ONE

1. Macaulay, J.C. Cited in G. Campbell Morgan. *Studies in the Prophecies of Jeremiah*. Jeremiah 9.
2. Michael, B. (2010). Longman, T., & Garland, D. E. (Eds.). *The Expositor's Bible Commentary* (Revised ed., Vol. 7). Zondervan. Page 52.
3. Harris, R. L., Archer, G. L., & Waltke, B. K. (1980). *Theological Wordbook of the Old Testament* (Vol. #2). Moody Press. Page 787.
4. Henry, M. *Matthew Henry's Commentary on the Whole Bible*. 2 Chronicles 36. e-Sword.
5. Maclaren, A. *Expositions of Holy Scripture*. 2 Chronicles 36. e-Sword.
6. Bee, L. (2013, August 16). *The Stats on Internet Pornography* [Infographic]. Posarc.com. Retrieved June 12, 2020, from https://www.posarc.com/blog/the-stats-on-internet-pornography-infographic-1

CHAPTER TWO

1. Bonar, H. Cited in *2 Timothy 2:15 Commentary*. (2019, November 8). Preceptaustin.org. Retrieved May 14, 2020, from https://www.preceptaustin.org/2_timothy_215-19#t.
2. Pascal, B. Cited in *Quote by Blaise Pascal: "Truth is so obscure in these times, and falseho...".* (n.d.). Goodreads.com. Retrieved March 2, 2020, from, https://www.goodreads.com/quotes/140550-truth-is-so-obscure-in-these-times-and-falsehood-so
3. *Expositor's Bible Commentary*. 2 Peter 2. e-Sword.
4. Booth, W. Cited in *Quote by William Booth: "The chief danger that confronts the coming cent...".* (n.d.). Goodreads.com. Retrieved February 27, 2020, from https://www.goodreads.com/quotes/291048-the-chief-danger-that-confronts-the-coming-century-will-be
5. Gallagher, S. (2006) *Intoxicated with Babylon*. Pure Life Ministries.
6. *The Pulpit Commentary*, 2 Thessalonians 2, e-Sword.
7. Lenski, R. C. H. *The Interpretation of St. Paul's Epistle to the Romans*. Cited in Longman, T., & Garland, D. E. (Eds.). (2010) *The Expositor's Bible Commentary* (Revised ed., Vol. 7). Romans 1. Zondervan.

NOTES

8. Robertson, A.T. *Word Pictures in the New Testament*. Romans 1. e-Sword.
9. Tozer, A.W. (2012) *The Dangers of a Shallow Faith: Awakening from Spiritual Lethargy*. Gospel Light Publications. Page 14.

CHAPTER THREE

1. Pink, A.W. (1942). *The Life of Elijah* [Sermon]. Gracegems.org. Retrieved March 2, 2020, from https://gracegems.org/Pink/life_of_elijah.htm
2. *The Pulpit Commentary*, Matthew 24, e-Sword.
3. Montgomery, B. Cited in *Quote by Bernard Montgomery: "Leadership is the capacity and will to rally me..."*. (n.d.). Goodreads.com. Retrieved March 2, 2020, from https://www.goodreads.com/quotes/713104-leadership-is-the-capacity-and-will-to-rally-men-and
4. Sanders, O.J. (n.d.). *Spiritual Leadership* [PDF]. *Moody Press*. Retrieved March 2, 2020, from http://spiritimpact.tripod.com/sitebuildercontent/sitebuilderfiles/spiritualleadership.pdf
5. Tozer, A.W. Cited in L. Ravenhill. (2004) *Why Revival Tarries*. Bethany House Publishers. Page 11.
6. Baxter, J. S. Cited in *2 Peter Commentaries & Sermons*. (2019, October 31). Preceptaustin.org. https://www.preceptaustin.org/2_peter_commentaries
7. Spurgeon, C. (n.d.). *A Prophetic Warning* [Sermon]. Spurgeongems.org. http://www.spurgeongems.org/sermon/chs3301.pdf
8. Barnes, A. *Albert Barnes' Notes on the Bible*. Matthew 7. e-Sword.
9. Brown, D., Fausset, R., & Jamieson R. Jamieson, *Fausett and Brown Commentary*. Matthew 7. e-Sword.
10. Gallagher, S. (2006) *Intoxicated with Babylon*. Pure Life Ministries.
11. Chambers, O. (1987). *The Best from All His Books*. Oliver Nelson. Page 79.
12. Guyon, J. (1984). *Experiencing God Through Prayer*. Whitaker House. Page 31.
13. Briggs, C. A., Brown, F., & Driver, S.R. *Brown-Driver-Briggs Hebrew and English Lexicon*. Shav. e-Sword.
14. Ironside, H. A. *Minor Prophets*. Kregel Academic & Professional.
15. Dictionary.com. (n.d.) Covetous. In *Dictionary.com dictionary*. Retrieved February 27, 2020, from https://www.dictionary.com/browse/covetous
16. Jones, D.W. (2015, June 5) *5 Errors of the Prosperity Gospel*. Thegospelcoalition.org. https://www.thegospelcoalition.org/article/5-errors-of-the-prosperity-gospel/

CHAPTER FOUR

1. Nee, N. (1972). *Spiritual Authority*. Christian Fellowship Publishers. Page 13.
2. Lloyd-Jones, D. M. *Studies in the Sermon on the Mount*. Wm. B. Eerdmans Publishing Co.. Pages 484 – 485.
3. Clarke, A. *Adam Clarke's Commentary on the Bible*. Matthew 7. e-sword.
4. Wesley, J. *Sermon on Several Occasions*. AGES Master Library.
5. Strong, J. *Strong's Hebrew and Greek Dictionary*. Planao. e-sword.
6. *The Pulpit Commentary*. Hebrews 2. e-Sword.

395

7. Murray, A. (1994). *The Holiest of All*. Fleming H. Revell Company. Pages 22-23.
8. Clarke, A. *Adam Clarke's Commentary on the Bible*. Hebrews. e-sword.
9. Bercot, D. W. (1998). *A Dictionary of Early Christian Beliefs*. Hendrickson Publishers. Cited in J. Bevere. *Driven By Eternity*. (2016). Messenger International.
10. Henry, M. *Matthew Henry's Commentary on the Whole Bible*. Revelation 13. e-Sword.

CHAPTER FIVE
1. Augustine. Cited in Wells, A.M. (Ed.). (1988). *Inspiring Quotations Contemporary and Classical*. Thomas Nelson Publishers. Page 76.
2. Burroughs, J. Cited in Wells, A.M. (Ed.). (1988). *Inspiring Quotations Contemporary and Classical*. Thomas Nelson Publishers. Page 77.
3. *Galatians 5:16 Commentary*. (2019, August 7). Preceptaustin.org. Retrieved February 13, 2020, from https://www.preceptaustin.org/galatians_516
4. Anxiety and Depression Association of America. (2018). *Facts & Statistics*. Anxiety and Depression Association of America. Retrieved February 13, 2020, https://adaa.org/about-adaa/press-room/facts-statistics
5. Suicide in the United States. (2020, February 10). In *Wikipedia*. https://en.wikipedia.org/wiki/Suicide_in_the_United_States
6. Drug Overdose. (2020, February 10). In *Wikipedia*. https://en.wikipedia.org/wiki/Drug_overdose
7. *The Pulpit Commentary*. Jeremiah 42. e-sword.
8. *Number of committed crimes in the United States in 2018, by type of crime*. (n.d.). Statista.com. Retrieved February 13, 2020, from https://www.statista.com/statistics/202714/number-of-committed-crimes-in-the-us-by-type-of-crime
9. Anxiety and Depression Association of America. (2018). *Facts & Statistics*. Anxiety and Depression Association of America. Retrieved February 13, 2020, https://adaa.org/about-adaa/press-room/facts-statistics
10. Winerman, L. (2017, December). *By the numbers: Our stressed-out nation*. American Psychological Association. https://www.apa.org/monitor/2017/12/numbers
11. Advisory Board. (2016, December 14). *An estimated 40 million Americans take psychiatric drugs. Here's what they're taking*. Advisory.com. https://www.advisory.com/daily-briefing/2016/12/14/what-psychiatric-drugs-are-americans-taking

CHAPTER SIX
1. Katz, A. (2008). *The Spirit of Truth*. Art Katz Ministires. Pages 10-11.
2. Mounce, W. D. *Mounce's Complete Expository Dictionary of Old & New Testament Words*. Zondervan. Cited in 2 Timothy 2:15 Commentary. (2019, November 8). Preceptaustin.org. Retrieved May 15, 2020, from https://www.preceptaustin.org/2_timothy_215-19#t.
3. Merriam-Webster. (n.d.) Osmosis. In *Merriam-Webster.com dictionary*. Retrieved February 29, 2020, from https://www.merriam-webster.com/dictionary/osmosis
4. Dictionary.com. (n.d.) Osmosis. In *Dictionary.com dictionary*. Retrieved February

NOTES

29, 2020, from https://www.dictionary.com/browse/osmosis

5. Vincent, M. R., Vincent, *Vincent's Word studies in the New Testament*. Cited in *2 Timothy 2:24-26 Commentary*. (2019, November 8). Preceptaustin.org. Retrieved February 29, 2020, from https://www.preceptaustin.org/2_timothy_224-26.

6. Wuest, K., *Word Studies from the Greek New Testament*. Cited in *2 Timothy 2:24-26 Commentary*. (2019, November 8). Preceptaustin.org. Retrieved February 29, 2020, from https://www.preceptaustin.org/2_timothy_224-26.

APPENDICES

APPENDIX ONE

1. Harris, R. L., Archer, G. L., & Waltke, B. K. (1980). *Theological Wordbook of the Old Testament* [eBook edition]. Moody Press. Page 51.

2. Kittel, G., & Friedrich, G. (1985). *The Theological Dictionary of the New Testament: Abridged in One Volume*. (G. W. Bromiley, Ed.). Wm. B. Eerdman's Publishing Company.

3. Kittel, G., & Friedrich, G. (1985). *The Theological Dictionary of the New Testament: Abridged in One Volume*. (G. W. Bromiley, Ed.). Wm. B. Eerdman's Publishing Company.

4. *Complete Biblical Library Greek-English Dictionary*. Cited in *2 Timothy 2:15 Commentary*. (2019, November 8). Preceptaustin.org. Retrieved May 14, 2020, from https://www.preceptaustin.org/2_timothy_215-19#t.

5. Harrison, E., *The Importance of the Septuagint for Biblical Studies*. Cited in *2 Timothy 2:15 Commentary*. (2019, November 8). Preceptaustin.org. Retrieved May 14, 2020, from https://www.preceptaustin.org/2_timothy_215-19#t.

6. Chambers, O. (1987). *The Best from All His Books*. Oliver Nelson.

7. *Biblical Theism Pt 3/4 The Attributes of God - Bibliotheca Sacra*. (Vol. 96). Page 14-16, 1939. Cited in *2 Timothy 2:15 Commentary*. (2019, November 8). Preceptaustin.org. Retrieved May 14, 2020, from https://www.preceptaustin.org/2_timothy_215-19#t.

8. Detzler, W. A., *New Testament Words in Today's Language 2 Timothy 2:15 Commentary*. (2019, November 8). Preceptaustin.org. Retrieved May 14, 2020, from https://www.preceptaustin.org/2_timothy_215-19#t.

9. Martin, R. P., & Davids, P. H., *Dictionary of the later New Testament and its developments*. Cited in *2 Timothy 2:15 Commentary*. (2019, November 8). Preceptaustin.org. Retrieved May 14, 2020, from https://www.preceptaustin.org/2_timothy_215-19#t.

10. Tozer A.W., *Renewed Day by Day: A Daily Devotional*. WingSpread. Cited in *2 Timothy 2:15 Commentary*. (2019, November 8). Preceptaustin.org. Retrieved May 14, 2020, from https://www.preceptaustin.org/2_timothy_215-19#t.

11. 2 Timothy 2:15 Commentary (2019, November 8). Preceptaustin.org. Retrieved May 14, 2020, from https://www.preceptaustin.org/2_timothy_215-19#t

BOOK THREE: APPENDICES

APPENDIX TWO

1. Harris, R. L., Archer, G. L., & Waltke, B. K. (1980). *Theological Wordbook of the Old Testament* (Vol. #2). Moody Press. Page 2462.
2. Harris, R. L., Archer, G. L., & Waltke, B. K. (1980). *Theological Wordbook of the Old Testament* (Vol. #2). Moody Press. Page 435.
3. Harris, R. L., Archer, G. L., & Waltke, B. K. (1980). *Theological Wordbook of the Old Testament* (Vol. #2). Moody Press. Page 742.

APPENDIX FOUR

1. Murray, A. (1985). *Abide in Christ*. Barbour and Company. Page 112.
2. Finney, C. (1985). *Crystal Christianity*. Whitaker House. Page 95.
3. Kittel, G., & Friedrich, G. (1985). *The Theological Dictionary of the New Testament: Abridged in One Volume*. (G. W. Bromiley, Ed.). Wm. B. Eerdman's Publishing Company. Pages 583-584.
4. Henry, M. *Matthew Henry's Commentary on the Whole Bible*. Revelation 13. e-Sword.

OTHER BOOKS AVAILABLE
BY PURE LIFE MINISTRIES

At the Altar of Sexual Idolatry
At the Altar of Sexual Idolatry DVD Curriculum
At the Altar of Sexual Idolatry Workbook
A Biblical Guide to Counseling the Sexual Addict
Create in Me a Pure Heart
Entering His Courts
From Ashes to Beauty
He Leads Me Beside Still Waters
How America Lost Her Innocence
i: the root of sin exposed
Intoxicated with Babylon
A Lamp Unto My Feet
Living in Victory
Out of the Depths of Sexual Sin
Pressing on Toward the Heavenly Calling
Selah! The Book of Psalms in the Richest Translations
Standing Firm through the Great Apostasy
The Overcomers Series (12-DVD set)
The Time of Your Life in Light of Eternity
The Walk of Repentance
When His Secret Sin Breaks Your Heart
Wisdom: Proverbs & Ecclesiastes in the Richest Translations
The Word of Their Testimony

Pure Life Ministries helps Christian men achieve lasting freedom from sexual sin. The Apostle Paul said, "Walk in the Spirit and you will not fulfill the lust of the flesh." Since 1986, Pure Life Ministries (PLM) has been discipling men into the holiness and purity of heart that comes from a Spirit-controlled life. At the root, illicit sexual behavior is sin and must be treated with spiritual remedies. Our counseling programs and teaching resources are rooted in the biblical principles that, when applied to the believer's daily life, will lead him out of bondage and into freedom in Christ.

BIBLICAL TEACHING RESOURCES

Pure Life Ministries offers a full line of books, audio CDs and DVDs specifically designed to give men the tools they need to live in sexual purity.

RESIDENTIAL CARE

The most intense and involved counseling PLM offers comes through the **Residential Program** (9 months), in Dry Ridge, Kentucky. The godly and sober atmosphere on our 45-acre campus provokes the hunger for God and deep repentance that destroys the hold of sin in men's lives.

HELP AT HOME

The **Overcomers At-Home Program** (OCAH) is available for those who cannot come to Kentucky for the Residential Program. This twelve-week counseling program features weekly counseling sessions and many of the same teachings offered in the Residential Program.

CARE FOR WIVES

Pure Life Ministries also offers help to wives of men in sexual sin through our 12-week **At-Home Program for Wives.** Our wives' counselors have suffered through the trials and storms of such a discovery and can offer a devastated wife a sympathetic ear and the biblical solutions that worked in their lives.

PURE LIFE MINISTRIES

14 School St. • Dry Ridge • KY • 41035
Office: 859.824.4444 • Orders: 888.293.8714
inform@purelifeministries.org
www.purelifeministries.org